All in a Day

Also by Mihir Bose

Keith Miller: A Cricketing Biography
The Lost Hero: A Biography of Subhas Bose

# All in a Day

Great Moments in Cup Cricket

## Mihir Bose

Robin Clark Limited

*To Bantu and Abhijit,*
*who already know the game*
*and to Raphael, Daniel and Buntun,*
*who will learn to love it.*

Published by Robin Clark Limited 1983
A member of the Namara Group
27/29 Goodge Street, London W1P 1FD

British Library Cataloguing in Publication Data

Bose, Mihir
   All in a day.
   1. Cricket—History
     I. Title
   796.35'8        GV913
   ISBN 0-86072-066-7

Typeset by MC Typeset, Chatham, Kent
Printed in Great Britain by
Mackays of Chatham Ltd, Kent

# Contents

# Acknowledgements

Any book depends on many people and this is no exception. I am indebted to my friends and colleagues at the *Sunday Times,* particularly Jim Pegg, Assistant Sports Editor and David Robson, Sports Editor. Asif Iqbal, Ted Dexter, Brian Johnston, Gordon Ross, M.J.K. Smith, Andrew Stevens of Prudential, Liz Stanbury of John Player, the Marketing Department of Benson & Hedges, Karen Earle and Fiona Foster of West Nally, Jack Prosser of Rothmans, Tony Pawson, Bagenal Harvey, Mike Brearley, Ron Roe – Promotions Office of TCCB, Andrew Longmore – Assistant Editor of *Cricketer International,* all provided me with their time, memories, useful facts and, in some cases, invaluable photographs.

Stephen Green, Curator of Lord's, was, as ever, extremely helpful and the Limited Overs Information Group provided the sort of statistical backup that is not found even in *Wisden.*

*Wisden* was, of course, a constant guide and both *The World of Cricket* (which ceased publication in 1980) and the *Benson & Hedges Cricket Year* (formerly the *Pelham Cricket Year*) were handy sources of reference.

I also found the *Playfair Cricket Monthly* (as it then was), the *Cricketer,* the *Wisden Cricket Monthly* and the official records of the 1975 and 1979 Prudential World Cup very useful.

Sandra den Hertog typed the manuscript cheerfully, Sue Cairncross took up the bits and pieces, Margaret Browne very patiently sustained my spirits, and Janet and Yehuda Mokades provided inspiration in their very different ways.

# Introduction

I do not, cannot, never have complained about the financial
benefits it [one-day cricket] has brought to the game. I do not,
cannot, never have accepted that its effect upon county championship and therefore Test cricket has been anything but
seriously damaging.

   Brian Close, former England, Yorkshire and Somerset captain

For the spectators it is a superb game. Personally I can't bear to
watch it – it's too desperately stereotyped. I won a few man of the
match awards but I couldn't tell you what they were.

   Ted Dexter, former England and Sussex captain
   in the early years of the Gillette Cup

In the beginning, so we are told, was the word. For most dedicated
cricket followers that spells three-day and, more particularly, five-
day Test cricket. As 1982 slid away and England won a dramatic
Test victory in Melbourne – by just 3 runs – almost the first reaction
of the joyful commentators was to pour obloquy on one-day,
limited-overs cricket. The final day of this crucial Test had dawned
with England needing just one wicket to win. Yet a stubborn –
classic – last-wicket stand between Border and the no. 11 – Thomson
– seemed likely to frustrate all English plans. As a combination of
chancy and good strokes – and some questionable England tactics –
took Australia nearer to victory, at least one cricketing pundit
argued that England's inability to prise out the last batsman, and
no. 11's ability to stay put showed the baneful influence of one-day
cricket. With Australia just four short of victory Thomson was
caught at the second attempt and the commentator, having
overcome his understandable excitement, used the occasion to
draw the appropriate moral: 'This game showed up one-day cricket

for what it is – an instant game which has little intrinsic worth.' In the beginning the good Lord had said, 'Let there be cricket,' and Lord's had responded with the five-day Test.

In that sense one-day cricket bears the same relation to the three-day/five-day game as, say, a Barbara Cartland or Harold Robbins novel does to the winner of the Booker prize for fiction. The public read the former, yet the literary pages of our newspapers and periodicals rarely mention them, while devoting acres to discussing the latest trends in the serious novel. One-day cricket does get a lot of media publicity – being ideal for television – and is well covered even in the serious papers, but it is interesting to reflect that twenty years after the first limited-over competition was sponsored by Gillette there has been precious little study of this type of game; what writing there is is more a summary of the scores interspersed with occasional hallelujah comments about this or that particular innings. The end of every English season brings forth a sizeable crop of cricket books but – apart from the annual statistical digests – few of them have anything worthwhile to say on the one-day game. Even players' autobiographies race through the one-day matches in a few uninformative paragraphs. And while this may reflect the prejudices of the 'ghost' – very likely a cricket writer who does not particularly like the one-day game – it is sobering to reflect that so far there have been only two books that have specifically dealt with this type of cricket. Maybe, as Jim Pegg, Assistant Sports Editor of the *Sunday Times,* suggests, one-day cricket does not lend itself to literature in the way traditional cricket does.

In July 1969 Sir Neville Cardus, who was rarely at a loss for words – or at least a cricket word – confessed in his monthly column for *Playfair Cricket Monthly* that like the artist in *Don Quixote* he felt barren. Rain had been partly responsible for his sterility but he was also 'handicapped' by the abundance of one-day matches.

> The pace and brevity of time conditioning one-day matches put a premium on the free exhibition of a great player's personality . . . One-day cricket depends *entirely* on competitive appeal. And frankly, cricket is at its least *consistently* appealing whenever the appeal is wholly competitive. For one thing weather interferes too frequently with results. The great glory of first-class cricket has always been the fascination of personality – the game played within the game – Larwood bowling at Bradman, Keith Miller and Lindwall bowling at Hutton, Douglas Wright bowling at Compton, George Gunn 'taking a walk' out of his crease to

render null and void the fastest ball of E.A. McDonald . . . In one-day cricket there can be no long symphonic planning of batsmanship or bowling . . . The writer on cricket, if he wishes to be more than a reporter, depends for inspiration on personality, which won't reveal itself in breathless 'bright' snatches.

If cricket's literature barely acknowledges it, then in cricket's Bible – *Wisden* – it occupies a very curious limbo.

In the twenty years since the Gillette Cup was started only one cricketer could be said to have earned the coveted title of one of *Wisden*'s Five Cricketers of the Year through his success in the one-day game: Jack Bond who captained Lancashire in the late sixties and early seventies through some of their most memorable matches. But even today cricket's statistical storehouse, *Wisden's Cricket Records,* does not list any statistics relating to the one-day game. Though these matches are played according to the rules of the first-class game, peformances in these games make no difference to first-class statistics, a paradox that has worried many a cricket follower.

In November 1965, David Drabble, a member of the Sheffield Cricket Lovers Society, wrote to *Playfair Cricket Monthly*:

At present I fail to see just what value the national averages are, for in the 1965 Gillette Cup Final Boycott scored one of the best hundreds ever seen (not to mention all the other fine performances in the final or in the competition generally). These runs or wickets in Gillette matches are not included in the averages yet runs scored in three-day Festival matches usually are – surely Boycott's century scored in a final with something like Test atmosphere counts for more than 200 scored in a Festival game? I realize that Gillette matches are only one-day affairs and generally do not come into consideration for averages purposes. What a state of affairs! The very competition that is raved about means nothing in terms of figures. Now is the time for the powers that be to re-term the averages to read 'Three-day matches and Gillette Cup games'.

Eighteen years on the cry of the Sheffield Cricket Lover is yet to be answered (though the Limited Overs Information Group formed in 1977 has done valuable work). A double century against the Free Foresters could boost an average player's first-class figures, yet even the greatest one-day innings will not figure in a good player's record. Thus, in an otherwise characteristic appreciation of Mike Proctor by Alan Gibson, in the 1982 *Wisden,* there was no statistical mention – and little literary mention at that – of Proctor's feats in English one-day cricket, arguably among the finest performances of this wonderful cricketer.

Great cricketers of course habitually disdain any interest in statistics but figures play a vital part in cricket; no other game has erected such a massive edifice from such unlikely material. The 1982 *Wisden* testified to the power of cricket statistics when John Woodcock, editor of *Wisden* and cricket correspondent of *The Times,* explained at some length why he did not agree with the Association of Cricket Statisticians about altering the number of centuries scored by W.G. Grace. The record shows he scored 126, the statisticians claim he really scored 124, and the discrepancy arises from the first-class status of certain matches the great man played in. The argument of the statisticians is that fresh evidence shows two of those centuries were scored in one-day games.

Woodcock argued against the change – after inadvertently allowing it in the 1981 *Wisden* – on the grounds that to tamper with the figures of the patron saint of cricket would be 'unromantic'. He goes on, 'That one-day games played more than a century ago should have been termed first-class need not surprise us; there were no regulations in those days stipulating the minimum time for a first-class match.'

For a game quite so romantic about figures to ignore one-day statistics illustrates the limbo one-day cricket occupies: it is loved by a wide public, albeit one untutored in the intricacies of the three-day or five-day game, and its revenue subsidizes the three-day match, but it is regarded for the most part by dedicated cricket followers as something to be suffered rather than enjoyed.

A sense of nostalgia is vital to the cricketing enthusiast. Mention Botham as the greatest all-rounder, and thousands will recall the achievements of Garfield Sobers. When Sobers reigned, millions were willing to testify to the all-round prowess of Miller or Bailey or Mankad – and so on. Cricket thrives on perpetually contrasting the present with the past, in a way few sports can. Instant cricket by its very nature is anti-nostalgic, somewhat like today's football where managers proudly say 'you are as good as your last result'.

Like the FA Cup, the one-day game can bestow instant glory or instant death, but it lacks the key ingredient that makes the FA Cup such a romantic event: the possibility that a team made up of bakers, carpenters and electricians, enthusiastic and skilful but part-time players, could humble the mighty Liverpool or Arsenal. Cup football is littered with the deeds of amateur teams like Yeovil or Enfield, toppling first division teams. Yet it was only on 30 June 1973 – ten years after the Gillette competition had started – that a minor county beat a first-class county in the Gillette Cup. Though this was a famous triumph – Durham humbled Yorkshire in Harrogate of all places – there have been few such triumphs and none to match the glory runs of some of the amateur sides in the FA Cup. The very nature of cricket and the fact that the game takes so much longer to play makes it difficult for inferior sides to surprise the more skilful ones.

As Michael Davie has written, 'Excitement in sport, as in no other human activity, depends on ignorance. If you know the result you cannot be keyed up.' In one-day cricket the tactics have a certain sameness, the result is often predictable. This was perhaps inevitable. Now it is all too common for the bowling side to have their faster bowlers on for the opening six or seven overs, then rotate the other bowlers – generally medium-pace with the odd spinner bowling flat and tight – only for the fastest bowlers to return towards the end of the innings. For the batting side the objective is for the openers to build a sound base, though at reasonable speed, so as to allow the middle order and the tail the platform they need for a successful late thrash. Of course there are exceptions, and the truly brilliant like Vivian Richards, Clive Lloyd or Ian Botham can upset all calculations, but in the main the pattern rarely varies. Though two well-matched sides often produce exciting matches, one-day cricket can never accommodate the infinite tactical variations of the longer game.

And while one-day cricket has provided many memorable performances, purists complain that it does lack a certain aesthetic appeal. Like no other sport, cricket values quality above quantity. A batsman making 70, largely through nudging and pushing, will not be rated as highly as the man who makes 20 with five immaculate cover drives. In evaluating cricketers, class does matter. A good cricketer is a good cricketer in any form of the game. But in one-day cricket it matters not whether the four the batsman earns is snicked through vacant slips, or blasted past cover point. In fact, given most field-placings the latter stroke would be exceptional, whereas the snick is common and gratefully received, often at the expense of the sort of ball that would claim a Test wicket.

But, as Mike Brearley pointed out:

Although some subtleties of the game do disappear with limited-over cricket, there are many occasions for the exercise of tactical judgement. However, the crucial difference is not so much tactical as psychological. There are nowadays far more close games, crucial moments, hectic situations. Many more instant and pressurized decisions have to be made. County cricket used to be incredibly sedate. There was the slow rhythm of three-day matches, with close finishes rare. Play would be held up while aeroplanes passed overhead, or until the barracking died down. Bowlers rarely posed a physical threat. Aggression was low-key.[1]

While some of these changes reflect the wider changes in society, much of it is due to the prevalence of one-day cricket.

The purists argue that apart from sharpening up the fielding, one-day cricket has contributed little or nothing to the game. Jim Laker, a noted enthusiast for this type of game, admits that:

> The standard of outfielding has improved out of all recognition, and in reaching such a high peak proves conclusively that the present-day cricketer is fitter and more athletic than his counterpart of bygone days. There was a time when the cricketer would continue playing until he was about ready to drop and the club had no alternative but to end his contract. In those days it was always possible to hide a couple of fielders and the slips and gully provided a ready-made heaven. Even in my playing days I can never recall going through any serious form of physical training which is now an accepted part of pre-season build up. I was certainly fit enough to bowl forty-over spells and complete 1,500 overs in an English season which would shatter one or two bowlers at the moment. Having said that, there is no doubt that neither I nor my colleagues would have stood up to the physical demands of the one-day game without attempting to put a much finer edge on our accepted degree of fitness.[2]

Fielding, though commonly invoked, is not the only area that has been affected by the one-day game. This type of cricket has also led to the growth of what are called the 'bits and pieces' players: batsmen who can bowl a bit, bowlers who can bat a bit. They are not quite the genuine all-rounders of the old days: men who were supposed to find a place in the side merely on the strength of their batting or their bowling. In fact in the history of the game such genuine all-rounders have been rare. Barry Wood of Lancashire is a prime example of a player whose one-day bits and pieces added up to the whole of all-rounder, even at Test level. The special requirements of the one-day game: bowlers who can keep it tight and perhaps nip in with a wicket or two, batsmen who can score a few, have provided a great impetus to all batsmen who thought they also fancied themselves as bowlers, and all bowlers who did not like their image as hopeless rabbits. The result has been that few Test sides these days possess a genuine tail. England have often been rescued by their tail, so much so that they have gone on to win matches and most countries now possess nos. 9, 10 and 11 whose exposure to the one-day game has made them better, more confident batsmen. Certainly before the one-day game few would have imagined the former England opening batsmen Boycott or Gooch bowling in Test matches and taking wickets, or the feats of the Pakistan opening batsman Mudassar Nazar whose bowling played a crucial part in their success in the 1982 Lord's Test.

Yet for many this plus is outweighed by the many minuses of one-day cricket: that batsmen, particularly lower down the order, no longer have the time to build up an innings, that the need for defensive containing cricket – 0 for 20 being better than 2 for 32 – has all but killed the type of spinner who would tempt and tease batsmen out; if they have not been replaced by in-slant medium-pacers they have themselves begun to bowl like them, as for instance Eddie Hemmings of Nottinghamshire. Worst of all, the accent on one-day cricket has meant that the ills of that type of cricket have been visited upon Test cricket – the highest form of the game where success or failure has the most profound national impact.

Some years ago when England had a dearth of middle-order batsmen, and a surfeit of openers – leading Keith Miller to suggest that England should populate its middle order with opening bats – one-day cricket was blamed for such an imbalance. Yet, more recently, England's problems have been to find reliable opening batsmen while a number of young middle-order batsmen compete for the one or two positions available. Again the blame falls on one-day cricket, which has become a convenient scapegoat for all of England's Test problems.

The effect on spinners may have been exaggerated. Figures produced by John Stockwell in Patrick Murphy's book *The Spinners' Turn,* and updated for this one by Robert Brooke (see statistics) show that the spinner is often quite economical in one-day cricket. In the seasons from 1979 to 1982 they were consistently more economical than medium-pacers, the type who most threaten their existence. In the 1982 season slow left-armers were the most economical bowlers of all, conceding 3.81 runs per over compared to 3.91 by fast bowlers, 4.04 by off-spinners and 4.31 by medium-pacers. This has been more pronounced in the sixty-overs-a-side competitions. The first Gillette final in 1963 was to see a left-armer, Norman Gifford, win the 'Man of the Match' award for his bowling, and both of Yorkshire's Gillette victories featured good, tight spin bowling. Sussex's victory in the 1978 Gillette final owed much to the intelligent use of Barclay, an off-spinner, and Cheatle, a left-armer, by their captain Arnold Long.

That one-day cricket should occupy such a position in the game reflects more on the state of English cricket in general than the limitations of this type of game. One-day cricket came in just as the traditional type of English game was declining. Until a few years after the Second World War the English game was built round the leisurely three-day domestic match and the periodic Test series against Australia. Though pre-Second World War Tests had been played against all the major cricketing countries (Pakistan, then, was part of All-India and Sri Lanka's status as a Test nation was inconceivable to most people) internationally what mattered was the Ashes battle with Australia.

The very term 'Ashes' indicates how English cricket, in a way quite unique to sport, institutionalized defeat at the enemy's hands. Its origins lie in a little tale about a witty journalist and two sporty women. In the international sense English cricket had suffered its truly great defeat in 1882 when on 29 August of that year Australia defeated the full strength of England on English soil for the first time. The Australians won by 7 runs and the following day the *Sporting Times* printed a mock obituary notice which said that the body of English cricket would be cremated and the ashes taken to Australia. The following winter when the Honourable Ivo Bligh took an English team to Australia, some Melbourne women burnt a bail and presented the urn containing the ashes to him; this subsequently found its way to Lord's where it resides permanently (recent cricket research suggests that it may not be a bail that was burnt, but a ball – but that is another story). Since then England and Australia play regularly for this sacrosanct urn.

Contrast this with English football which only accepted that the rest of the world could play the national game in 1953, after the 6–3 defeat at the feet of the Hungarians – and though the 1966 victory in the World Cup did something to restore confidence in English technique, many in football see 1953 as the year that marked the loss of a particular English footballing innocence.

The 1950s changed much in cricket as crowds deserted the three-day game and countries other than Australia began to defeat England in cricket, even India. Defeats against Australia were fully explicable and accepted according to the Ashes code which had long been established. These other defeats were more difficult to explain.

They were to start a debate about the condition of cricket that continues to this day and many and wonderful were the proposals advanced for remedying the situation. About the same time economic realities forced the introduction of the one-day game, and as this became more popular, and the England team continued to have difficulty in winning international matches, so it attracted the brunt of criticism. One-day cricket had been created because the three-day game had grown sick and no longer attracted a great many people. Within a decade of the one-day game emerging, it was held responsible for all the ills of the game.

Such is traditional cricket's appeal that even its supposed revolutionary critics find change uncomfortable. In the *Willow Wand*, Derek Birley examined some of the myths that envelop cricket and did his best to expose the cricket establishment's efforts 'to preserve an eighteenth-century feudal dream'. But having dealt impressively and wittily with the foibles of such cricketing greats as Sir Pelham Warner, Lord Harris and Neville Cardus, he felt it necessary to sneer at the most revolutionary innovations of the limited-overs game. 'The new competitions were sponsored by tobacco and drinks firms, razor-blade manufacturers and so forth as an aid to selling their products.' Birley then made common cause with the most traditional followers of the game by concluding:

It would be wrong to put all the blame for the recent decline in cricket crowd behaviour in England on this type of cricket. Nevertheless spectators at over-limit games increasingly tend to behave like association football crowds, chanting and running on to the pitch, waving banners and so forth. Cricket, despite its ancient claim to superiority, appears to be coming to terms with the plebeian taste for tribal war-chants and with the vulgar apparatus of show business stars, agents, publicity, ballyhoo, mass media, adulation and hysteria.

Since then many of the ills of cricket have been laid at the door of one-day cricket. The effect of promoting Test cricket as Packer used to promote his one-day games produced scenes in Australia in the winter of 1982–3 which are more usually associated with football. Alderman, Australia's main strike bowler, was injured trying to tackle some unruly spectators. His absence was to have quite unforeseen, and for England, tragic cricketing consequences.

Many of the recent changes in one-day cricket have come from Australia, under the influence of Kerry Packer, the mediaman who for a time ran his own cricket matches in opposition to those of the authorities. These changes, at first resisted by English cricket, are slowly being accepted. They have, though, been accompanied by violence, or as in the Australia–New Zealand Benson & Hedges World Series Game of 1 February 1981, deeds that give an entirely new meaning to the words, 'It's not cricket.' On that day at Melbourne New Zealand arrived at the final ball of their fifty-over-a-side match needing 6 runs to tie. Greg Chappell, the Australian captain, instructed his brother Trevor to bowl the ball underarm – a form of delivery outlawed in this country. The New Zealander patted it back and then threw down his bat in disgust, which was the start of a furore that continued for months. Both the Australian and New Zealand prime ministers condemned the action, the New Zealand premier commenting that it was appropriate that the Australians wear yellow clothes for the one-day matches.

Though the Australian Board later outlawed such a ball it revealed the financial pressures of modern cricket, particularly the one-day variety where vast sums of money can depend on one ball. It also affected the *Economist,* where at that week's editorial conference its editor suggested that Australia's action should take precedence on the cover over every other international event. The *Economist*'s staff could understand such eccentric behaviour in an outwardly staid colleague only when they recollected that their editor was from New Zealand.

I must confess that my cricket upbringing – in Bombay – was based on the five- and three-day game. In fact we knew no other and the way Indian cricket was played then, the matches had a certain timeless quality. Like the Hindu epics they would go on forever, irrespective of such technicalities as who won or lost. The draw seemed a cherished Hindu goal and my earliest cricket memories are of watching Subhas Gupte, the greatest leg-spinner I have seen, match wits with Sobers, Kanhai, Butcher and others of that young but brilliant West Indian side of 1958 and the anguish at his failure to get all ten wickets in an innings.

Certainly, few sporting occasions can match the quite unique excitement of a thrilling five-day Test; the tensions slowly drawn out over the first four days produce a finish so taut as to be unbearable. And while much Test cricket appeals more to the connoisseur, a series like the 1960–61 Australia–West Indies Tests, which started with a tied match and ended with an Australian victory by two wickets, or the 1981 Ashes series in this country when Botham performed cricketing miracles, can lift peoples and nations in a way that few other events can. Mike Brearley may have been overstating the effect of the 1981 Test series when he suggested in *Phoenix from the Ashes* that the incredible results probably helped stop the riots of that summer, but there is no denying that it did reach out even to those indifferent to, or even ignorant of, cricket.

Of course the basis of the game, at the village or club level, has always been and still is one-day. A match beginning at 2 p.m., or perhaps later in high summer, would have to finish by seven or eight in the evening, evoking the sort of romance that made George Orwell describe it as a game 'where everyone plays in braces, where the blacksmith is liable to be called away in mid-innings on an urgent job, and sometimes about the time when the light begins to fail, a ball driven for four kills a rabbit on the boundary'.

A game limited not by overs but by the hours of light available, and social customs. The sort immortalized by the creations of Mary Russell Mitford, or Mr Pickwick and his fellow members of the Pickwick Club watching Dingley Dell play All-Muggleton (All-Muggleton made 54 and easily beat Dingley Dell, though we shall never know by how much). And, of course, the most famous of all fictional cricket matches in A.C. Macdonnell's *England, Their England* was a one-day match between the gentlemen of London and the Kentish village of Fordenden, which finished in a tie thanks to a remarkable catch off the last ball. Nowadays, no doubt, calculators would easily determine who had achieved the better run-rate.

Club one-day cricket has always had its own conventions. The side batting first would have to declare round teatime to provide enough time for the fielding side to bat. But this is far removed from the reality of the limited-overs one-day match that dominates our cricket season. Here the accent is not on time but on overs, and even this limitation varies considerably from competition to competition. The John Player League is restricted to forty overs for each side, and is genuinely one-day (in fact, one-afternoon). Each team in a Benson & Hedges Cup match can have fifty-five overs at the crease and, since the tournament is held at the start of the season, play often extends over the weekend into Monday. The games for the Nat West Trophy (formerly Gillette Cup) offer sixty overs a side and often have three days allocated to them. The Prudential Trophy matches between England and the respective touring teams have been played over fifty-five overs, while the Prudential World Cup is played over sixty overs.

Round the country there is now a host of such limited-overs competitions – twenty-seven, at the last count, including the North of Scotland League, the Tartan Bitter Trophy in Yorkshire, the Watney Mann Knock-Out Shield in East Anglia and the Cornwall Senior League.

Even the Orwellian village game has adopted limited overs and sponsorship. In 1972, John Haig, appropriately enough perhaps, sponsored the National Village Championship, a forty-overs affair with the finals played at Lord's. Since 1980 the sponsorship has been taken over by Samuel Whitbread and while much in this cricket would probably displease Macdonnell's hero, subaltern Donald Cameron, he could still comfort himself with the thought that some things do not change. As *Barclay's World of Cricket* recorded, with that unconscious male chauvinism that is so traditionally cricket: 'To end on a note expressive of the spirit of village cricket, in Wiltshire Mrs Amor and Mrs May have, between them, given eighty-two years of tea service to their husbands, sons, grandsons and others, in the Spye Park Pavilion.'

Club cricket, the other great bastion of the English game, has two sponsored limited-overs competitions, and even in friendly matches twenty overs must be bowled in the last hour – a regulation which, though now a Test requirement, could be identified as a spin-off of one-day cricket.

This book is not a history of all such 'one-day' competitions, since this would be both impossible to record and pointless to relate. It is an attempt to present concisely the story of this form of cricket, highlighting the major tournaments and some of their more memorable moments, as the cricketing world gears itself up for the third World Cup.

# I
# A Razor to Sharpen Cricket

We have had a highly successful experiment with one-day cricket played by first-class cricketers. Personally I feel we must tread warily in regard to future entrants but this does not prevent us from considering a small extension of the one-day match idea.

Billy Griffith, Secretary of the MCC, talking to the
County Secretaries at Lord's, 10 December 1963

Perhaps it would have all been different had a Cricket Cup really taken off in 1873. In cricket history it is the year which saw the first recorded instance of W.G. Grace scoring 1,000 runs and taking 100 wickets in a season. Yet on 9 and 10 June of that year Kent played Sussex in what the MCC had hoped would be the County Champion Cup.

The MCC had met the previous winter and thought a silver challenge cup would do much to promote county cricket. The MCC offered to bear all the expenses and initially five counties accepted. Matches had already been arranged when two of them withdrew, leaving Middlesex, Kent and Sussex. A cup tournament was clearly impossible but Kent did play Sussex at Lord's. Kent won by 52 runs before two o'clock on the second day, largely through the bowling of what *Wisden* called, a 'new and very fast bowler' named Mr Coles who 'battered and bruised several Sussex men', finally 'disabling George Humphreys' whose 32 'retired hurt by Mr Coles's bowling' was the highest Sussex score in the match. Mr Coles finished with 10 for 70. In an early exposition of cup cricket containment Wilsher, 'Kent's rare old bowler', took 4 for 16 in the first innings, bowling ten consecutive maidens, and 1 for 19 in fourteen overs in the second.

But at the time the County Championship was just being established (1873 is the commonly accepted starting date), and W.G. Grace was remaking cricket in his mould. Clearly the counties felt in no need of extra stimulus.

A cup competition is, however, intrinsically exciting, and in 1903 C.B. Fry, who had played in the 1902 FA Cup Final against Sheffield United, sent a circular letter to the counties proposing a series of matches along the lines of the FA Cup. He proposed that not less than eight first-class counties, and not more than sixteen, should take part in the first season – 1904. The tournament was to be run by a committee of management consisting of representatives from each competing county, and all matches, including the semi-finals, were to start at 11 a.m. and finish at 7 p.m. each day. Unfinished matches were to be decided by the first-innings scores. The final match was to be played to a finish on a neutral ground and, as *Wisden* recorded in 1904, '£75 shall be paid to each competing club to cover its team expenses'.

English cricket, however, was enjoying its long Edwardian summer and the recently formed Advisory County Cricket Committee showed little interest. It was not until the middle of the Second World War that the Advisory County Cricket Committee would look again at the idea of a knock-out cup. In the midst of debating how best cricket could start up after the end of the war, the thirty-seven members of the committee, including Sir Pelham Warner, Sir Julian Cahn, Stanley Jackson and H.D.G. Leveson-Gower, considered and rejected a knock-out competition. Though they did not rule out the idea, indeed the minutes indicate that they were sympathetic to it, they could see no way of holding such a competition under the 'existing method of three-day matches'. Departure from this model would mean 'innings limited by time, or number of overs', and this the committee opposed because:

(i)   It would be detrimental to the art and character of the game;
(ii)  A captain will be drawn towards placing his field and using his bowler not to take wickets, but to keep runs down. If, on the other hand, he pursues aggressive tactics, he may well be assisting his opponents.[3]

In October 1944 a sub-committee was appointed to report on the possibilities of a knock-out competition, and in June of 1945, just as the Victory Tests were getting under way, it came up with a detailed plan for the Cricket Cup which would be awarded to the winners of the four-day final held at Lord's each year. But the need for such a competition was hard to justify and three-day county cricket was now to experience its most astonishing period of health, as crowds starved of cricket for six years flocked back in large numbers. By 1947 – the golden summer of Edrich and Compton – the sub-committee's labours had been safely minuted and forgotten.

A decade later, a meeting of the Advisory Committee again considered and rejected a knock-out cup, the feeling being that there were no practical solutions for rain-ruined and other drawn games. There were some who felt such a competition might not be financially successful, and above all that it could not be meshed in with the County Championship programme. Within three years all such reservations seemed insignificant, for by then the County Championship itself was in mortal peril.

In 1947, 2,200,910 had paid to watch county cricket. In 1957 the numbers had dropped to 1,197,979, and by 1962 they were less than a million, and the trend was accelerating. Trevor Bailey, recognizing the impact of wider social changes, thought that the drop in cricket crowds owed something to the gogglebox mania, the 'national habit of car-cleaning', the attractions of learning 'to play the electric guitar' and 'other new pastimes'. Rowland Bowen, the eccentric historian of the game, who felt that the withdrawal from India meant the end of Empire and with it cricket, had, in fact, prophesied in the early fifties that 'factors such as full employment and the taxation of the well-to-do' would make the continuance of the first-class game as we knew it, and still know it, impossible.

There had been many and varied reasons for cricket's post-war popularity: the chance to catch something of the host of young pre-war players; the release from war; and the absence of alternative entertainment, at a time when television was in its infancy and the car still a luxury. But the cricket administrators had only one simple explanation: that county cricket was intrinsically popular. When the decline came, first-class cricket was not the only entertainment affected by changing social attitudes: attendances dropped at football matches, noticeably so in the third and fourth divisions, and cinemas all over the country were being converted to bingo halls.

What made it worse for cricket was its complicated structure. In addition to twenty-two, possibly twenty-four players, a whole host of people are needed to administrate a day's cricket. Furthermore counties are required to take cricket round their many grounds, accentuating the problem. Even today, much as out-station Surrey members may complain, cricket outside the Oval seldom pays for Surrey and rarely meets the recurring expense of the Oval.

Also, since membership is the lifeblood of the county clubs, members' wishes and needs predominate. In the halcyon post-war years when there was no shortage of members, county treasurers found little need to look at membership fees. Thus Yorkshire, the largest and most successful club in English cricket, saw its wage bill – traditionally increased in advance of other clubs' – treble between 1955 and 1970, yet its membership fee of two guineas was increased to three guineas only in 1958 and reached four guineas as late as 1969.

The MCC response to county cricket's decline was a series of petty changes to the laws of the game. Between 1945 and 1966 there were only three years – 1947, 1951 and 1953 – when there were no changes to the laws or the rules and conditions. They covered the entire gamut: new ball after fifty-five overs, increased two years later to sixty-five overs, and twelve years later, to eighty-five overs. In 1946 captains could declare the first innings closed only after 300 runs had been scored on the first day of a three-day match, but by 1950 they could declare at any time. The mid-fifties saw increasing concern about 'in-slant' medium-pace bowling and the first restrictions on the leg-side field. In 1960 the follow-on was abolished, only to return two years later in its old form. In 1957 all boundaries were standardized at seventy-five yards; in 1965 this was abolished. In 1963 the bowler's run-up was limited to twenty yards and in 1966 bowlers were banned from polishing the ball.

That was the year that also saw the introduction of sixty-five-over restriction in the first innings of some matches, though this never extended to all County Championship matches. Years later, when bonus points were introduced, first innings were restricted to a hundred overs (a restriction that still applies in the calculation of bonus points).

All the changes were meant to make cricket brighter and bring back the missing supporters, and they all failed. The MCC felt that there was nothing wrong with county cricket that a change of attitude would not put right. Attention focused on the first day of the three-day match. If the counties had a bright Saturday, then at least some of the crowds would come back.

The MCC were not short of advice. In 1957 the reigning England captain, Peter May, proposed that counties be abolished and replaced by zones, and the matches themselves be played over Saturday, Sunday and Monday with corresponding changes for international tours. Many thought this would not only bring the crowds back, but lift technical standards and C.L.R. James welcomed it as a means of once again linking cricket to contemporary society.

Intermittently in the fifties county clubs had used the proceeds of football pools to meet costs, following Warwickshire's example, but by 1962 Lord's could no longer avoid the question of sponsorship, and the need to do something more than pushing or pulling back the boundary line. A committee under the chairmanship of Colonel Rait-Kerr had agreed that a three-day cup was out of the question, but that a one-day cup could be feasible and at a meeting at Lord's on 20 December 1961 the Advisory Committee decided by a wafer-thin majority to inaugurate such a competition in 1963. However the fear still persisted that, although cricket's wider support may have been dwindling, as in 1873 the hard-core members might not care much for the gimmick of a limited-overs cup.

However, one young man who left the committee meeting that December night was determined to make it succeed. He was Michael Turner, then a very young Secretary of Leicestershire. He had given up playing the first-class game at a fairly young age to concentrate on administrative duties and already had made an impact on the Midland club. A study of the fixture card for 1962 showed that there was a period between 2 and 9 May when Leicestershire, Derbyshire, Northamptonshire and Nottinghamshire were without championship matches on the first two Wednesdays. The geographical proximity meant that there were no hotel expenses; and as ITV were prepared to film the first match he arranged between Leicester and Derby this not only covered all expenses but also left enough spare cash for Turner to acquire a second-hand cup and have it replated and polished by a local blacksmith.

On 2 May Leicester played Derby at Leicester, while Nottingham played Northants at Nottingham in a first round that doubled as the semi-finals of the Midlands Counties Knock-Out Cup. The cricket at Leicester could hardly have been bettered: 493 runs were scored, fifteen wickets fell and Leicester won by 7 runs. Though Leicester's defeat at the hands of Northants by five wickets in the final disappointed Turner, the competition had served its purpose.

The match had been held in characteristically cool May weather, yet it had provided just the stimulus needed to convince faint hearts that a one-day cup competition was possible. The special rules introduced for the knock-out had worked; each innings limited to sixty-five overs, no bowler to bowl more than fifteen overs (except in the final), leg-side field restricted to six men. The old fears about batsmen not playing sound strokes, or spinners proving redundant, had not come true; in the semi-final a left-arm spinner had turned the tide for Leicestershire, and Ron Roberts reporting it for *Playfair Cricket Monthly* found that 'the game's subtleties as well as its more obvious attractions were paraded, and all in all, the appearance was of first-class cricket as it is often approached on the third day, but, regrettably, not on the first'.

There was one major doubt: the attendances had been no better than mid-week championship matches in May, leading Roberts to propose a cup competition that coincided with 'late summer, when holidaymakers are out in force'. And there were other worries. What if it rained? Who would guarantee the expenses? As luck would have it, there was a commercial firm which was looking for a nice sporting outlet to smooth its own marketing problems.

Gillette, an American company that had sponsored the first base-ball series in the United States and since 1952 the Gillette Sports Show over Radio Luxembourg, had just begun to face intense competition from a new stainless steel razor blade manufactured by Wilkinson. Gillette needed something truly English to counter Wilkinson's native appeal and cricket seemed ideal. Even then, the sponsorship of the cup competition was one of those chance things that start great adventures.

In June 1962 Alan Campbell-Johnson, Gillette's PR man, and his partner were discussing with Jim Dunbar, MCC Assistant Secretary, ways in which the company could help cricket when, quite by chance, Dunbar mentioned that a one-day cup competition was being planned. For Gillette this was a Godsend and with Alan Campbell-Johnson and Gordon Ross, the company's sports consultant, acting as eager and energetic midwives, the competition easily shaped itself. The rules have changed little over the years except that the number of overs has been reduced from sixty-five to sixty, and each bowler is now allowed no more than twelve overs as opposed to fifteen in the early years.

Henry Garnett, managing director of Gillette, was aware of the susceptibilities of the traditional cricket supporters.

There were those in Gillette who thought that sponsorship of such an English game as cricket, particularly of a radical new competition, would do Gillette little good, but rather much harm. This awareness probably prompted Garnett to promise, in a letter to Billy Griffith, then Secretary of the MCC, that 'Gillette would expect to pay such promotional costs as would be incurred for the purposes of identification with the competition (purchase of trophy, printing, entertainment costs, etc.)' – a phrase that would cause a few problems.[4] Gillette were also providing £6,500 as a 'block grant' which was seen largely as insurance against possible losses due to rain or other hazards. As this was going to the administrative pool, Garnett felt that there ought to be something for the players in the shape of 'Gillette awards to the man (or men) of the match'. This was soon skilfully shaped into a Man of the Match Award, but Garnett's sponsorship terms had been so modest that in 1963 Gillette were technically sponsoring the cup not the competition. The full title, 'The First-Class Counties Knock-Out Competition for the Gillette Cup' was a mouthful both for newspaper sub-editors and the public and inevitably it was shortened to 'KO Cup'. It was only days before the 1963 final when Gordon Ross mentioned to Lord Nugent, then President of the MCC, that Gillette's only quarrel with the sponsorship was that nobody seemed to give the company any credit, and the name was changed to the one it bore till 1980 (when Nat West became the sponsors), and eventually signified a cricket revolution. The real irony was that this was brought about by a company selling razor blades when the game's patron saint, W.G. Grace, never seemed to acknowledge the existence of one.

History always sounds neater than the contemporary record, but then most cricket followers would have said the real revolution in 1963 was not the start of the Gillette Cup but the abolition of the distinction between Gentlemen and Players. The issue of *The Cricketer* that announced the draw of the 'Knock-Out Competition' featured an article by Michael Melford headlined 'Hard decision could set a fashion':

If the French habit of naming places after the dates of revolutions or momentous events were followed in this country, there would surely be a gate at Lord's known hereafter as the Porte 26 Novembre. The Advisory Committee meetings have ranged over a lot of ground in recent years but never have they reached a decision as far-reaching and seemingly irrevocable as the abolition of the amateur.

The same meeting had also announced the rules for the cup but for Melford this was, 'A novelty, generously supported by Gillette and given the flavour of excitement by the knock-out element. It may well be a success, though an immense amount depends on the luck of the draw, the weather and [how] it is . . . publicized.'

The 1963 *Wisden,* celebrating its centenary, had carried an article by John Solan, which looked forward to the 200th birthday of *Wisden.* And though the author was convinced that annual holidays to the moon would be commonplace in 2064, he saw few drastic changes in the way cricket was played. County cricket would be reduced from six days to a Saturday, Monday, Tuesday match, with the Saturday corresponding 'as closely as cricket ever can to the urgency and excitement of the big football arenas', Test cricket would remain unaltered, and the cricketer would return from his 2064 moon jaunt to oil his bat pining:

> for a return to the 'old lbw law' if he is a leg-spinner, and executing in his mind's eye, the drive past 'old-fashioned point'. He will be the only sporting figure in the world, or in outer space, to be dressed in long trousers and, in moments of introspection, will be harbouring dark thoughts that cricket is not what it was.

So, the Gillette Cup arrived quietly, almost surreptitiously, on 30 April. The first match pitted Lancashire against Leicestershire at Old Trafford on a bitterly cold, damp, disagreeable day. Frank Woolley, the adjudicator for the Man of the Match Award, sat for two days behind the bowler's arm well covered in sweater, overcoat, scarf and gloves. The match, which was interrupted by rain after lunch on the first day, finished on the second with a comfortable Lancashire victory. Despite this, J.L. Manning's fears of a beer-and-skittles game were dispelled, and man of the match Peter Marner scored a century in 109 minutes displaying a technique that would hardly have disgraced three-day cricket.

Yet for the players and spectators this was still a thing that you treated with care. Mammon had fathered the competition and in that first year, in order to keep costs down, players generally stayed with committee members or friends. Trevor Bailey, leading his beloved Essex against Lancashire at Old Trafford, recalls arriving at Altrincham police station shortly after midnight after what was a long drive in those pre-motorway days. He was met by Geoffrey Howard, the Lancashire Secretary, and some of the side. They were then ferried to various homes for the night which 'may not have been the ideal preparation for a vital knock-out game but it saved money, which after all was the main object at that time'.

The competition proper, as it were, began on 22 May and produced, at Cardiff and Bournemouth, just the sort of result this type of cricket needed: victory for Glamorgan by 10 runs with two overs left; victory for Derbyshire by 6 runs with three balls left. The more significant match, at least tactically, was played between Kent and Sussex at Tunbridge Wells. It was attended by perhaps the most impressive cricket notables to be collected on one ground: Lord Nugent, President of the MCC; the Duke of Norfolk, manager of the previous winter's tour to Australasia, and his assistant, Alec Bedser; the captain on the tour, Ted Dexter, and his vice-captain, Colin Cowdrey. Led by a Suttle century, Sussex made 314, and though Peter Richardson made 127, Kent were in the end rather easily beaten by 72 runs. But the real significance lay in the early realization by Ted Dexter of the tactics to be employed in this sort of cricket.

Dexter had reasoned that no particular heroics were called for when batting and his advice to his batsmen was not to treat this as a cross between a benefit game and a slogging match with sixes flying all over the place. His bowling tactics were to an extent dictated by his resources: Thomson, Bates, Buss, Snow and Dexter himself, all right-arm-over bowlers varying from quick to quickish medium pace. Thomson was a master of line, length and control and regularly took 100 wickets a season; Buss was more dangerous than he appeared, while Bates, Snow and Dexter were all able to bowl with the routine that the competition required. Dexter had not been impressed with the pre-competition theory in the air that the best way to contain the batsmen would be to bowl down the leg-side or wide of the off stump.

He instructed his bowlers to aim at the wickets all the time, bowling to a field with a man close in on the off side, a third man fine for the 'nick' and five on the leg side. The batsman would not be able to pick runs off his legs, but would have to make room on the off side to score, a difficult thing for most right-handers to do. In the match against Kent, as Richardson began to get into the groove and play 'quite wonderfully', Dexter gave him a single and bowled tightly to the other batsmen. Such tactics are very common nowadays, but then the emphasis was very much on providing excitement and Cowdrey, who had been more conventional in his approach, agreed with the Kent crowd (who had been booing Dexter) that the England captain's tactics were 'not entertainment'.

But they worked, and this was the first victory in a remarkable Sussex run that would see them unbeaten till 23 June 1965 when

Middlesex vanquished them by 90 runs. Interestingly, they fell chasing a target – only the second time in their first ten games that they had done so. The first eight of their nine Gillette victories had come after batting first. This gave Dexter additional satisfaction for it upset one of the cherished theories advanced most noticeably by Trevor Bailey, already established as the thinking player's guru. For one of his 'random thoughts' before the competition began had been that, 'In these cup matches there is much in favour of inserting the opposition on both good and bad wickets, and I expect this to become standard practice as is often the case in club cricket.' Later, when Lancashire replaced Sussex as Gillette kings, they often preferred to bat second, though in a side of their strength it would not have made much difference.

Crowds had averaged around 2,000 for the first round, but it was three weeks later when Sussex met Yorkshire at Hove that the competition attracted the sort of crowds that made the sponsors happy. Gordon Ross, Gillette's historian, would later see it as the moment Gillette arrived on the cricket scene: 15,000 people packing Hove to watch the match against the reigning champions, Yorkshire, in an atmosphere evocative of the best of the FA Cup matches. The match was played with waves of sea mist sweeping over the ground all day, on which surprisingly Trueman failed to capitalize (0 for 40 after fourteen overs). Though Close took 4 for 60, Sussex's 292 seemed enough, especially when Yorkshire were 100 for 4. Then a certain Geoffrey Boycott, who had made his modest debut the previous season, albeit playing only four innings, came in. Though support from the others was patchy, Boycott's excellent strokeplay kept the Tykes in the hunt and only when he was run out in the sixty-second over for 71 out of 262 for 9, did Hove feel secure.

After a commanding century by Dexter – the only one he hit in the competition – and a 160-run stand in ninety-five minutes with Parks produced an easy victory over Northants, Sussex met Worcestershire in the final. The Midland county's batting, led by Tom Graveney, and their bowling, spearheaded by Jack Flavell, had proved too much for Surrey, Glamorgan and Lancashire by wide margins. The final promised much that was fascinating: the power of Dexter against the elegance of Graveney, the tight seam of Buss and Thomson in contrast to the genuinely quick Flavell (whose 101 wickets in eighteen matches effectively won Worcestershire the championship in 1964). In the event, the principals did little. Dexter made 3, Graveney 29, and though

Flavell took 2 for 31, it was the spin of Horton and Gifford, who ultimately won the Man of the Match Award, that kept Sussex within bounds.

In subsequent years the final always seemed to fall on one of the best days of late summer, leading to much talk about Gillette weather, but 7 September 1963 was grey and cold and rain was an ever-present threat. The previous day a match between Derbyshire and Middlesex had been abandoned at twelve o'clock with pools of water on the turf. The pitch was soft, and Sussex, batting first, did not find it easy to score quickly – or in quantity. Dexter's belief that a good start – 62 for 1 – leads to better things was not borne out and only a characteristic 57 by Parks took them to 168. Worcester, required to get 2.5 runs an over, were odds-on favourites, and Alec Bedser was quite convinced they would win. So it seemed at 80 for 2, but Dexter for the first time in these matches began to use his spinners. Oakman, coming on as first change, bowled thirteen overs for 17 runs and the wicket of Graveney, and Worcestershire were caught in the now-familiar one-day vice: as you fall behind the clock you try hard to get abreast of it; the harder you try the more wickets you lose, and eventually you fall foul of the overs/runs equation.

But as in all good cup competitions, there was a twist. At 133 for 9 Worcester looked dead. Then Booth was joined by Carter and in light drizzle and darkness so intense that one cricket writer would call it 'cricket in the deep of the night', Booth and Carter inched the Midlands side back. They had added 19 for the last wicket, and the fielders were all on the boundary when, going for a second run, Carter was run out.

The choice of the man of the match proved a further complication, for the two adjudicators – Herbert Sutcliffe and Frank Woolley – could not agree whether Parks or Gifford should get it; eventually, helped by the advice of the Duke of Norfolk, it was Gifford who climbed the steps on to the platform (specially designed to make the presentations more like Wembley) to accept his piece of gold. Gordon Ross had had Wembley much on his mind when planning the Gillette Cup and his overall concept met with the approval of Peter Wilson in the *Daily Mirror*:

A year ago, anyone suggesting that, on a cold, damp September Saturday afternoon, Lord's, the temple of tradition, could be transformed into a reasonable replica of Wembley on its Cup Final Day, would have been sent post haste to the nearest psychiatrist's couch. Yet that's what happened – a sell-out with rosettes, singing, cheers and counter jeers. Plus a hark-away on a Worcestershire hunting horn when England and Sussex captain Ted Dexter was dismissed by a fine diving slip catch by Broadbent.

Not everybody was so convinced. This was Sussex's first triumph in any class of cricket for 140 years and Jim Pegg, very much a traditional Sussex supporter, had come to the final more out of county loyalty than from the prospect of seeing good cricket. To him this sort of competition was still a bit of fun on the side – rather than proper cricket – and he was all the more convinced of it after the final. Both the nascent football-style atmosphere and the appalling playing conditions had made him feel that he was in terrain foreign to cricket.

But apart from the similarities with a Wembley occasion, there had been two other pointers to the future. Dexter, caught by a diving Broadbent at slip, had stood his ground and only gone after given out by the umpire; then in his victory speech he had praised his own team but said not a word about the rivals. Both incidents indicated to some how quickly cricket had begun to accept the ethos of football.

The competition, however, was considered a great success – as indeed it had been – and by the winter of 1963 all sorts of teams saw themselves as the Yeovil Town or the Enfield of cricket: Minor Counties, Scotland, Ireland, the Services, Universities, even the Lancashire Leagues, which with the wealth of overseas talent could undoubtedly have mounted a major challenge. But though MCC were happy to admit a few of the Minor Counties, the competition was meant to shore up the coffers of the major ones, and, since the moneys coming in were sliced up per county according to the number of rounds it played, more teams meant somebody had to put in more money. Gillette offered an extra £1,500 to allow five Minor Counties to compete and in 1964 Wiltshire, Durham, Hertfordshire, Cheshire and Cambridgeshire, once a great cricketing power in the land, took part.

The early start to the Gillette in those days – first-round matches were sometimes played by the last week of April – and the peculiarities of the draw often led first-class opposition to destroy each other while minor counties survived to prosper to the later rounds – till they met a first-class county. This caused some chagrin, and in 1964 Don Kenyon, the Worcestershire captain, was particularly upset that the very first match of the competition that year saw his team beaten by Glamorgan by one wicket, almost a week before the start of the first-class season.

Kenyon's only consolation was his part in one of the most exhilarating finishes of the season, even if, as Gordon Ross commented, 'the game wasn't real cricket'. There had been heavy overnight rain at Neath, the mud in the outfield came over the welts of the shoes, there was rain during the day, and it was cold enough for fires to be lit in the dressing rooms.

Though many of the matches produced interesting results, the early ones were more noted for curiosities. In the Yorkshire–Middlesex match at Lord's Yorkshire had to requisition the services of their scorer, Ted Lister, to take the place of John Hampshire who had been taken ill following an anti-tetanus injection.

Two of the best matches of 1964 took place at Taunton. Somerset and Notts produced the first tie of the competition and one of those results when cricket turns to mathematics to solve its problems. Nottinghamshire made 217, almost wholly due to a brilliant 107 by Maurice Hill in just under two hours. Somerset, after beginning well, fell away and still required 4 to win with one wicket in hand, when Bomber Wells began the last over. The first ball produced a near run-out and a single; the next three were kept out – just. The fifth was snicked for a single, and then off the last Langford scored a single sending Somerset through because they had lost nine wickets, while Notts had been bowled out. Just about a month later, Somerset promised even bigger things against Sussex. Nine thousand spectators were packed in, some of whom had been queueing to get in for two hours. They saw Geoff Hall and Fred Rumsey rout Sussex in ideal bowling conditions: a pitch that was fast and still had some early-morning dew and heavy cloud cover. Dexter, with his usual luck, won the toss and batted. He was bowled by Hall for 6: Sussex, from 29 for 4, stuttered to 141. But Somerset could do little better and despite 54 by Virgin, they were bowled out for 125 by Bates, 4 for 28, and Snow, 3 for 28.

This was, perhaps, just a hiccough for the champions, for Sussex fairly steamrollered their way through the semi-finals, beating Surrey by 90 runs. In the final they defeated Warwickshire by eight wickets in one of the most one-sided finals ever, helped by the fact that when Warwickshire batted Ian Thomson swung the ball so much that the match was decided by lunchtime.

Finals rarely live up to the occasion, though Gillette, on the whole, had more good finals than most other competitions. But the inequality of the 1964 match was all the more surprising, given that it pitted Dexter against another England captain, M.J.K. Smith, a man who had acquired a reputation for having mastered the art of one-day cricket. In the process he had also acquired the sort of notoriety that was never far from instant cricket. At the end of July, Warwickshire were involved in a semi-final with Lancashire that has been described by Gordon Ross as 'highlighting one of the worst faces of one-day cricket'.

M.J.K. Smith, who thinks his rather improvised style of batting was particularly suited to this new form of cricket, had given some thought to tactics. Unlike some of the traditionalists, Smith had welcomed the innovation. He had seen how county cricket had atrophied. 'When I started playing first-class cricket, by the end of May most sides did not have a cat-in-hell's chance of winning the championship and if you were not competing for a place in the England side, then you just played out the season rather peacefully, almost ritually.'

The new game reminded him of the fourth innings of a three-day championship match, except, of course, it happened on the first day. The side batting first need not go too quickly, since a good start meant you could always get runs by crash, bang and wallop. As it happened, in 1963 Warwickshire, in their very first match, did go crash, bang, wallop and lost, though Smith could claim that injury deprived his side of his guiding hand. In the 1964 semi-final against Lancashire, Smith was very much in evidence and his one-day ideas were put to the test – with some unexpected results.

Warwickshire, who reckoned runs in hand were worth more than two in the chase, won the toss and batted, making 294 for 7. Lancashire, led by their young openers Green and Worsley, had made 60 for no wicket in the first ten overs when Smith decided to dispense with the more conventional field and move back to the strategically defensive field positions, with one man in front of the wicket saving one, but a deep point, deep extra and deep mid-wicket and three others on the boundary. The Warwickshire bowlers were instructed to pitch it up straight and M.J.K. Smith recalls, 'The intention was to put pressure on, so that they didn't hit fours. It caused a lot of fuss at that time. Quite honestly, if you saw the television replay today, nobody would raise an eyebrow about the field-setting.'

But for Lancashire it was a disaster: they slid to 161 for 5, needing 134 from twenty overs. The light had deteriorated and the new batsman, the Lancashire wicket-keeper, Clayton, appealed against it. When this failed, Clayton decided there was nothing left to play for and, in the words of a contemporary report, 'took it upon himself to flout all cricketing tradition and conventions and ignore the enthusiasm of a very large and happy crowd by stubbornly defending to pick up 19 runs in three-quarters of an hour'. He even refused Harry Pilling's calls for easy singles at the other end. 'Slow hand-clapping developed into stormy booing and amid a welter of unpleasant barracking, the match fizzled out into a disgraceful exhibition of bad cricketing manners. There can be no excuse for Clayton unless he was acting under instructions.'

One Lancastrian actually ran on to the pitch to remonstrate with Clayton, and when the Lancashire wicket-keeper returned to the pavilion he found the committee in an unforgiving mood. He was dropped for the following match against Yorkshire and at the end of the season sacked. The committee argued that his retention 'was not in the best interests of the playing staff of the club'. Though Herbert Sutcliffe awarded the Man of the Match Award to M.J.K. Smith, he gently wigged him for having six men on the boundary. The Warwickshire committee did not view Smith's part in the affair quite so seriously and in fact supported their captain. *The Cricketer* magazine headlined its report, 'To Warwickshire the end justifies the means.' Cricket still had not come to terms with the right tactics to be adopted – spinners in those early matches often bowled the final overs – and crowds were yet to accept that defensive field-placings were integral to this type of cricket. They still saw cup cricket in terms of the FA Cup where teams often raise their drab league performances.

It was another M.J.K. Smith fielding innovation that was to have equally far-reaching consequences – and further fuel the cricketing rivalry between England and Australia. On 20 August 1972 Middlesex met Warwickshire in a middle-of-the-table John Player League clash. Warwickshire, through a vigorous 44 by Smith and an explosive 60 by Kanhai, made 182 off forty overs. Middlesex made a good start but then in deteriorating light fell behind until they required 11 at the start of the final over, and 4 off the last ball. Before this ball was bowled, Smith pulled all the fielders – including the wicket-keeper, but barring the bowler, of course – on the boundary line. Middlesex could get only 2 and lost by one run. By then the crowds in this country – even the ones at Lord's, were used to one-day tactics but for Mike Brearley, the Middlesex captain, this seemed worthy of note.

On 28 November 1979 England met West Indies in the first of a series of one-day triangular international matches that have been a feature of Australian cricket ever since Packer and the cricket authorities made their peace in the summer of 1979. England had rarely beaten the West Indies but with resolute batting and some luck – the West Indies were batting under floodlights, and their innings was interrupted by rain – they appeared to have created a splendid opportunity. When the final over began West Indies still needed 10 to win with just one wicket in hand. Garner got 5 off the first four deliveries, Croft 2 from the next, and requiring 4 to win from the last ball, Brearley recalled Smith's 1972 Lord's field. As Botham prepared to bowl, Brearley sent everybody back on the fence, including Bairstow, the wicker-keeper, and Croft, attempting a six, was bowled. England had beaten the world champions.

Throughout the match – indeed throughout that series – Australians had vociferously supported the West Indians and Australian children used to run on to the pitch to celebrate West Indian achievements, a sight that was ironic in the light of Australia's own racist past. Brearley's field confirmed the old Australian fears and prejudices about the 'Poms'. Brearley and England bore the brunt of criticism for what were considered unsporting tactics and the next day the *Sydney Sun* ran a story about the match under the headline: 'Poms sabotage series.'

As it happened, Mike Smith did not rightfully claim the Gillette Cup until the summer of 1966 when Warwickshire beat Worcestershire by five wickets in another low-scoring final dominated by the bowling of Tom Cartwright and the batting of Bob Barber. This former Lancashire opener was the first of several players who found one-day cricket a useful catalyst for changing his style. Originally rather stodgy, getting his runs mainly from deflections and nudges, and rarely from the aesthetically pleasing front-of-the-wicket strokes, his one-day experiences made him one of the most attractive batsmen of his day, and Mike Smith is convinced that limited-overs cricket played its part in that.

Warwickshire, of course, should have contested the 1965 final but failed to reach it because of a series of suicidal run-outs in the semi-final against Yorkshire. At that stage, the major shocks of the 1965 Gillette had been the dethroning by Middlesex of Sussex, for the first time in the competition, and Fred Trueman's confidence to Gordon Ross that he had misplaced the cheque of £50 awarded to him as man of the match for 6 for 15 against Somerset at Taunton – a revelation that quite shocked Ross. In the Yorkshire–Warwickshire semi-final play did not begin until the third day, a Friday. Close won the toss and chose to bat. Yorkshire reached a disastrous 85 for 6 and though they recovered to 177, at tea Warwickshire were 64 for 1 and it looked all over. Close would not concede defeat and decided to bring his spinners on. They bowled in the tight, mean fashion Close expected of them, but more significant was the quality of Warwickshire running. As Don Kenyon said afterwards, they ran like 'a lot of little prep-school boys'. From 64 for 1 they slid to 97 for 5, after four run-outs of amazing stupidity, and never recovered.

Yorkshire's opponents in the final, Surrey, had come through a semi-final at the Oval which had earned ringing plaudits from *The Times*. Its cricket correspondent, sheltering under pre-Thomson anonymity, wrote: 'One of the best and most dashing games of cricket seen at the Oval for many a day ended on a golden evening with Surrey beating Middlesex. A crowd of 8,000 had watched a game crowded with challenging strokes and virile fielding and adventurous running between wickets.'

A total of 502 runs had been scored and both Middlesex and Surrey had hit furiously, with Surrey's Edwards making 53 and putting on 92 in ten overs with Barrington deservedly to win the Man of the Match Award.

The final was again disappointingly one-sided. But it will be remembered as the final in which Geoffrey Boycott played what is still reckoned to be the greatest single innings in a final, and possibly of his own career. There are two photographs that illustrate the innings. One shows Boycott swinging Sydenham hard and high to leg: the short leg has just taken evasive action, slip and wicket-keeper are just beginning to register amazement; the second, taken just after he reached his century, shows Close whispering mid-pitch congratulations in Boycott's right ear: a slow blush seems to form on the callow features. Yet the irony was that Boycott may never have had the chance but for Billy Griffith's prodding and the help of the entire Oval ground staff, specially requisitioned to augment the Lord's men.

For twenty-four hours before the match the rain had been so incessant and heavy that Gordon Ross was convinced there could be no play on the Saturday. He advised Reg Simpson, the adjudicator, not to bother to travel up from Nottingham. But Simpson heard on the radio while shaving that Saturday morning that the MCC expected play before lunch. He set off immediately for Lord's, where the ground was being so heavily layered with sawdust that Ian Peebles was to feel he had come to a Bertram Mills circus rather than a cricket match. In the committee rooms, Billy Griffith was twisting the arms of the two captains, Brian Close and Micky Stewart. The umpires thought play might begin after teatime but, when the captains emerged from Griffith's study, a twelve o'clock start was announced.

Stewart, fully aware of his success in chasing Middlesex's semi-final total, was confident that the pitch would not become difficult (which it did not), and that the outfield would progressively dry out and help his batsmen. He put Yorkshire in.

The plan seemed to be working. In July Surrey had beaten Yorkshire in a county match, won effectively by David Sydenham's bowling. He had taken 7 for 32 in Yorkshire's first innings of 147 and Yorkshire had never recovered. At Lord's in September Boycott and Ken Taylor seemed haunted by that memory and just could not get Sydenham away. Doug Padgett suggested to Close that he ought to pad up and go in next to show the way. Almost immediately Taylor was out – with the score at 22 – and Close joined Boycott. After surviving a snick between first and second slips when on 3, Close got Boycott to take quick singles. Then he suggested Boycott should play some of his strokes. What followed was a revelation to him: 'No one had ever seen anything like it from Boycott. He was hitting the off-spinner over mid-wicket and long-on. Over mid-wicket and long-on: how often do you see Geoffrey hit shots like that, twelve or thirteen years later? At that time no one had ever seen him do it.'[5]

When Close was out at 214 for 2, Boycott had played in such a fashion that John Woodcock among many was 'startled' by his performance. In just three and a half hours he made 146 with three sixes and fifteen fours. He was helped by the fact that Stewart kept up attacking fields, and even when Yorkshire were 200 for 1 he had a slip, a short leg and a mid-wicket in a fairly orthodox position. But on that day any tactics Stewart might have tried were just as likely to fail – and after Yorkshire had scored 317 for 4, Surrey folded.

John Woodcock, pleased that Surrey's medium-paced attack had been thrashed and that Yorkshire's magnificent style had 'made the day-to-day approach seem careworn and unnecessary', hoped that:

The Boycott who fastens his seat-belt at London airport next week [for England's 1965–66 tour of Australia and New Zealand] is the same man who made 146 against Surrey and who won the award as man of the match. It is quite likely that Boycott will open England's innings for a decade to come. The prospect of his doing so in his ascetic mood is hard to entertain. If prepared, as at Lord's, to chance his arm, he would give far greater pleasure to others as well as himself.

Though Surrey would soon learn new one-day tricks, Boycott, alas, would forget the lessons of 1965 – and only in the winter of 1979–80, facing the jibes of the Australians, and even some sceptical Englishmen, did he reproduce some of that vintage '65 wine. Driving Lillee and Thomson in front of the wicket – the most effective answer to a fast bowler – with great panache, he gave fitting answer to the Australian banners that mocked that watching Boycott was like going to a funeral. But he had left it so late that many felt he was trying to clothe a ghost.

The 1967 cricket season was considered one of the poorest of recent years. *Wisden* found it could report no improvement on the 'general low standard of batting and bowling' in the championship, or even a welcome change in the attitude of the players. The Indians, the first visitors of the dual-tour summer, suffered the wettest May since 1773, and despite the efforts of their captain, the Nawab of Pataudi, never really got going. While the Pakistanis had better luck with the weather, their performances were not all that much better. Asif Iqbal did, however, play one of those exhilarating innings that would have won many a one-day match – an innings moreover in a lost cause, so endearing to cricketers and their followers. He went out to bat in the third Test at the Oval when Pakistan were 53 for 7 requiring another 167 to make England bat again; the talk all round him was of arranging a twenty-over exhibition match to compensate the Monday crowd. He saw Pakistan lose another wicket then took charge in such a spectacular fashion that in three hours, ten minutes he made 146 out of 202 with two sixes and twenty-one fours. Pakistan still lost but Iqbal wrote himself indelibly into English cricket history. Later, playing for Kent, he would play many wonderful innings, almost winning them a Gillette Cup some years later, but nothing matched this performance.

No innings in the 1967 Gillette Cup was of this quality. However, the competition had many exciting finishes, including an astonishing Surrey collapse at the Oval, and a thrice-arranged match that was finally played as a ten–over thrash in the mud and rain of a Yorkshire League ground. That game pointed up the difference between the Gillette Cup and the rest of cricket: the competition had acquired a distinct character because cup matches must be played to a finish, regardless of whatever else happened in the championship and the Tests.

Yorkshire had been due originally to play Cambridgeshire at Bradford on 13 May. But the players had little luck with the weather and for the next three days they amused themselves in the traditional fashion with cards while Park Avenue filled with rain. The match was rearranged a few days later for Headingley, but the ground was flooded the night before play by a violent thunderstorm. It was decided to try one of the Yorkshire League grounds and the groundsman at Castleford – more famous for its rugby league team – assured the organizers that a start would be possible at two o'clock. The adjudicator had just walked out to the Castleford pitch when a violent thunderstorm flooded it and even fused the lights in the pavilion. The groundsman, however, was determined not to miss this tale of a lifetime – that he had prepared the wicket on which mighty Yorkshire had played – and despite yet more rain a ten-overs-a-side match began at four o'clock. Trueman bowled the first ball, David Fairey hooked it for six and one of the most bizarre cricket matches was under way. The amateurs of Cambridgeshire, living up to their billing as farmers, slogged their way to 43 for 8 and when Yorkshire had reached the score with four wickets down, the players of Cambridgeshire left the field looking, Gordon Ross recorded, 'like Spurs coming off the pitch on a wet day at White Hart Lane in November'.

If the rest of the Gillette season did not produce anything quite as bizarre, it did provide a final whose colour and atmosphere would make it a most memorable occasion – and give proof of the revival of a once great county. Until 1967 Kent had done little in this competition. In fact, their only victory had been against minnows Suffolk in 1966. So sorry was their state that when they lost to Hampshire in the next round, Robin Marlar, in his usual pugnacious fashion, wrote that Kent 'have now become the sick man of Gillette. Suffolk, minor in cricket if in nothing else, have been their only victims these last four years. This must hurt.'

A county with such a proud heritage could not suffer such agonies for long and in 1967 they fashioned the first of many winning cup teams. In Luckhurst and Denness they had one of the best opening pairs in the country, Underwood was already rewriting some of the Kent bowling records, Knott was inviting comparisons with Godfrey Evans, and Dixon, a skilful all-rounder, could switch easily from seam to off-spin (his seam-bowling destroyed Surrey in the second round). They were supplemented by the considerable talents of the West Indian, John Shepherd, in many ways the ideal one-day cricketer.

And while the Yorkshire and Cambridgeshire players were watching the rain at Bradford, Kent in the semi-darkness of Brentford (the match finished at quarter past eight) recorded their first win over a first-class county in the Gillette: they defeated Essex by 42 runs. If Dixon with 7 for 57 was the Kent hero against Surrey in the next round – Surrey collapsed from 31 for no wicket to 74 all out – the semi-finals confirmed a new one-day county power. In front of 16,500 at Canterbury, which was looking as delectably traditional as only that ground can, Colin Cowdrey effectively won the match. Coming in after Luckhurst and Shepherd had laid the foundation with an 135-run second-wicket stand, Cowdrey made 78 in only eighteen overs and might have had even more but for some fine fielding by Sussex. A target of 294 was always going to be difficult and became quite impossible once Sussex had lost their first three wickets for 27 runs.

The Cowdrey innings had wider repercussions. For Cowdrey had not been picked for the summer's three Tests against India, or the first against Pakistan. This innings earned from Alec Bedser, adjudicator and chairman of the selectors, the Man of the Match Award and three weeks later Cowdrey returned to the England side. The tale does not quite finish there. For at the end of that summer Close, who had looked good as England captain for many more years, had another of his famous brushes with authority, this time over delaying tactics used against Warwickshire in a championship match. He was selected, then sacked, as England captain and Cowdrey took the side to the West Indies – a turn of events that could hardly have been expected in mid-July. Close would later claim that he thought the knives were out the moment he heard Cowdrey was back. Ironically, three years later in another one-day competition – the John Player League – Cowdrey would damage his Achilles tendon, rule himself out for much of the 1969 summer and lose the captaincy to Ray Illingworth – starting another saga in English cricket.

Though *Wisden* christened the 1967 final the 'best of all the five final ties' it was more notable for its colour, the clash of two teams that had never won the competition, for what Gordon Ross called 'the sheer joy of it', than its cricket. Some of this joy, no doubt, was due to the sight of Sir Alec Douglas-Home, then President of the MCC, presenting the Gillette Cup to M.C. Cowdrey for whom the English cricketing public have long had the sort of delicious, yet infuriating, love that the English cinema reserves for, say, Susannah York.

Somerset touched different chords. The county revels in its West Country yokel status (this is not meant unkindly) and among the 20,000 crowd at Lord's that day were Somerset supporters complete with pitchforks, straw and barrels of cider. The days before the final the bars and pubs round Taunton rang with cheerful Somerset songs: 'Drink up thy zider. Vor tonight we'll merry be. We've knocked the milk churns over. An' rolled 'em in the clover. The corn's half cut and so be we.' A group of them thus equipped were photographed marching purposefully around Lord's and it seemed to do the heart of cricket a world of good. As if to suggest, 'Well, they might not win, but isn't it good to see them here at the headquarters?'

Not that Somerset disgraced themselves. Kent, having won the toss, got away to a great start, but were then pegged back; though their total of 193 was the second highest in the final at that time, Somerset looked capable of scoring 3.21 an over to win. More so, when they had reached 50 for no wicket, but they were up against one-day specialist bowlers like Underwood and Shepherd, assisted by some wonderful fielding. In the end the Kent victory was more comfortable than the margin of 32 runs suggested.

The final reflected another theme that would become more prominent in years to come: a single county attempting the 'double': winning both the cup and the championship. In 1966 Worcestershire had played in the final, on the day after losing the championship to Yorkshire. Now Kent spent the week after their victory awaiting the result of the match between Yorkshire and Gloucestershire at Harrogate. Yorkshire won and Kent had to be content with being runners-up, their highest position since 1928.

The 1967 final also marked another turning-point, for in some ways it was the first final in which an overseas star played a significant part. The West Indian all-rounder John Shepherd had scored 30 and, despite a damaged hamstring muscle, taken 2 for 27 in twelve overs, to become a worthy contender for man of the match. From 1968, as English cricket relaxed its rule prohibiting overseas cricketers from playing county cricket, many more established overseas players became associated with one-day cricket.

The 1968 season itself began with intense speculation about the effect Gary Sobers would have on Nottinghamshire. Though it is fashionable nowadays to blame the importation of overseas stars as much as one-day cricket for all the ills of the English game, in the late sixties there was almost unanimous agreement about the need for overseas players. The two West Indian visits of 1963 and 1966 had produced some marvellous cricket, drawing large crowds. It was believed that a Sobers or Kanhai on display six days a week would do much to restore the prestige and the authority of the domestic county season. As the editor of *Wisden* put it in 1968:

> This bold move could be the salvation of the three-day County Championship and I am only surprised that the plunge was not taken sooner. The numerous provisos safeguard the welfare of English-born players and the very fact that a heavy responsibility will now rest upon the star cricketer should help the promising youngster to take his place in first-class company without the worry that any temporary failure will weigh heavily against the side.

The 'Big Prize', as *Wisden* put it, was Sobers. Seven counties vied for him, before Nottinghamshire, who had not won a county match in 1967, announced he was not only to join them but also lead them. (He was not the first overseas player at Trent Bridge, for the Australian Bruce Dooland had been a prominent member of the fifties sides.)

The prospects for Sobers could hardly have been less inviting. For the 1968 summer was one of the wettest and worst cricket has ever experienced. Mike Proctor was photographed wielding a bat on an April snow carpet in Bristol and the story of the summer was summed up in the memorable scene from the Oval at lunchtime on the last day of the final Test against the Australians: Cowdrey, hands in pocket, gazing wistfully at the lake that had formed at the Oval following the thunderstorm. That story had a happier ending, and for a time Sobers, too, promised miracles at Trent Bridge.

In the first round of the Gillette against Lancashire, he took a wicket before conceding a run, and finished with 3 for 28, helping bowl out Lancashire for 168. Then with 75 not out he saw Notts to victory.

The second round was hit so badly by the weather that five of the eight matches did not start, and it was mid-June before Sober-shire (as Notts had been christened) played their match against Worcestershire. Again the hero followed the script faultlessly. Notts, batting first, lost 3 for 29. In walked Sobers and scored 95 not out in a final score of 226. Then he took three wickets in two spells without conceding a run, first with the help of Frost to reduce Worcestershire to 6 for 3, then breaking a threatening stand between Graveney and Hemsley, and finally dismissing the aggressive Booth. Not surprisingly he won the Man of the Match Award for the second time in succession, and arguably might have done so for a record third successive time when Notts met Gloucestershire in the quarter-final.

Though Gloucester had acquired the South African Mike Proctor they had not yet become Proctorshire. But that day his 53 in just half an hour was as explosive an innings as any seen in the Gillette, and consolidated the splendid start provided by David Green and Arthur Milton in a 164-run partnership of which Green made a vigorous 90. A target of 297 seemed beyond even Sobers, more so when Proctor helped reduce Notts to 78 for 3. But, helped by Smedley, Sobers put on 114 in twenty-one overs 'in a sparkling display of controlled hitting'. At 224 however, both fell and when the end came Notts were still 25 short. Cyril Washbrook named Green as the man of the match, though in his view almost everybody was a winner – he would remain convinced that it was greatest Gillette match he had seen.

Just two weeks later Rohan Kanhai, Sobers's colleague, and in some respects his great rival, was steering Warwickshire to their fourth semi-final in five years. The Midlands side, too, had acquired West Indian stars in Kanhai and Gibbs, and Kanhai might have felt that only Alec Bedser's well-known prejudice towards bowlers stopped him getting a second successive Man of the Match Award for his 53 against Middlesex in the semi-finals. The match was meant to start on 7 August, but rain held it up for a week. In the event Warwickshire won a low-scoring match by three wickets. Bedser gave the award to Middlesex bowler Hooker who took 4 for 20 and made 43 not out – one of the growing number of capable losers to be awarded some compensation.

The final against Sussex was a repeat of 1964, though this time the hero was a very unlikely candidate and the villain, rather more predictably, was television. Though Sussex no longer had the aura of invincibility that cloaked them in the early days they were still, on paper, a formidable side, and apart from a quarter-final scare against Northants (when they won by 7 runs with ten balls left) they had progressed smoothly enough to the finals. Much of the old team remained and although Thomson, after a wonderful career, was difficult to replace, Tony Greig had begun to show his undoubted promise and John Snow was at the peak of his talents.

The problem, as so often in team games, was leadership. Dexter's withdrawal from the captaincy had led to a succession of interim captains including Jim Parks and the Nawab of Pataudi before Mike Griffith, son of Billy, took over. Dexter, looking back, feels that 'under Mike Griffith cricketing discipline did slip', though he is not inclined to blame him overmuch for what happened at Lord's that day, arguing that in one-day cricket the tail-ender is often the equal of the class batsman. John Snow, whose name had often been linked with the players' revolt in the late sixties, was convinced that the Sussex committee had made a dreadful mistake in preferring Griffith to Buss, a carpenter's son and not 'part of the Sussex syndrome', as Griffith was:

> I had nothing against Mike. I'd spent many a pleasant evening with him before his appointment but I would have preferred Tony purely on cricketing grounds. In talking to him I never felt Mike had the type of cricketing brain a captain requires. He showed very little tactical flair and lacked vision. He did not understand the way people played, the fields required, or which bowlers were best for certain situations, and could not assess the way a game was shaping. The events in the Gillette Cup final that summer seemed to prove me right.

For a long time, in fact, things seemed to be going Sussex's way. Though Dexter made only 3, Parks (57) and Tony Greig (41) helped Sussex total 214 for 7 against a Warwickshire attack which, lacking Cartwright and Bannister, had to use twelve overs of Amiss at a cost of 63 runs. With Barber making 15 and Kanhai 3, Warwickshire, despite 59 by Stewart, seemed to have left themselves too much to do at 155 for 6. They still required 60 in thirteen overs, and only Amiss of the recognized batsmen was left, when captain Alan Smith came out to join him. It was here that John Snow's worst fears started to come true:

> He [Smith] started to hit out boldly, slicing the ball repeatedly over and through the covers . . . We helped him considerably by not setting the right field or using the right bowlers in an effort to contain him. It was a clear indication of Mike's lack of understanding of the way batsmen played and inability to assess the way the game was shaping.[6]

Most people reckoned Smith would hold one end up and leave the scoring to Amiss but Bates was just the bowler Smith liked. His normal line was just outside the off-stump and Smith, combining the good tail-ender's virtues of luck and guts, assaulted the Sussex bowling. Amiss and Smith ran their singles adventurously, rattling the Sussex fielders – they dropped Smith twice – and Griffith seems to have got so confused that when the end came Snow still had two overs left to bowl. A perilous 155 for 6 had become a winning 215 for 6, with Smith on 39 not out and man of the match.

The television villainy was odd. This was the only Gillette final – come to think of it, the only major cricket occasion – not to be televised by the BBC. ITV had won the contract and already caused alarm in the way they had been televising that year's Gillette but worse was to come. Just as Smith had launched his winning assault, ITV's 'World of Sport' decided that they had had enough cricket for the day and the television company switched to the David Frost programme. It was perhaps not surprising that this was the first and last major cricketing occasion to be televised by the commercial channel.

The Gillette Cup in 1969 provided some indifferent cricket. The first-round weather was so bad that for the first time the competition actually lost money, but the second round produced better weather and better cricket. Surrey in particular won a splendid game of cricket at Southampton and Leicester a thrilling victory against Kent. But for real cup fervour and excitement we had to wait until the third round and the clash between Notts and Essex at Trent Bridge. Though Sobers had bowled in his usual style in the previous match against Middlesex, he was now engaged in trying to shore up a rather weak West Indies side against England. In his absence, however, Nottinghamshire's bowlers performed well enough to restrict Essex to 180. In fact, Essex had been 100 for 5 after forty-five overs but Fletcher was missed and he went on to make 74. Notts, however, never seemed to come to terms with the Essex attack of Boyce, Lever and Edmeades and at 148 for 7 Halfyard joined Frost. While the tail-ender chanced his arm, Frost kept one end going. He had damaged a hamstring while fielding and Trent Bridge's natural anxieties were now tinged with the glow of pride that only a semi-invalid can evoke. Off the fourth ball of the last over, Frost, appropriately enough, hit a four and Notts scrambled to a famous two-wicket victory. Frost was instantly engulfed by supporters wanting to acclaim their hero.

The other third-round matches were less dramatic. Yorkshire repeated their 1965 final victory over Surrey by almost as convincing a margin, 138 runs. Again Surrey had no answer to Boycott and Close. The Yorkshire captain, coming in after Sharpe had gone with the score on 0, made 96 out of 159 in thirty-three overs; Boycott was steadier and finished with 92. Only 5,500 turned up as Surrey crowds, painfully aware of the mauling their team received in the 1965 final, stayed away.

Though probably not popular in the South, the semi-finals provided the most apposite of pairings. Yorkshire v. Notts at Scarborough, Derbyshire v. Sussex at Chesterfield.

The Queens Park ground at Chesterfield is one of the loveliest grounds in the country. It seems so far removed from the hustle and bustle of ordinary life, let alone the hectic goings-on of a cup match, that it could well have been the model for the village green in Eric Linklater's tale of the two young soldiers who reach the Elysian Fields and find a cricket match in progress. We were in the middle of a heat wave that had begun, after a dreadful May, during the first Test against the West Indies. On that hot July day 11,000 crammed in to watch a quite extraordinary match. On a slow, stopping wicket a patient innings by Gibbs took Derbyshire to 136. It did not seem much but that was before Eyre got among the Sussex batsmen. Ward and Rumsey had already reduced the former champions to 12 for 3 when in ten overs Eyre took 6 for 18, only Parks getting into double figures (16).

The Derbyshire miracle had long been fact while the struggle at Scarborough remained unresolved. Over 15,000 had gathered in this seaside town – so many in fact that quite a few were turned away when the gates were closed at twelve o'clock. Sobers, back with Notts after his sojourn as West Indies captain, won the toss. With the score on 2 Boycott was caught behind for 0 and the large crowd was silenced. But though Leadbeater fell one run later, and Sobers in twelve overs conceded only 12 runs, he could not prevent Sharpe and Padgett from pushing Yorkshire to respectability. The target of 191, however, seemed within Nottingham's grasp, and the more so as Bolus and Harris put on 40 for the first wicket. But Sobers did not seem quite his majestic self at the crease. Every time a Yorkshire bowler approached the wicket the crowd went completely quiet. But his somewhat tentative play gave them satisfaction and on 20 he edged Old to Binks and Notts were, effectively, beaten.

After all this we were due for an anticlimactic final and in glorious weather Yorkshire defeated Derbyshire by 69 runs in the same way that they thrashed Surrey. In the previous championship match

Boycott had broken a bone in his hand and was not playing; Leadbeater had also taken a blow on his thumb but not quite broken it. Close insisted that Leadbeater had to play, but both injuries were well publicized. Close had an intuitive feeling that Derek Morgan, the Derbyshire captain, was looking to put Yorkshire in. Though this was meant to help Derbyshire's strong suit of seamers, Close desperately wanted to bat first. Yorkshire had been to the Lord's final before, could soak up the pressure better, and Close was convinced that Derbyshire's players facing their biggest cricket moment for many years would crack. Close recalls:

> Derek and I approached the toss tight-lipped and tense; we tossed and he won. Suddenly it occurred to me that on this brilliantly sunny morning he might back down and decide to bat first after all – so I tried a bit of reverse psychology on him. Instead of giving him too much time to think about his choice, I didn't hang around waiting for him; I turned and walked straight back to the pavilion, as if to imply that by getting out of his way quickly I certainly didn't want Yorkshire to bat. Whether my action had anything to do with it or not, a moment later Derek chased after me, catching up before I'd gone twenty yards, and invited us to bat. I hope that my face didn't betray the relief I felt inside. I turned back, ordered the roller and then went in to tell the lads.[7]

And goaded by Close, the 'lads', particularly Leadbeater, responded well. Close played much the same guru role with Leadbeater as he had done with Boycott, four years previously. They put on 50, then Close got Leadbeater to quicken the tempo. His thumb was still extremely painful and as Close saw him take his hand away while playing shots he advised him to get himself out. 'You've done your job. It's no use wasting overs with the others to come.' Leadbeater made 76, Close himself 37, and Yorkshire finished with 219. The Derbyshire openers put on 37, but once that stand was broken – and with Page, their most talented hitter batting no. 7 instead of no. 3 because of a strained side – Derbyshire meekly folded.

From Close's point of view the only disappointment was provided by Cowdrey – adjudicator for the match. He told Close that though he deserved the Man of the Match Award (37, 3 for 36, two catches and his overall generalship) it was going to the youngster: Leadbeater.

In retrospect, though, that date marks quite an historic moment. For since then Yorkshire, the county that has won the championship more often than any other, has never won a competition.

Fourteen months after winning the Gillette, Close was summoned to a meeting with Yorkshire supremo, Brian Sellers, and given ten minutes to decide whether he wanted to resign or to be sacked. It eventually emerged that a primary reason for this abrupt dismissal of one of Yorkshire's most successful captains (four championships and two Gillette Cups in his eight years in command) was Close's alleged lack of enthusiasm for one-day competitions. Since then Yorkshire have never been out of the news – not because of cricketing achievements, but of non-cricketing rows and persistent failures. These have led to repeated changes of captaincy, the appointment of a cricket manager and lately, the recall of the veteran Illingworth to the captaincy.

Though Yorkshiremen believe that only their internal bickerings keep them from rising again, the plain fact is that alone of the seventeen counties, Yorkshire do not employ any overseas players – or even any players not born within the county borders. And by 1969 overseas stars were the key to success in English cricket. Yorkshire's deadliest rivals, Lancashire, had never had such parochial restrictions, (the Australian Ted McDonald had been a vital member of their great sides of the twenties) and had just acquired two Test stars: the Indian wicket-keeper Faroukh Engineer and the West Indian Clive Lloyd. 1969 was to mark the beginning of the great years of Lancashire revival when, at least in one-day cricket, they seemed capable of doing everything.

# 2
# The Team that Hated Mondays

> On bad days and good days Bond never read the riot act. He was
> shrewd enough to know that no cricketer fails on purpose. There
> were times when plain speaking was necessary, and Bond seldom
> failed to make his point. He dreaded cricket on a Monday morn-
> ing, often before rows and rows of empty seats, after a Sunday
> match in front of a big crowd tense with atmosphere. It was this
> aptitude for understanding men and the way they reacted that
> made Bond such a remarkable leader.
>
> Notes by the Editor, *Wisden* 1973

On 30 August 1970, Lancashire met Yorkshire at Old Trafford. The
previous day the two rivals had begun the traditional Roses match
in front of 9,000 people – not as great as the many thousands that
had thronged such matches between the wars, but still quite good
considering that across the road, at the other Old Trafford,
Manchester United were at home. But by midday that Sunday it
was clear that Old Trafford was going to see something special.
Some time before Brian Close and Jack Bond, the respective
captains, went out to toss, it was announced in tones of awe that the
Old Trafford gates had been closed. This had not happened there
since 1948 and the visit of Bradman's Australians. A crowd of
33,000 people were packed into Old Trafford to witness a forty-
overs-a-side match between these two ancient rivals.

For those with memories of the classic Roses struggles of these
two teams it brought back vivid impressions of the twenties and
thirties. The crowds, though, had been attracted back not by

atavistic memories of those grim battles, but to see Lancashire win the John Player Sunday League trophy for the second year in succession. This brand new one-day competition demanded a special approach to cricket and drew a particular type of spectator. When at the end of a rather poor match Lancashire won, the crowd sporting banners, rattles, and scarves, even including some early skinheads, acclaimed Bond with the sort of emotion that must have made him feel he was George Best. It was, said Jim Laker, 'the day when Lancashire supporters returned to Old Trafford'.

If the crowds at Old Trafford in the early seventies reflected the particular fervour the county felt for one-day cricket, these forty-overs-a-side matches designed to finish in an afternoon were meant to attract families back to the game nationwide. In 1969, the first year of the competition, almost as many people watched the Sunday League – as it is popularly known – as had watched all championship cricket in 1968. And by the end of summer Frank Bough, who presented BBC2's regular Sunday coverage of these matches could be understandably euphoric:

> In 1969 the Sunday League persuaded the British family to climb into the car, drive to the local ground and watch a game of cricket in greater numbers than at any time since those balmy artificial days immediately after the war. Many drove to the next county to do it, others went even further afield. This summer half a million people weighed all the attractive alternative ways of spending a modern Sunday, a day which is going more conti-nental year by year, and decided to watch a cricket match.[8]

The half a million who watched the Sunday League that summer set a standard of attendance that has been maintained ever since. But despite its popularity it is perhaps the least considered of one-day competitions. For the traditional cricket follower it is an irrel-evance, the more so when rain reduces matches to a ten-overs-a-side slog seemingly more suited to farmers than cricketers. Much as the crowds flock, particularly if their team is winning, the players generally loathe it. Peter Roebuck, the Somerset batsman and an elegant essayist catches well the mixture of despair and senselessness that afflicts most players when faced with the prospect of another Sunday League game.

Somerset are playing Middlesex and Roebuck has sorrowfully confirmed that it is not raining. As he drives to the ground, wild thoughts pass through his mind. Perhaps Middlesex will invade

Libya and he can boycott the game. At the ground his captain approaches him. 'He looks worried and forlorn. My heart leaps; obviously he is dreading breaking the news to me that I'm not playing. Remind myself to look a broken man.' But, alas, he has to play.[9]

Yet despite the professional's distaste the origins of a Sunday League lay in measures to improve the quite inadequate benefits that players were receiving in the early sixties. Its conversion to a properly sponsored competition revealed the growing financial skills of the cricketing authorities; in this case Lord's showed the kind of ruthlessness more appropriate to a tycoon planning a City takeover.

For all the undoubted success of the Gillette, by the late sixties one-day cricket was still considered something foreign to the traditions of the game. The debate about the future of county cricket was as heated and confused as ever. Everybody had their own thoughts on how county cricket matches could be made more of an event than a ritual. Clubs were encouraged to make every effort to welcome spectators and convert their grounds into leisure centres. The specialist cricket magazines were deluged with suggestions ranging from the practical to the bizarre. One cricket follower thought that there was an intrinsic dichotomy between a match that could please the players and one that would delight the spectators, and blamed dull cricket 'on the inability of the spectator to realize and appreciate the situation of the game'; another thought that more West-Indian-style exuberance in the members' enclosure might awaken county cricket from its somnolence. 'We have heard a lot about brighter cricket recently, but not so much about the need for brighter spectators. Who better to set an example than the readers of *The Cricketer*?'

Even if the readers of *The Cricketer* were not quite willing to become West Indians, they were eager to express their views on the future of cricket. At the beginning of the 1966 season *The Cricketer* took a sample eight-point poll of its readers and found that while 69 per cent were still as interested in county cricket as before, 60 per cent wanted fewer three-day championship matches. Nor were the readers in favour of four-day matches: only 24 per cent in favour, 76 per cent against. And though 63 per cent did not want an extension of one-day matches along the Gillette pattern, there was a considerable majority (70 per cent) in favour of first-class cricket on Sundays.

In 1982 a poll in the same magazine showed that 64 per cent

thought there was the right amount of one-day cricket, 28 per cent too much of it, while 4 per cent wanted more.

This was of course the voice of the informed, dedicated cricket follower. A *Daily Mail* investigation about the same time showed that the general public did not share their views. Cricket seemed to have broad support among the general public; more than 300,000 actually played cricket, every weekend. Of the country's then population of sixteen million males, just over six million expressed an interest in cricket. (Only soccer and boxing had greater appeal and it should be noted that the survey was carried out just as Henry Cooper was fighting Muhammed Ali.) But the general public were keen for a change. They not only wanted Sunday cricket (53.1 per cent), but 65.2 per cent wanted more one-day cricket, a proportion that rose to 78 per cent among the 45–54 age group.

The lesson that the powers that be drew from all this was interesting. Doug Insole, then chairman of the selectors, felt that it would 'be right to introduce additional one-day cricket for a trial period' but he was still concerned about the perennial headache of county clubs: how to satisfy both the members and the general public:

> Counties at present substantially depend for their revenue upon membership income. Members in most counties like to have the opportunity of watching cricket – even if only for an hour or so at the end of the day, and at weekends. One match a week, as is sometimes proposed, would mean one home match for each county every fortnight. If it happened to rain over the weekend, this would be reduced to one match a month. Members like to watch: the public likes to read about the game six days a week: the counties depend upon subscriptions.[10]

So what was the way out? Billy Griffith, who had masterminded the introduction of one-day competition, was convinced that the way forward was radically to change the structure of the game. The *Daily Mail* survey had shown that while six-million-plus males were interested in cricket, only 29 per cent went to a first-class match. It meant a potential four million spectators waiting to be attracted. If county cricket could get one in twenty of that pool it would be viable, one in ten and it would be laughing all the way to the bank. Griffith's plan was to have one three-day match per week (Saturday, Sunday, Monday), an additional mid-week one-day competition, less television and more amenities at the ground. Despite his position as President of the Cross Arrows Club, which played at the Nursery End at Lord's, Griffith, Secretary of the MCC, was quite happy to contemplate building a swimming pool at the Nursery End of the ground. 'Over the next ten years county clubs have simply got to turn their grounds into social centres with amenities to attract wives and children. They must be clubs, twelve months a year . . . where cricket is played five months a year.'

But even as Griffith became the radical of the Nursery End, most players still saw nothing wrong with the present structure. Replies to a questionnaire sent to players by the Cricket Advisory Committee showed that the restricted introduction of limited overs in county cricket had proved unpopular. In 1966, in some county matches, the first innings was limited to sixty-five overs, and ninety-four out of 112 players voted against it. Two-thirds of the 125 players who responded to the questionnaire thought that the existing three-day structure was good, and a substantial majority rejected any idea of more limited-overs matches.

County cricket was their livelihood and most players polled thought it important to produce reasonable figures and averages (limited-overs matches did not – as now – count for anything) in order to safeguard their futures. Micky Stewart, then captain of Surrey, even felt that 'the public must be educated to accept that a draw is a right and proper result in a lot of matches played, and it need not be anything to do with dull cricket whatsoever, just as a draw at soccer can be the most exciting match played'. However, the players were convinced that Sunday play would be popular.

Many county players did, in fact, play on Sundays, often in charity matches or to help a fellow player's benefit. Generally, these were the traditional beer-and-skittles matches but they did earn the beneficiaries a bit more money – another three hundred or four hundred pounds. The sad fact was that in the sixties cricketers' incomes had slipped down the wages ladder. Once, professional cricket was an escape from the drudgery of going down the pits. In 1949, when Brian Close signed for Yorkshire, he was paid £1,000, three times as much as the average wage of a working man. By the mid-sixties the differential had been reversed. About this time Bill Voce offered a position on the Notts staff to a young fast bowler. He was told, 'Nay, nay, why, ah can mek twice as much as that in t'pit.' The only succour was provided by benefits – granted at the discretion of the committee, but even then they hardly fetched more than £3,000 or £4,000 in total. Leading cricketers like Compton, Laker or Dexter did much better, largely because their reputation earned them money outside cricket. Most of them had also acquired agents. The most prominent was an Irishman called Bagenal Harvey. And he thought there might be a way of improving players' benefits and providing the public with the entertaining Sunday cricket they wanted.

Harvey had a lot of players on his books, including some who had retired but still had a lot of good cricket left in them. For some time Harvey had been associated with Rothmans in various promotional activities and they seemed keen to sponsor a one-day cricket match that would match talent with money and, as Harvey recalls, 'improve the miserable money that players were receiving'. Rothmans had produced a *Cricketing Almanac* in 1961, the following year they had sponsored well-attended receptions at cricket clubs, and in 1963 the first of the Rothmans Cavaliers charity matches. But suddenly in the winter of 1964–65 the whole concept took off and Ted Dexter, who had given up the England captaincy to try and enter Parliament, received a telegram from his agent, Harvey, asking whether he would be interested in playing Sunday-afternoon cricket. Dexter returned to find that Harvey, along with Sir Learie Constantine, had already set up a club called International Cavaliers.

It was in the back room of Harvey's London office that Ted Dexter worked out the rules for this new competition. BBC2 had showed interest in televising the matches and Dexter had to tailor the rules to fit an afternoon's viewing. The most important constraint was timing: the televising of matches would begin at two o'clock and end at about six. For two innings to finish in four hours, no side could have more than forty overs. Long run-ups were out and Dexter thought that fifteen-yard run-ups would be a proper compromise. So with £5,000 from Rothmans and a further £6,000 from BBC2 International Cavaliers were launched. Very quickly for millions of television viewers Sunday would not be Sunday without a Cavaliers match. But before the Sunday Trinity of Harvey, Rothmans and the BBC got together, first the God factor had to be sorted out. Though the matches were due to finish by 6 p.m., this was perilously close to that part of Sunday evening which was known as 'the God spot'. If the matches were to be televised then Bryan Cowgill, BBC's Head of Sport, would have to encroach into this sacrosanct area. The BBC Governors were reluctant but eventually persuaded that the public would not mind dwelling on spiritual matters a bit later provided their other senses were satisfied by the cricketing exploits of Sobers, Graveney, Pataudi, Dexter or Compton.

In television terms the programmes were innovative, as Frank Bough, the first presenter, recalls:

The programmes were to have a presenter at the match. Someone who, in vision, would welcome viewers to the game, set up the characters, the personalities, and what is more talk to the players as they came off after an innings, or during the interval. This had never been done before. In Test matches plus the Roses game between Yorkshire and Lancashire, which was about the only county three-day game televised, the commentator remained out of vision, purely as a commentator. An interview with a player apart from possibly the England captain after the game was unheard of. It was also decided that in the Sunday series we'd stay on the air during the tea intervals, to talk to interesting people at the match – not necessarily the players – or to feature the ground, the county whose guests we were, the club's foundations and history. The presenters were also required to stage-manage the presentation of the winning cheque at the end, talk to the heroes of the day, and say goodbye.[11]

BBC2 gathered together a commentary team that included John Arlott, Peter West, Richie Benaud, and Brian Johnston, with Sir Learie Constantine, who had made his initial reputation in similar matches in the Lancashire League, as summarizer. Suddenly, for a mere £6,000 the BBC found that it had chanced on wholesome, popular, family entertainment. As Brian Johnston recalls, the matches 'attracted large and enthusiastic crowds. They came to see the great Test cricketers from all the countries playing together in one team and these Sundays became a family occasion. The matches not only brought money into the game, but also a fresh approach, with the gay dynamic cricket which was played.'[12]

So great was the impact that one ardent church-goer wrote complaining to Peter West that 'he always missed the final result of the cricket due to the claims of Evensong'. Could the BBC announce the results later?

The cricket, if light-hearted, brought together the stars of today and yesterday, such as Compton, Evans, Graveney, Trueman, Dexter, Sobers, the South Africans Pollock and Dennis Lindsay, the Australian Bobby Simpson, the Pakistani Hanif Mohammed and the Indian Nawab of Pataudi.

The Cavaliers with reason can claim to have discovered Clive Lloyd. Though he had made his Test debut for the West Indies in

1966, and had been playing for Haslingden in the Lancashire League, it was really an explosive innings for the Cavaliers one Sunday at Southport that made his name. 'By the time it was televised people had heard of this big black man who hit the ball so hard,' recalls Harvey. Later that summer he was approached by Lancashire Secretary, Jack Wood, about joining the county.

The Cavaliers also demonstrated – if demonstration was needed – that when it came to influencing people television was the medium. Though the press rarely reported their matches, and considered them a bit of a joke, television effectively tapped the home audience that the Sunday League now exploits. If the initial matches were mostly against Sussex – because of the Dexter connection – later the Cavaliers would play most counties and produce some memorable cricket. Counties often used the matches to introduce younger players: Tony Greig made a strong impression in one match by taking a remarkable catch. The combination of television and prize money (£100 a side) seemed to produce cricket that was both competitive and entertaining. By 1967 International Cavaliers were firmly established. That year 115,000 spectators watched the matches and £13,250 was raised – nearly all of it going back into the game through Players' Benefits and County Development Funds. The Clive Lloyd match had been watched by 8,000, and 10,000 had gathered at Worcester. But the really crucial match for the future of Sunday cricket was at Lord's when 15,000 watched the Cavaliers play Middlesex and contributed £2,300 to the Middlesex Colts Cricket Association and the Middlesex Youth Appeal Trust.

Before this match, the Cavaliers' organization had warned the Lord's authorities that given the popularity of the Cavaliers a large crowd was quite likely and that the necessary catering and other logistical arrangements ought to be made. But Lord's rarely had more than a couple of thousand for Sunday matches and cricket's headquarters kept to their leisurely Sunday arrangements: only three gates were opened.

As a result, half an hour before the match thousands were clamouring outside Lord's to get in, extra gatemen had to be suddenly requisitioned, inside the catering arrangements were proving inadequate, and as the day dissolved into chaos the authorities realized that they had a winner on their hands. They had expected at best 5,000; there were more than 15,000 that Sunday at Lord's. As Ted Dexter says, 'That was when the penny dropped that this Sunday business could be very profitable.'

The real significance of the unexpected crowd was seen in the light of the half-hearted experiment undertaken by some counties that season, of playing county cricket on Sunday, as the second day of a three-day championship match beginning on Saturday. The law would not permit a start till 2 p.m. and the Sunday five-hour session had proved an abysmal failure – at least at Lord's. In mid-July, in glorious weather, Middlesex had played Northants and drawn a minute crowd. Admittedly there were mitigating factors: Middlesex were a poor side then, Northants without their stars, and on two previous occasions Middlesex had bored the pants off their supporters with some sublimely dull play. The amazing popularity of the Cavaliers' type of Sunday cricket did seem to point a moral: that the public would not come to watch Sunday county cricket, but if there was a match with the possibility of genuine entertainment, and almost guaranteed result, then they might be tempted.

In the winter of 1967 the counties met and decided that all televising of cricket which required the participation of registered county cricketers, should be controlled by one authority – the newly formed Test and County Cricket Board. The television company should negotiate directly with this body, and there could be no televised cricket involving registered players outside the context of a Sunday League. This dealt a body-blow to the International Cavaliers, effectively introducing a Sunday League competition for which only the first-class counties would be eligible.

For a time it seemed that the BBC and Rothmans would brazen it out on their own; the BBC felt a great deal of paternal pride in the creation of Cavalier Sunday cricket and Brian Johnston, then its cricket correspondent, wrote:

> I hope the counties will think again. When everyone is saying that county cricket is sick and losing support they cannot afford to do away with one of the two good ideas which have proved so successful [the Gillette Cup is, of course, the other]. If they do so they will antagonize many thousands of their supporters. They and their beneficiaries will be giving up something without any guarantee that the replacement which they are being offered will be as successful. [13]

The BBC, having started Cavaliers television cricket by putting in £6,000, now offered so to increase its fee that each county would be guaranteed at least £2,000. The Cavaliers worked out a fixture list for 1969 that would enable them to play on any Sunday the seventeenth county not engaged in one of the eight league games. They also promised to enlist additional overseas stars if because of the league it became difficult to raise a side of the usual standard. John Arlott, Jim Laker and others thought that a possible solution would be to make the International Cavaliers XI the eighteenth team in the competition with the Cavaliers match against the respective county the one to be regularly televised. But Lord's were looking for a clean break, and though there was some talk of a commercial television company broadcasting the matches, eventually a lucrative contract was signed with the BBC.

For Rothmans this was a cruel blow. After Gillette, they had been perhaps the most enthusiastic supporters of cricket, organizing not only the International Cavaliers but various other cricket matches between England, the Rest of the World and the tourists of the season. They had not even been given the opportunity to bid for the sponsorship, and watched their rivals, the Nottingham-based John Player Company, sneak in and land a market they had created. Even years later Bagenal Harvey still felt like the wife who discovers her husband has been carrying on behind her back. Even more unpleasant were the accusations that Harvey was feathering his nest out of cricket, when the money really belonged to the players:

> Without so much as a by-your-leave the counties voted not to allow any further televising of Cavaliers matches. We were not in it for the money. It was because of the matches that several players made money: £2,200 for Ken Taylor, £3,300 for Tom Cartwright, upwards of £4,000 for Don Wilson. If we had anything left, after expenses, then this was handed over to the MCC – something like £10,000 in three years. We were not competing with the authorities. This was not business for us. Our whole motive was to maximize the benefit received by the players. After all that has been said I feel sorry I did not put the money in my pocket, which I could have done quite easily.

A decade later, when Packer came along, Harvey felt a pang. 'When I saw what Packer had done, I realized how soft I had been. We never tried to compete with the authorities.'

If it was any compensation, the International Cavaliers' last match at Lord's in 1968 packed the ground. But while the Cavaliers did play their matches in 1969 deprived of television, interest died, and with it Rothman's association with cricket. In retrospect, it is clear that the International Cavaliers as an eighteenth team in the

Sunday League would never have worked – but the ruthlessness with which Lord's acted to cut out Rothmans indicated the new mood, both on the field and in the committee room. Cricket was not to see anything else like it until the authorities themselves were at the receiving end of Mr Kerry Packer's revolution.

The first few weeks of the new competition certainly gave the impression that the gods themselves were weeping for Rothmans and Bagenal Harvey. May was so dismal that only five of the thirty championship matches produced a result, and the John Player was reduced almost to a non-event: twelve matches were abandoned. This particularly affected Warwickshire who had looked to have the ideal team combination: a strong array of stroke-players in Barber, Kanhai, Jameson and Mike Smith and plenty of useful seam or containing spin, in Cartwright, Brown and Gibbs. But they lost a quarter of their matches to rain and never really got going. They developed such a jinx about the competition that it was a decade before they finally won it.

The early pace-setters were Essex, who had the explosive West Indian Keith Boyce, who was capable of turning a match with either bat or ball. The competition seemed designed for him. By the end of the first season he had hit sixteen sixes in the league, winning £44.11s.4d (from a sixes-pool of £1,000); and the BBC donated £50 for the fastest fifty of the season, which he scored (he also took twenty-five wickets at 12.04 each). The Boyce fifty had come on 4 May at Chelmsford when Essex had beaten Lancashire by 108 runs and looked like world-beaters. Ward, Taylor, Barker, Fletcher and Irvine all made runs and, after they had softened Lancashire up, Boyce in twenty-three minutes made 50 with two sixes and seven fours. This left Lancashire 266 to get. Boyce took two wickets in his first two overs and Lancashire caved in. If anybody had suggested then that this competition would mark the start of Lancashire's great one-day successes, they would have been laughed out of court.

Lancashire's sixties were just as bad as Yorkshire's seventies were to prove. Things had reached their nadir in 1964 when three players were sacked and the incumbent Grieves was removed from the captaincy. In the winter the county advertised in *The Times* for an experienced new captain. There had been complaints by other counties about Lancashire players and a special meeting of the members, in turn, expressed dissatisfaction with the committee. In the next few years captains came and went – and their one modern immortal retired: Brian Statham.

Then in one of those flashes of inspiration that occasionally visits committees and officials, the county appointed a certain Jack Bond as captain. Though he had made his debut in 1955 his struggles had coincided with those of the club and by 1968, at thirty-six years old, he was not even a regular member of the first team. Lancashire had already signed the Indian wicket-keeper Faroukh Engineer, who brought flair behind the stumps and occasionally played the sort of innings that had nearly brought him a Test century against Hall and Griffith in Madras; in 1969 Clive Lloyd joined – and by then the Lancashire team of something new, something old, something borrowed had knit together splendidly. Pilling, perhaps the shortest player in the country, was a consistent no. 3; Hughes and Simmons were effective spinners and late middle-order batsmen; Wood and David Lloyd extremely useful openers, with Wood a valuable one-day bowler besides. If Statham's retirement had meant opponents found runs easier at one end, there was the pace promise of Shuttleworth and the maturing worth of Lever.

A religious man, who owed his early cricket coaching to Edwin St Hill, a West Indian in the Lancashire League, Bond was one of those cricketers who had the knack of getting the best out of players far more gifted than himself. As Clive Lloyd recalls:

He could hardly be described as a great player, nor a brilliant tactician, just an efficient middle-order batsman who had never quite secured his place in the Lancashire first team. Yet he had the quality of leadership. His own enthusiasm and dedication proved infectious. He understood his fellow players and they understood him and, until he retired from the game in 1973, I do not believe it was possible to find a more popular captain anywhere.[14]

Lloyd vividly remembers the first match he played for Lancashire and made 0 and 2. Bond came up to him and said, 'Look, Clive, you don't have to prove yourself to us or anyone else. We know you're a fine player and you've got the record to prove it. You'll come good soon.' Simple words, but they meant a lot to Lloyd.

Bond's attitude to the Sunday League was admirably pragmatic. It was a useful way of 'letting off steam', and while first-class cricketers would understandably baulk at sacrificing first-class principles in order to provide a spectacle, he told his team the league could be the making of cricket and urged them to give it a try. 'Let us go out there and enjoy ourselves; if we do that the crowds must surely enjoy themselves too.' They so enjoyed themselves that soon thousands packed Old Trafford on Sundays – and Bond came to hate the loneliness of an empty ground on Mondays.

In that inaugural season, after the initial defeat against Essex, Lancashire lost only twice, once after they had won the title, and their main disappointment was that the match against Yorkshire at Old Trafford, which might have provided revenge for the 1969 Gillette first-round defeat, was totally ruined by rain.

The final John Player averages showed the all-round strength that Bond had harnessed. There were three Lancashire players among the top fifteen batsmen in the league: Sullivan, Pilling and Engineer. Interestingly, the league's first two batting places were occupied by a twenty-year-old from Northants, Peter Willey, followed by Greg Chappell, then playing for Somerset. It demonstrated that good batting was not redundant in this type of competition, though the bowlers do seem to have suffered from the fifteen-yard run-up; some of the country's leading bowlers like John Price, John Snow and Peter Lever occupied lowly positions – 28, 44 and 45 respectively, while occasional bowlers like Sullivan finished fifth with an average of 12.21, and Green fourth with an average of 12.13. On the whole bowlers did rather better than batsmen, many of whom failed to pace themselves in the early part of the innings. In fact, only one, Peter Willey, averaged over 40, while the first eleven bowlers all captured wickets at a cost of less than 14 runs per wicket.

If the first year had seen a narrow one-point victory over Hampshire – with Essex another four behind – 1970 was to see Lancashire winning the league in the most commanding fashion. Though Kent were only five points behind, Lancashire began the campaign with a massive eight-wicket victory over Middlesex and never looked back. The only two defeats they suffered, at the hands of Kent and Surrey, were freak results that are part of the competition. Against Kent, Lancashire made 202 for 7 in thirty-five overs. Then the rain came and reduced Kent's innings to ten overs, leaving Kent 58 to get, which they did. The Surrey defeat is more complicated – and tells a lot about the nature of the competition. Surrey met Lancashire at the Oval on 26 July 1970. Lancashire won the toss and batted, but rain interrupted their innings and after thirty-four overs they finished on 162 for 6. It began raining just as Surrey were starting their sixteenth over with the score 48 for 2. At that stage Surrey were behind Lancashire in their run-rate and so during the sixteenth over tried to score another 7 to get ahead; they only succeeded in scoring 3 by the end of the over, when heavy rain forced a stop. Had the rain continued for another fifty-five minutes, the game would have finished and Lancashire would have won. But it did stop and with Surrey's innings now reduced to twenty-five overs, they required another 56 in the remaining nine overs. This they duly scored to produce the memorable headline: Surrey 106 for 8 beat Lancashire 162 for 6. Though this is probably an extreme example, ever since its inception the John Player League has produced such matches, leading to cries that a game won on mathematical formulae is no game at all. Still it thrives and when your favourite team is winning it seems to matter little how they do it – even if microchips have to be used to determine a winner.

But it was the triumphs in the Gillette of 1970 that all Lancashire savoured in particular. The players, of course, wanted the 'big one', the championship, but Lancashire, after a good challenge, finished third. Till then they had done little of note in the cup. They held the dubious record of being at the wrong end of the quickest finish: 2.20 p.m. in the 1963 semi-final against Worcestershire. They had been in another semi-final the next year, then again in 1967, but in both 1968 and 1969 they had been knocked out in the first round, in 1969 in a humiliating defeat at Old Trafford by the ancient enemy Yorkshire, by seven wickets.

It was perhaps a good omen that they received a bye in the first round in 1970, and met Gloucestershire at Bristol in the second. This was the third time the two teams had met in this competition (they were to meet four more times with Lancashire winning every time). Though this match was not a classic, as the 1971 match would become, victory turned on an unfortunate accident. Lancashire, thanks to steady contributions by all their batsmen, including a breezy 53 from Lloyd, made 278 for 8. Gloucestershire seemed to be well on course when, at 126 for 2, Ron Nicholls on 58 flicked a ball on to his face and had to leave the field. By the time he returned Gloucestershire had slumped to 154 for 5, and though Nicholls earned the Man of the Match Award for his 75, and an eighth-wicket stand of 51 caused a few hearts to flutter, Gloucestershire never quite looked likely to overhaul Lancashire.

The only moment of doubt for Lancashire in the next round against Hampshire came when, chasing 142, Engineer ran himself out with the score on 12. Then, after Wood provided a solid rallying point with 63 not out, Clive Lloyd and Sullivan with useful contributions saw the red roses to their fourth semi-final, this time against Somerset. It promised to be a match of high drama and in the early afternoon the gates were closed with 10,000 inside – Taunton's largest crowd since the visit of the 1948 Australians.

The crowd photograph of the match captured the atmosphere well: a long line of solid, anxious, West Country supporters standing on a low wooden bench, amidst them a small boy with his back to the game: tired of trying to peer over the heads of the ten rows in his way, and probably a little afraid for the fate of his beloved Somerset. The cider county had, in fact, begun brilliantly – or at least opener Roy Virgin had. In thirty-four overs to lunch, Virgin, helped by Clarkson and Robinson, had taken Somerset to 134 for 1 – the ideal launch-pad for a late assault. But, just after lunch, Virgin was bowled by Hughes for 65 and Lancashire, working the one-day formula to perfection, diddled the next six wickets for 51 runs, with Wood, who was already being acclaimed as a specialist in this sort of thing, taking three wickets. Somerset finished on 207 which did not seem much against a batting side of Engineer, Pilling, Lloyd and the rest.

Lancashire's response revealed the depth of their cricketing strength. Engineer after four fours tried to hit one too many, then Lloyd hit powerfully for 43, but suddenly Lancashire were 130 for 5 after thirty-eight overs with the main batting gone. In the next seventeen overs Sullivan, who made 50, and Bond, 35 not out, put on 74 playing sensible one-day cricket, enabling Lancashire to reach their first Gillette final.

Their opponents Sussex – four times finalists and twice winners – knew all about big-day nerves and, if anything, had had a tougher path to the final. Their victory against Essex had been comfortable enough even if it had required a single-stealing stand between Mike Griffith and Langridge. In the quarter-finals a remarkable all-round performance from Tony Greig had turned a match all Kent expected to win: his 54 rescued Sussex when they were 35 for 3 with twenty overs gone, and his 5 for 42 in ten overs and five balls prompted a sensational Kent collapse from a serene 88 for 1 to 152 all out – the last seven wickets going for 25 runs.

The semi-final between Sussex and Surrey was the match of that year's Gillette Cup. Long after the Taunton crowd had wearily wended homewards after their defeat by Lancashire, millions were gathered round their television sets watching one England bowler trying to bowl out another. Though Surrey had spluttered and wheezed their way to 196 this looked more than adequate when the thirty-ninth over saw Sussex at 102 for 5. Then Pataudi, helped intelligently by Graves, launched a crucial assault, and, when Arnold's last over began, Sussex needed three to tie. Only one run came off the first five balls, but off the last ball bowled by Arnold, his England bowling partner John Snow clumped it to deep extra cover and set off for two. In the sort of mad finish this sort of situation produces, the batsmen just kept running, the fielders panicked a bit, and Sussex got two runs and were home – on a technicality. The scores were tied, but Sussex had lost two fewer wickets.

The final was not half as exciting – unless you happened to support Lancashire. Despite their prowess in this competition, and with players who knew all about the atmosphere of a Gillette final, Sussex found themselves out-generalled and out-fought. As the Lancashire supporters brought a touch of the other Old Trafford to Lord's with their chanting, 'Lan-ca-shire-tra-la-la, Lan-ca-shire-tra-la-la,' the team displayed at cricket the qualities that Alf Ramsey considered essential to footballing success: teamwork and running. If fielding alone could ever be said to have won a final, then it did that day. Three men were run-out in the Sussex innings at that crucial stage when they were looking to accelerate, and Lloyd's cat-like prowling, Pilling's immaculate throwing and Engineer's ebullience behind the wickets never seemed to furnish Sussex with any easy runs.

Lancashire, chasing a modest 184, were struggling in their turn and with only twenty overs left there was little to choose between the sides. Lancashire were 113 for 4, with Clive Lloyd out for a mere 29, where Sussex had been 115 for 5. This was where Lancashire's mastery of one-day batting was revealed. Over the next ten overs Pilling and Engineer in their very contrasting styles put on 42 (Sussex had managed only 33), and that left just 3 runs an over required from the last ten. Only five of those overs were needed before Lord's became a bit like Old Trafford and Harry Pilling, 70 not out, went up to receive his Man of the Match Award.

Wonderful as the limited-overs double success was, it served only as a prelude to the 1971 season when three wonderful matches created a resonance that would always associate Lancashire with the Gillette and with one-day cricket in general.

The very first round of the 1971 Gillette against Somerset revealed that like all great champions Lancashire had the ability to bounce back from a bad position: they often looked down, they seldom went out. The match, spread over two days because of rain, saw Virgin and Kitchen provide their usual forthright start: 100 in thirty-two overs, Virgin finally making 105. But Wood and Simmons did their by-now-familiar claw-back and Somerset slowly slid down to 206 for 8. Lancashire at 8 for 2 were in some trouble but their batting again proved its depth and they ran out comfortable winners by six wickets. Lancashire's victory over Worcestershire was by an identical margin – six wickets – and if anything it was easier, despite a century by Glen Turner. This took Lancashire to a quarter-final against Essex.

The two teams had fought some interesting duels in the John Player League, but this one overshadowed every game that had gone before. The match pitted Lloyd against his West Indian team mate Keith Boyce, and when Lloyd came out to bat, Boyce seemed well on his way to destroying the innings. He had bowled Barry Wood for 2, and had had Pilling caught behind for 0. Then came probably the turning-point of the match and, who knows, Gillette Cup history. Clive Lloyd tried to steal a foolish run and his partner, David Lloyd, unselfishly sacrificed his wicket. While Clive Lloyd benefited from this, all around him Lancashire collapsed and only at 59 for 6, when Simmons joined him, did the West Indian receive any support. All Chelmsford was hushed waiting for the kill. They had to keep waiting as Simmons helped Lloyd put on 91, and, after Simmons had been bowled by Turner, Hughes helped add 23. Lloyd made 109 and Lancashire 203 – a fighting total. It seemed a winning total when Lever, Shuttleworth and Hughes reduced Essex to 34 for 4. But the ebullient Boyce and Saville added 51, and after they had gone Turner and Robin Hobbs put on 74 in thirteen overs for the seventh wicket.

Already the tension was telling on the players – and it was instantly communicated to the crowd. The Turner–Hobbs understanding, like all these partnerships, was based on quick running and the crowd began to feel that Barry Wood was impeding Turner from running between the wickets. However at 186 for 6 it seemed Essex could relax. Then suddenly Lever bowled Turner, Shuttleworth bowled Hobbs and Essex nose-dived from 186 for 6 to 191 all out – beaten by 12 runs, with four balls of the last over left. So high had the emotions run that one Essex player, going out to bat, left the dressing room without his willow.

But this was a mere appetizer to the epic that was to follow a month later against Gloucestershire at Old Trafford – amazingly the only time that year Lancashire were drawn at home. Gloucestershire, too, had had a narrow quarter-final squeak. They had won by 15 runs against Surrey although Surrey, coasting at 167 for 4, required just another 48 to win. But Roger Knight had his future cricket manager Micky Stewart caught for 82, and then took four more wickets in ten balls for one run: Surrey were doomed.

The Lancashire v. Gloucestershire semi-final is such a legend that it is only surprising it hasn't been made into a film by David Puttnam. For here was a cricket match that even the Americans could appreciate. They may not have followed the intricacies, but they would undoubtedly feel the fervour, the passion and the sheer romance of a match beginning in brilliant sunlight and ending in virtual lamplight.

This is in many ways an historic television story as well, for the final moments were televised live on the BBC nine o'clock news. Though the BBC have cameras at both semi-finals, they choose one particular match on which to concentrate their resources. David Kenning, then in charge of BBC1 cricket, decided that Kent v. Warwickshire would provide more thrills and excitement as a match between two well-balanced sides. So the BBC heavy-weights, Peter West and Richie Benaud, went off to Canterbury, and Jim Laker was sent to his old hunting-ground at Old Trafford to cover the auxiliary game. As luck would have it, rain played havoc with the Kent match – it took two days and produced an easy Kent victory – and a little after 10 a.m. that late July day Laker climbed into the commentary box with debutant Tony Lewis to assist him.

A total of 23,250 paying spectators were packed inside Old Trafford (there were probably many more free-loaders) when Gloucester won the toss and were given a solid start by Nicholls and Green, returning to his old haunts. The innings, however, came to life when Mike Proctor held centre stage with a brilliant 65. He was dropped twice by Wood and eventually went to a marvellous catch by Engineer. By then the visitors were well positioned at 150 for 3, but in their characteristic way Lancashire slowly hauled themselves back with Jack Simmons bowling his 'flat' off-spinners to good effect. Despite a 29 by Bissex, Gloucester finished on 229 for 6. Lancashire seemed right on course when Wood and David Lloyd put on 61 for the first wicket, a trifle more slowly than Lancashire would have wished but nevertheless solid. Wood and Pilling had taken the score to 105 when Wood was run out and Pilling bowled by Tony Brown.

Worse was to follow. For in quick succession John Mortimore bowled Clive Lloyd and caused Engineer to hit his wicket. Though Mortimore has the dubious distinction of being the most infrequent wicket-taker in the history of the competition (87.5 balls per wicket: twelve wickets in 1,050 balls), that evening he looked like a match-winner. The light had begun to deteriorate – it was now after 7.30 – as Bond and Simmons began to repair the damage. Bond felt that they had reached the stage when the only way to victory was by playing shots and this is what he and Simmons began to do. From 163 for 6 they took the score to 203 when Mortimore struck again, clean bowling Simmons for 25. Lancashire still needed 27 from the last five overs and the light had been bad for some time. The incoming batsman, David Hughes, had been sitting in a dark corner of the dressing room just to accustom himself to the light. Up in the commentary box Jim Laker wondered if the match could continue: 'It was now very, very dark, the pavilion light casting shadows on the enclosure and in the background Old Trafford station had been ablaze with lights for some time. The umpires only needed a nod from Jack Bond for the play to be suspended . . . The focus was on Bond. Would he now decide to call it a day?'[15]

The joke goes that as Hughes came out to bat one of the umpires took him aside and asked him to look up at the sky, 'What do you see?' he asked. Hughes replied, 'The moon.' The umpire retorted, 'Well, how much further do you want to see?'

Bond of course wanted a finish that night. The crowd had been large, excitable, and very noisy, and they would be extremely disappointed if they had to go away and come back the next day. This, at least, was what Bond later claimed swung his decision. He may also have been persuaded by the fact that Gloucester had spent very nearly four hours in the field – one of the longest sessions any fielding side has had to face – and they had time neither to rest nor rethink their options.

Bond and Hughes consulted and worked out their strategy. Of the five overs left, one was from Mortimore, two each from Proctor and Davey. The Lancastrians decided they had to get the runs off Mortimore, as in that light the quickies would have been impossible. Bond advised Hughes, 'If you are hitting over the top, hit straight.'

Hughes recalls what happened as Mortimore bowled that crucial fifty-sixth over:

I picked up the first ball quite easily because with the arc it came over the top of the heads of the crowd behind the bowler's arm. I cursed that I had no sight-screens; these had been taken down to allow more people to get in. The first ball was a good length. I moved a couple of yards to it to make it into a half-volley and hit it over extra cover for four. Morty then pulled a man from the leg-side to deep mid-off. I hit the second ball over long-on for six, and the third through extra cover for two. John then bowled more middle-and-leg, and I got underneath the ball a bit and found the gap at mid-wicket for another two. Having had success with dancing down to the first ball, I decided to do it to each remaining ball. The fifth ball was on the off-stump and I played what I think was the best shot of the over through the covers for four. I shall never forget the crowd noise and it seemed that thousands of small boys kept charging on after every ball and I kept shouting to them to go back. The last ball I played the same shot as the second but I remember as I made contact that it felt good – and it went for six. Only one run left to win from four overs.[16]

In the next over Bond nudged Proctor wide of gully for a single but even as they ran the crowd, which had several times come over the barriers – in fact, had inhabited parts of the ground for some time – now took it over completely. Meanwhile, back in the BBC box, Jim Laker was quietly going mad. The match had been shown on BBC1 earlier, now Paul Fox decided to cancel a ten-minute Robert Robinson letters programme and began broadcasting the match live. Ten minutes remained before the prestigious nine o'clock news but nine minutes thirty seconds later the match finished and Laker had made television history and the BBC maintained its news slot.

Inevitably, Hughes was made man of the match, and he very thoughtfully took a consolation glass of champagne to Mortimore. The crowd though kept singing and dancing till 10 p.m. and in quite an unintentional way Lancashire had taken part in the first night cricket match – long before anybody had heard about Kerry Packer.

It is a measure of the intrinsic merit of the final that even after this extraordinary match – televised live to the people back home, to quote Tony Benn's picturesque phrase – Lancashire and Kent produced a match that, as *Wisden* opined, 'was possibly the best and most exciting of all the nine Gillette Cup finals'. In some ways it was an even better cricket match than the Lancashire–Gloucestershire semi-final. Asif played an innings of such quality that it would have graced any class of cricket anywhere, and Bond's catch to dismiss him, and effectively to win the match for Lancashire, was one of those historic fielding exploits that have rightly become part of cricket's folklore.

Kent had had a much easier ride into the finals. They had had fairly comfortable victories over Northants by 45 runs, Yorkshire by 6 wickets, Leicester by 78 runs, and then in a rain-ruined semi-final against Warwickshire by 129 runs. They looked an all-round side of immense power with the batting, bowling and fielding to match any situation.

Bond won the toss and batted – in contrast to the more common Lancashire policy of batting second whenever possible. Dye had Wood lbw to the second ball of the match and after that the batsmen were always struggling. Though Clive Lloyd opened his scoring by hitting a six off Asif, who had bowled five maiden overs, his 66 was not vintage stuff and after forty-five overs Lancashire had just reached 179 for 7.

Enter Hughes. Since the semi-final he had regularly found him-self at the crease when a large score was needed off a few balls and won the match by striking sixes. He had done just that against Leicestershire in a John Player Sunday match, hitting Davison for a six and a four to win the match.

So as he walked out a wag shouted, 'Fetch Mortimore.' Kent fetched Underwood, a different type of bowler altogether, and while Hughes did not smite sixes he and Simmons put on 45, a priceless 39 coming in the last four overs: good, clean hitting. The total, 225, was the largest set in a final for a side batting second since the 1965 Boycott final when Yorkshire made 317. And with the England bowlers, Lever and Shuttleworth, doing much of the early damage, Kent were soon a disastrous 64 for 4. This, however, was just the cue for Asif. He had made his mark in English cricket when he had played an incredible innings for Pakistan in a lost Test. Now, as he recalls, 'I thought I must do something for my side. We were in trouble, and I wanted to do something for Kent. Suddenly my concentration seemed to be right, and I began to enjoy it. After Alan Knott got run out I was even more determined to see us to victory and I wanted to make sure I stayed.' With support from Shepherd and Woolmer (batting no. 8) he began to bring the game round. Pulls, drives and cuts, square and late – all followed in textbook profusion. Never once did Asif lift the ball and at 197 for 6 one could sense that Lancastrian heads were drooping. They still kept at the task in the field but just did not seem capable of undoing Asif.

Throughout his innings Asif had concentrated more on placing the ball than on hitting it. Runs came steadily, but suddenly Simmons tightened things up and for an over or two the runs dried up. Asif, just a trifle worried, now tried to hit the ball hard for the first time in his innings and he crashed Simmons for what seemed a certain four. In fact he had failed to middle the ball, had just got a thick edge and at extra cover Bond leapt to his right, pulled the ball down and a forlorn Asif was wending his way back. For the thousands on the ground, and the millions watching on television, it was perhaps the most memorable Gillette scene ever.

Though Asif did get the Man of the Match Award, he was inconsolable – as were Kent, whose last three wickets meekly surrendered as if accepting the inevitable. Lancashire had won their second Gillette Cup by 24 runs.

The only unsavoury element in the final – and a pointer to the future – concerned Arthur Fagg of Kent, one of the umpires. As he went up to receive his umpire's medal, he was booed by a section of the crowd. He had given two Lancastrians lbw – one of them Wood who actually had a mark on his bat, as Robin Marlar pointed out – but for these knock-out matches now the crowds were more partisan, and the Lancastrian one was particularly affected by the ethos of the other Old Trafford. To them there was no such thing as a neutral umpire. (Fagg was so incensed that he never again spoke to Marlar.)

In time, regrettably, Test crowds have come to believe that all umpires are wrong unless proved right. But that was still some time off in 1971.

The season of such surprises had to end with one, albeit of an unpleasant kind for Lancashire. Although they had been beaten five times in John Player matches, the pleasure of really humbling them fell to the most unlikely county: Glamorgan.

A week after the Gillette final Lancashire played Glamorgan at Old Trafford in the final John Player League match. In order to hold on to the trophy and complete the double they needed not only to beat the Welsh county but to do so with a run-rate of 4.680. Thirty thousand packed Old Trafford, confident that the John Player title was theirs. Lancashire had begun to acquire an aura of invincibility in one-day matches and when Glamorgan managed only 143 in thirty seven overs and four balls some Lancastrians were inclined to begin the celebrations. But they reckoned without the shrewdness of Tony Lewis of Glamorgan who shortly after took on the England captaincy. His astute field-placings cut down both fours and singles, and Lancashire, always struggling, lost the match and the John Player title by 34 runs. In that summer this was as much a sensation, if for Old Trafford of a somewhat embarrassing kind, as Bond's catch.

Although John Player matches had continued to pull in the crowds, the committed cricket follower still had reservations.

There were many who thought that the ten-over slog to which these matches were reduced when rain intervened produced farces, and in 1971 Lancashire could perhaps claim just such a farce prevented them from retaining the title. For the match before the crucial clash with Glamorgan had been against the eventual champions, Worcestershire. Rain had reduced it to ten overs a side and Lancashire lost by 10 runs.

But despite this, as the years went by more and more spectators were attracted to this type of competition. In 1970 an additional 30,000 spectators attended; in 1971 there was a further 18 per cent increase, bringing the gate to 340,000. Between 1969 and 1976 John Player gates doubled and BBC2 reported a quadrupling of viewing figures. Of particular significance was the fact that this was an armchair or lounge-chair audience who had possibly never watched a cricket match before, or at any rate seen one completed in an afternoon's viewing. As Jim Laker later wrote:

> No one would have dreamed twenty years ago that it would be possible to watch a game of cricket in your own home lounge from beginning to end on a Sunday afternoon from a perfect vantage point, and that if you should happen to be in doubt as to a batsman's dismissal, then the action would be replayed again for you in slow motion.[17]

Anyway, despite what the purists said, there had been some memorable matches and innings. We have already heard the story of the day when Lancastrians once again felt attracted to attend cricketing Old Trafford. But up and down the country there were other memorable matches and innings. In 1970, on 24 May at Bramall Lane, Yorkshire met Nottinghamshire in front of 10,000. In weather characteristic of that summer they saw 471 runs scored at the rate of almost 6 runs an over throughout. John Hampshire led the way with a century in seventy-three balls, his 108 including three sixes. Notts, chasing 235, seemed to have lost the game when Sobers fell for 10. But Hassan, that all-purpose cricketer, made 46 improbable runs and when the last over began Notts needed 10 to win. Off the third ball Taylor hit a six off Hutton and Notts claimed victory by two wickets.

Not all the Sunday League cricket offered excitement at the expense of technique. The final match of the 1970 season produced an innings from Barry Richards of Hampshire that *Wisden* called 'perfect batting, aggressive but correct'. In reply to Kent's 220,

Richards in thirty-three overs made 132, an innings that Jim Laker was convinced was 'not only the greatest I have seen in the John Player League, but one of the finest centuries it has been my profound pleasure to watch'.

Against an expertly placed defensive field, Richards hit three sixes and fifteen fours, without once hitting a cross-bat shot, or slogging in any way. As *Wisden* noted, he 'rarely allowed the ball to pass the bat . . . used all the strokes in the book, many deployed with almost arrogant ease, others defiant, some savage and fierce'.

The 1971 season showed that more counties were getting the hang of this competition. Somerset had some exciting victories in June against Northants and Surrey. Against the Midlanders the scores were level with one over left, and Somerset had three wickets in hand. But two Somerset wickets fell off the second and third balls, and only a scrambled single – with the batsman just beating the throw – gave Somerset victory. The next match against Surrey was even more pulsating – and produced an even more improbable victory. With seven balls of the match left, Surrey seemed to be coasting: five wickets in hand, 8 runs to get. But Virgin, who had himself made a remarkable 101 (dropped four times, two sixes and eleven fours) took a good boundary catch, and, in the last over, Burgess took three wickets including that of the dangerous Younis to conjure up a victory by 4 runs. Somerset, who made a determined challenge for the title, only faded when they lost to the eventual winners Worcestershire in late August by 8 runs.

Another relatively successful county was Glamorgan who had risen from tenth in 1969 and second from bottom in 1970, to a better place in 1971 thanks to the batting of Majid Khan and some explosive innings from Roy Fredericks. Yorkshire were to feel the full brunt of his power in early August when he made 84 in eighty-eight balls, hitting seven sixes and eight fours.

No John Player season could be without statistical oddities and sure enough the Hampshire v. Yorkshire match at Bournemouth in early September 1971 produced a most curious result. Boycott, so often blamed for slow scoring (he was dropped in 1967 from the England side for scoring a double century too slowly) was now blamed for bowling his overs too slowly.

Yorkshire had made 202 with Boycott himself making 61, and John Hampshire 62. Hampshire had reached 176 for 4 off thirty-four overs when to the astonishment of the 5,000 crowd, the umpires pulled up the stumps and strode towards the pavilion. It was only after much confusion that it was announced that according to the rules play must end by 6.30 if more than five overs remain to be bowled. Had Boycott squeezed in one more over before 6.30, this rule would have come into play and Yorkshire, with the main Hampshire batting gone, might still have won. As it was, the match was decided on run-rate, and Hampshire won on a faster scoring-rate – 5.17 runs from thirty-four overs as against 5.05 from Yorkshire's forty overs.

Of course, for the traditionalist things could never be quite the same. A Mr Drake from Leeds, having cheerfully decided to attend one Sunday League match between Yorkshire and Lancashire, found himself becoming a snob: of the 18,000 spectators there, 75 per cent, he thought, had come 'because of the liquid refreshment'.

> The Lancashire contingent, seven or eight busloads I should think, were shouting encouragement in idiotic chanting similar to that heard at football matches. The beer-drinking 'supporters' of Yorkshire shouted back with their own brand of slang humour. I can assure you that this was my first and last visit to the 'splosh' game. If I thought for one moment that this type of cricket would attract spectators to a genuine game of cricket there may be some hope. But I do not believe this. It attracts the undesirable element and will surely kill the game that we have grown to love. I am aware of the importance of sponsorship but, I repeat, it will kill cricket. Don't be misled by the optimists – three-day cricket is being cut – the next step will be the axe.[18]

Mr Drake and many other like-minded citizens were soon in for even ruder shocks, as cricket's traditional enemy – rain – helped usher in further changes.

# 3
# A Different County Every Day

Fans 'Dig' Pop-age Cricket . . . A cricket revolution in which players would be air-lifted by helicopters to make one-day County League games possible each Saturday, as well as Sunday, could be on the way. The success of this year's Sunday competition has hit the three-day game for such a huge six that a completely new format for county cricket is now being proposed.

Crawford White, cricket corrrespondent of the *Daily Express*: summer 1969

Our age will probably be remembered more for the prediction of doom or revolutionary glory, than either actually taking place. We have probably seen more revolutions on television than in our everyday lives, and it is perhaps appropriate that television coverage of one-day cricket should have had to use modern technology much more than cricketers do. In 1976, on the final Sunday of the John Player League, five counties had a mathematical chance of ending up as John Player champions. The helicopter carrying the trophy and the John Player officials waited at the BBC's Pebble Mill studio till well past 5.15 before a producer took a calculated gamble and sent it to Maidstone where Kent were playing Gloucester. Happily he was proved right.

Such a finish would have been inconceivable in the County Championship. Though 1969, 1970 and 1971 produced close, even exciting, championship results, it remained an event that was read about in the papers rather more than it was actually watched. The connoisseurs were devoted to it, but among the wider public it attracted little interest. While there were no sponsors willing to take the championship on, one-day cricket was still exciting commercial interest.

The involvement of John Player had already tightened the commercial screw. Their sponsorship of cricket was not quite as laid-back as Gillette's. For their one-day matches they insisted on having their company's banners on the ground. And Gillette sales-men, watching another commercial company's banners displayed so prominently, insisted that their own company get some recog-nition. Thus, in July 1969, Gordon Ross, up at Scarborough for the Yorkshire–Nottinghamshire semi-final, suddenly found himself in the middle of a bitter dispute between the BBC and Gillette. The company's salesmen had plastered the ground with advertising banners and, the BBC, who were more sensitive than they are now about televising events on grounds littered with advertising slogans, refused to televise the match unless the banners were removed. A compromise was eventually worked out but the episode indicated how the commercial winds were blowing.

The relationship between commercialism and sport is a complex one – and outside the scope of this book. Yet it is interesting to see how, in the early seventies, cricket, and particularly the one-day game, suited the interests of many companies. For Gillette in the sixties it had provided an opportunity to associate with something typically English, to counter the claims of a purely English rival; for the tobacco companies, like John Player and others that were to follow in their wake, it provided a means of combating the in-creasingly powerful and popular anti-tobacco lobbies that were lobbying the Government with increasing success to issue public health warnings on cigarette packets, and ban television advertising.

And in 1970, association with cricket seemed just right for one of the country's best-established institutions: the Prudential Insurance Company. The Pru, as it is known, had made its reputation special-izing in industrial life insurance. The man from the Pru came along every week to collect the premiums from industrial workers, and also acted as the family's counsellor. So strong was this association that his symbol, the umbrella, had become part of the country's industrial landscape and the phrase 'Man from the Pru' passed into the language. But if this approach had worked very well in the early part of this century, by the 1970s the Pru needed, in the ubiquitous phrase of the PR men 'to reappraise its publicity posture'. In other words, appeal more to white-collar, middle-class clientele. Unlike, say, Cornhill who before their sponsorship of Test cricket were virtually unknown outside the City, Pru's PR advisers found that the company had a 64 per cent 'umprompted market awareness'. The next best-known insurance company was hardly a threat with only 16 per cent market awareness.

So what Prudential wanted was not just blanket, undifferentiated television coverage, but a structured programme that would reach out to the sort of middle-class professional clients they were seeking. In this type of insurance and pension selling much of the work is done by making the right contacts, and cricket provided just the platform the Pru needed. Instead of inviting their brokers to an expensive, and perhaps fruitless, seminar, it seemed more subtle to invite them to watch a day's cricket. The guests would be flattered to be accommodated in a box next to the one occupied perhaps by the Duke of Edinburgh; the whole day could be passed plying the important contacts with food and drink while they watched their favourite sport – ideal conditions for the creation of the right image and the development of business. In the early seventies insurance companies were also worried that a Labour Government might nationalize the industry, and the Prudential matches often gave a useful means of bringing influence to bear on the right politicians, namely those both interested in cricket and in listening to the arguments that a leading insurance company had to offer against nationalization.

Prudential were already seeking new promotional outlets when in the winter of 1971 they were approached by Jack Bailey, Promotions Secretary of the TCCB. Would the y be interested in sponsoring a new series of one-day internationals being planned between England and Australia in the summer of 1972? In one of the great ironies of the game the idea for such matches had been prompted by the activities of cricket's ancient enemy – rain.

On 2 January 1971, after three days of continuous rain, the fourth Test between England and Australia in Melbourne was abandoned. The captains had tossed, and Illingworth, the England captain, had put Australia in, but no play was possible. An additional Test was added on to the programme and, on the last day of the abandoned Test, England met Australia in a forty-overs-a-side match. Australia, as it happened, won easily by five wickets, but of great interest was that 46,000 spectators turned up – and Melbourne was traditionally conservative both in politics and its cricketing tastes. (Years later it was successfully to refuse Kerry Packer use of the

Melbourne Cricket Ground for his rival World Series Cricket matches.)

The English cricket authorities, by now fully aware of the value of sponsorship and the sort of cricket that a modern public might want, immediately realized that there was scope for a new, and potentially profitable, international development of the one-day idea. It is worth recalling here that even in the winter of 1970–71 too much one-day cricket was held responsible for cricket's problems – but one-day cricket of a rather different nature. That winter in Australia, England played nine one-day matches of the traditional kind with up-country opposition, meant to show the flag and bring glamour and Test stars to the cricket-starved Australian outbacks. But in these matches several members of the team were injured, others were exhausted by the travel and, by the end of the tour, E.M. Wellings – certainly no cricket revolutionary – was to write in the 1972 *Wisden* that 'the fixture list was bad . . . the last four Tests were due to be played with only one other first-class match intervening in which to exercise the reserves. An international side should consistently meet worthy opposition, and not be asked to frolic with up-country teams of club standard. One-day games in future should be restricted to over-limited games such as the one in Melbourne.'

Jack Bond, something of a guru on this type of cricket, had already suggested that old-style one-day matches should be dispensed with and instead there should be: 'Three five-day Tests, and three one-day Tests, in short an amalgam of county and Gillette Cup cricket. Hands may be thrown up in horror, at the idea of so summarily dispensing with five-day Test matches. But the best out of the two might well capture the imagination of the cricketers and the public alike.'[19]

With the Prudential ready to put in £30,000 the summer of 1972 did see just such a pattern. In time this outlay was to grow, reaching £130,000 for the 1982 international Prudential Trophy matches. For the 1983 Prudential World Cup the total outlay will be £500,000, in the final year of an index-linked three-year contract. (These expenses do not include Pru's exploitation costs which in a sponsorship of £100,000 is often of the order of £80,000 to £120,000, catering for the expense of entertaining clients, etc.)

In the summer of 1982, however, Prudential announced that the 1983 World Cup would be their last sponsorship of limited-overs cricket – as a consequence of another shift in its marketing strategy. Cricket had helped Pru reach out from the industrial inner-city areas to the leafy suburbs. Now the company wanted to strengthen this base. Cricket, the company's researches found, no longer had the broad base for the marketing strategy it wished to develop. In the last three or four years of the Prudential Trophy competition there have been increasing complaints from regional Pru offices, who could never get sufficient tickets to cater for their small-town clients. The matches were being hogged by the big city metropolitan branches where they were held. Prudential now seeks smaller, more regional sporting events which can more effectively combine the pursuit of Mammon with the appeal of sport.

Although the Prudential World Cup made an undoubted impact – as we shall see later – the company must have felt that despite their subsidy these internationals never quite had the cricketing impact they hoped for. Before 1977 they were always held at the end of a dead series, though between 1977–82 they were a gentle rehearsal before the main Test event. Despite some wonderful individual performances they never quite came alive or acquired a distinct flavour in the way that the other limited-overs competitions did. They did, however, provide the English selectors with opportunities to try out new players and reassess the merits of experienced, if rusty, regulars.

In that sense the first Prudential Trophy series against Australia in 1972 set the trend. The rules for the competition were broadly along Gillette Cup lines, except each side was restricted to fifty-five overs, each bowler to eleven, and generally only two days were allowed for rain-affected matches to be completed.

The 1972 Prudential Trophy matches saw Brian Close return to the England captaincy after Illingworth injured himself in the final Test of the summer. Played over the August bank holiday, the matches attracted 55,000 crowds and established the pattern of English dominance over Australia in this form of cricket. Between 1972 and 1982 England played Australia eleven times, won seven and lost only four. The matches gave the selectors another useful look at possible Test players. Thus Amiss, disappointing in the previous summer's Tests, re-established himself by winning the England Man of the Series Award with 103 in forty-seven overs at the Old Trafford international, the very ground where in 1968 he had made a pair against the Australians.

Some games in the series have had to be finished in a day; the most famous occasion was in 1977 when Australia beat England by two wickets with ten balls to spare at 8.15 p.m., the final stages played in heavy rain with a blinding low sun at the Vauxhall End and pools of water in the middle. A picture of the scene might give the uninformed the impression that mid-winter cricket had returned to England.

The series that year produced some remarkable individual performances. In the first 1977 international, England needlessly got into a muddle and scraped home by only two wickets. In the second, Chappell took 5 for 20 and Cosier was even more successful, taking 5 for 18, bowling England out for 171. But these efforts were undone by Lever who took 4 for 2 in fifteen balls and Australia were bowled out for 70 – a defeat by 101 runs. In the final rain-sodden match, despite the conditions Chappell made a brilliant 125 not out – the highest individual score in Prudential Trophy matches ever. This more than offset Amiss's 108 and Brearley's 78, producing a narrow victory.

This year was the first time the Prudential Trophy matches were played as a prelude to Tests. Brearley's fine innings of 78 in that last match finally clinched him the captaincy for the 1977 series; and, in 1981, the unexpected victory by Hughes's team in the second and the third of the summer's Prudential internationals were to hammer further nails into the coffin of Botham's captaincy. The second match produced a thrilling victory by two runs for the Australians who proved that, as England had often done, they too could come back from the dead, and in a run–chase England could get rattled.

The individual innings of the decade in these matches was, probably, played by Majid Khan for Pakistan in their frustrating summer tour of 1974. Rain had prevented a result in the first two Tests – wiping out an excellent Pakistani position in the second – and in the third the flattest of Oval wickets had produced a high-scoring draw. But for the first Prudential match at Nottingham Majid Khan, opening the innings and still wearing the dirty sun-hat that became a trademark of his cricket, put on 113 in eighteen overs and two balls for the first wicket with Sadiq. He eventually made 109, including one six and sixteen fours. England had made a seemingly competent 244, but lacerated by this assault England lost by seven wickets, Pakistan getting the runs in 42.5 overs. The next match saw another heavy England defeat by eight wickets when in damp, helpful conditions, England were reduced to 28 for 8 and ultimately 81 all out. Not surprisingly they never got back into the match. Not even the West Indies, who won five of their seven matches – and all the three series – inflicted quite such a crushing defeat as did the 1974 Pakistanis. In 1978, faced with a Pakistan minus its Packer players, England exacted revenge: victories by 132 and 94 runs respectively. In 1982 with Pakistan, now back at full strength – and with probably their best side in years – England still notched up decisive victories: by seven wickets in the first match and 73 runs in the second. The matches underlined the brittle brilliance of the Pakistani batting and gave Gatting, who had made a hatful of runs in the championship, the opportunity to force his way into the Test side with some sumptuous stroke-play in the second international. Decisive one-day scores sometimes are a better way of impressing selectors than championship hundreds.

Despite the cricketing dominance of the West Indians, some of the Caribbean matches, particularly the ones that produced English victories, were among the most exciting of the series.

The best cricket matches are those that produce a result so unexpected as to be utterly improbable. This was certainly the case in the first Prudential Trophy match between England and the West Indies in 1973. It took place at Headingley, at the end of a Test series which had seen the revival of the West Indians, after a long period in the doldrums. After failing to win for seven years they had anni-hilated Illingworth's England, sending the captain to his retirement and breaking up the team that a year earlier had retained the Ashes. The West Indies, who won the Tests by massive margins, seemed even better equipped for the demands of the one-day game: the batting strength of Fredericks, Kanhai, Lloyd, and Kallicharran, the all-round skills of Julien and Boyce, the useful quick bowling of Holder and, of course, the incomparable Gary Sobers.

But that day at Headingley England, under their new captain Mike Denness, restricted the West Indies to 181 – after reaching 132 for 3 at one stage. Though England began disastrously, Denness himself made 66, Greig 48 and as the fifty-fourth over of the match began, England were in with a very good chance: 7 wanted with three wickets in hand. A run later England had lost two wickets in two balls. Underwood stopped the hat-trick but with the last over to be bowled 4 runs were still needed.

Sobers bowled to Willis: the second ball of the over was swung back over his head for two, the third ball edged down to third man for two more – and England were home by one wicket.

The 1976 and 1980 Test series with the West Indies again resulted in impressive wins for the visitors but in the one-day internationals England bridged the gap opened up in Tests. In 1976, after some of the most devastating defeats suffered by England since the visit of Bradman's Australians in 1948, England salvaged part of their reputation with some fighting cricket. In the second international a marvellous 88 by Randall, who dealt with the West Indian pace attack more severely than any England batsmen had managed in the Tests, nearly produced an England victory. England eventually lost by 36 runs.

In 1980, when the series was played before the Tests, the West Indies won the first match – spread over two days because of rain – by 24 runs. At Lord's, for the second match, in front of a full house of 24,000, England did well to restrict a strong batting line-up to 235. A marvellous opening partnership of 135 between Boycott and Willey seemed to point the way to victory but four wickets fell cheaply in the middle of the innings and it needed some character-istic hitting from Botham to set matters right at a crucial stage. He hit his Somerset colleague Garner, probably the most difficult bowler to get away in this type of cricket, for six and then with three balls left made the winning boundary. It seemed to promise much for Botham, who had just been appointed captain of England, though as so often happens, the demands of captaincy in Test matches were to prove rather different from those of one-day internationals.

Neither India, nor New Zealand, had come close to stretching England in this competition, though in 1974 after heavy defeats (including 42 all out in eighty-seven minutes in the Lord's Test) India in the first Prudential Trophy match at Headingley made 265 – a record score until England replied with 266 for 6. These remained the highest match aggregates until they were bettered in the England–Australia match at Edgbaston in 1981.

The 1978 matches against New Zealand did produce some of the erratic individual performances that are a hallmark of this type of cricket. In the first 1978 match, four wickets for 5 runs in nine deliveries by Cairns tore the heart out of the England batting and gave New Zealand a glimmer of hope, but they lost by 19 runs. In the second match Cairns, whose final figures in the first were 5 for 28, was hit for 84 runs in his eleven overs as England totalled one of the highest scores in the competition: 278 for 5. But with the bat, Cairns salvaged some honour by making 60 of his side's last 67 runs, pulling Edmonds for four sixes. To compensate him further, he received £250 as New Zealand's man of the series.

The successful formula of one-day cricket was now attracting commercial sponsors in significant numbers: brewers sponsored single-wicket competitions, Ford offered cars to the three fastest century-makers. But in some ways cricket had missed its most exciting opportunity. In 1967, after much anguish and fervent debate the counties rejected the Clarke Report on the future of first-class cricket. This revolutionary committee acutely diagnosed the problems of championship cricket and proposed a two-tier structure of sixteen championship matches that would cut down six-day cricket to four days a week, supplemented by sixteen one-day matches. But the counties rejected this proposal, still believing that the first-class game could be rescued if pitches were better, batsmen scored faster and everybody had a more positive attitude.

By the early seventies the power of positive thinking had clearly failed on the county circuit and the authorities began looking round for another sponsored one-day competition – in effect accepting the Clarke findings but without acknowledging them and acting on them in a haphazard fashion. In 1969 Nottinghamshire proposed separate Saturday and Sunday one-day matches with normal county matches confined to mid-week. The counties, still fearful of making too many changes, imposed a moratorium until the end of the 1971 season. Then cricket found a new even more generous sponsor – and a new competition that would provide the final twist in the restructuring of cricket.

In March 1971 the TCCB, the new controlling body of the game, accepted its structure sub-committee's recommendation of a County Championship reduced from twenty-four to twenty matches, and a new sponsored League Cup played along the lines of the soccer World Cup: first, four league areas would be drawn up, each comprising five teams. The top two teams from each league would then play in a knock-out with a final, of course, at Lord's. It was the old idea, in a somewhat different form, of a Saturday one-day competition. In the 1972 *Wisden,* in fact, the editor in his notes actually christened it the Saturday League Cup, though as it has worked out in practice, not all the matches are played on Saturday. It did bear, at least initially, the same relationship to the Gillette (now Nat West) as the football League Cup (now Milk Cup) bears to the FA Cup and meant a later start for the Gillette which, given their experiences with fickle early season weather, pleased the sponsors immensely.

By the autumn of that year the cricket authorities had found a sponsor for the competition. To the surprise of nobody it turned out to be another tobacco company. Gallagher, parent company of Benson & Hedges, were seeking an outlet for the television advertising money they could not spend. Like the Prudential, they too had been 'reappraising their marketing and PR activities'. This had led to the appointment of Peter West and his company, West and

Nally, as their public relations consultants. The new cricket competition had quickly acquired a name, rules and lots of money.

Largely to distinguish it from Gillette each side was restricted to fifty-five overs. This meant a corresponding reduction in the number of overs permitted to each bowler: eleven, instead of twelve. Otherwise the rules were identical to the Gillette.

The money, of course, was much more generous and clearly showed how far cricket had come from 1963 when £6,500 bought Gillette a cup. Benson & Hedges pledged £160,000 over the 1972 and 1973 seasons; £80,000 a year, of which £65,000 went to the TCCB and £15,000 to the players for team and individual awards.

Nor was there any shortage of razzamatazz. Gold was the Benson & Hedges colour and the cricketer who produced the 'outstanding individual performance' in a match got a gold award. The grounds where the Benson & Hedges matches took place were decked with Benson & Hedges gold; a coach decorated in the company's gold colours was both flagship and general hospitality area for players, officials, guests and the press. And in all sorts of weather, blonde ladies, their golden hair immaculate, gracefully perambulated round the grounds advertising the product and attending to the needs of players, officials and press. In general there was an air of bustle and concern that impressed everyone; here was a new sponsor who could expel some of the stuffiness of the old game, yet produce good cricket.

Yet for all that, it was only in the late seventies that the competition really caught fire. For much of the early and mid-seventies, like the Football League (Milk) Cup, it suffered as the poor relation of Gillette. It did not help that it had inherited the old – and unwelcome – Gillette spot in the season, late April and May. Often the early zonal matches were ruined by rain and ran over two or three days – and there is nothing worse, not even the flattest of Tests, than a one-day limited-over match struggling to die on the third day in murky, damp weather.

In the very first year of the Benson & Hedges, forty zonal matches were scheduled between 29 April and 3 June, the traditional time for overcoats, a thick sweater or two heavy rugs and something more warming in the flask than just coffee. An analysis of the first ten years of the Benson & Hedges, prepared by the Limited Overs Cricket Information Group, shows that of the 470 scheduled games, only 329 finished in one day. Sixteen of the Benson & Hedges matches were abandoned without a result, six without a ball being bowled, mostly in 1981, the year when Middlesex inadvertently set up a dubious record with three of their matches abandoned, two without a ball bowled. This after they had lost the first match of the season by one wicket to Hampshire – the south coast's side first victory for two years – with a finish at 8.20 as Hampshire scored a single off the third ball of the last over.

The competition was not helped by the zone structure. The initial system saved travel and expenses by grouping teams on a geographical basis, but the need to round up numbers meant the seventeen first-class counties were joined by two representative teams from the minor counties and Oxford or Cambridge in alternate years. (Since 1975 Oxbridge have played in a joint team called Combined Universities.) But the makeweights made little impression on the competition: only six victories in ten years between 1972–1981, and none of them once progressed to the knock-out, quarter-final stages.

Also in the early years Kent, Essex, Middlesex, Surrey and Sussex had to fight it out in the South Zone; three would fall by the wayside, although all were potential winners. The North Zone invariably found Lancashire and Yorkshire qualifying at the expense of Derbyshire, Nottinghamshire and whoever the minnows in their group happened to be.

By 1976, after further changes, the Benson & Hedges finally set the pattern that prevails now. The geographical zones were replaced by four better balanced zones: A, B, C, D. This has provided both more variety and rather more interesting zonal matches. A further change for the better was the rescheduling of the start of the zonal matches from the last week of April to the second and third weeks of May, which brought the matches closer together and has led to more spectator interest, largely because the preliminary matches can now be finished in reasonable weather.

However, once the competition moved into the knock-out stages it attracted both better weather and better crowds. In fact the early years of the competition allowed the also-rans of other limited-overs competitions to win a share of the glory. No team was more successful in this than Leicestershire.

Like Sussex, in the years of the Gillette Cup, Leicestershire established an easy dominance by winning their first nine matches, and in the first four years they won two finals and lost a third to Surrey by 27 runs. Yet when Benson & Hedges started in 1972 nothing could have been more unexpected. Until then, Leicestershire had never proceeded beyond the quarter-finals of the Gillette. But in the three years of the John Player they had finished eleventh, seventh and fourth. This suggested they were on the way up and it was largely the work of one exiled Yorkshireman: Ray Illingworth.

Illingworth, in fact, had started the exodus from Yorkshire in the sixties that led to the break-up of their championship-winning side of that era, and he found himself in 1969 captaining lowly Leicestershire. They had won nothing for years and were quite conditioned to defeat. Illingworth, himself, could remember the time when Yorkshire would book in for only two nights at Leicester, so confident were they of success. Within a few years Illingworth had acquired eight new players, and built a team that was a nice blend of youth and experience: some seasoned professionals who had retired from their original counties but were still full of useful cricket, others young and raring to go. Victories in one-day competitions were no fluke, for Illingworth saw his first task as acquiring the habit of winning:

> We consciously set out to do well in the one-day game because it was as good a way as any to get a team used to winning. When I first went to Grace Road, like most experienced players I suppose I was rather against the one-day stuff. But I said to the side, 'If we've got to play it, we might as well play it properly and get some rewards for winning. You will get a bit of money out of it and it will do everybody a bit of good in every way.' There was another reason for our concentration on success in the one-day game: in 1969 the pitches at Grace Road were slow, 'nothing' wickets, and it was going to be damn near impossible to win a three-day game there. In the one-day game the pitch was obviously to have substantially less effect on the course of the game; we had as much chance of winning as anyone else and that was what the team had to get into their heads – that we were capable of beating anybody, provided we played it right.[20]

1972, the first year of triumph, was quite remarkable: Leicestershire not only vanquished all their opponents in the Midlands section of the Benson & Hedges by comfortable margins, but defeated Lancashire in the quarter-finals at Leicester by seven wickets, and this to boot a Lancashire that six weeks later were to create Gillette history by winning the trophy for the third year in succession.

If that triumph was largely the work of Dudleston, who made 65 not out, the semi-final victory against M.J.K. Smith's Warwickshire was wholly the doing of Illingworth who won the Gold

Award for his 3 for 19 (Kanhai, Smith and Murray) and his brilliant leadership. As Lancashire had found, the victories were having their effect on the Leicestershire gates: 7,000 for the quarter-finals and 10,000 for the semi-finals, mid-week gates not seen there for years. The final, against Yorkshire in somewhat murky weather, in front of a crowd of 18,000, was tense rather than spectacular. Yorkshire batted first, making a poor 136, and Leicestershire – after a slump – won by five wickets. They might even have emulated Lancashire's 'double' of 1970, for they led in the John Player League for much of the season, until injuries to Illingworth and other players in the crucial closing stages allowed Kent to pip them by just one point.

In the realm of one-day cricket, 1972 of course belonged to Lancashire. Whatever their form in other competitions Gillette seemed to belong to them. Often they came close to defeat: they beat Somerset by 9 runs in the second round, Kent by 7 runs in a semi-final that had echoes of the night semi-final against Gloucestershire of 1971. Kent, chasing Lancashire's 224, thrice refused the umpires' offer of bad light. Denness and Cowdrey, the Kent batsmen, felt they could not deprive the 24,000 present of the entertainment they had come to see, even if it meant defeat for their county.

The final belonged to one adopted Lancastrian: Clive Lloyd. He had had a rather indifferent season before the first Gillette match against Somerset in July, when his 86 was crucial to the Lancashire victory. On that September day at Lord's he easily surpassed that score in playing the first of his many fine Lord's final innings. Warwickshire, batting first, set Lancashire 235 to win, a target that a side batting second in the final had never before reached. Lancashire began sedately, were 26 for 2 after ten overs, and Lloyd himself made only 6 runs in the next eight overs. But then he hit the Warwickshire seamer Brown for a four and a six in successive balls and suddenly the floodgates opened. Fielders found drives whizzing past them and the guests in one Gillette box near the Tavern scoreboard suddenly found a Lloyd six landing amidst them. He made 126 not out, and by the end, even the dispirited Warwickshire players applauded. 'How,' asked Norman McVicker, 'can you argue about an innings like that? Tremendous.'

But all good things must come to an end and 1973 saw the departure of Jack Bond to be succeeded by David Lloyd. The 1973 *Wisden* asked prophetically:

Now that Jack Bond has gone into retirement and David Lloyd

has taken over will the red rose representatives retain their flair and power at one-day level? Many studious followers of the game believe it was the inspiring leadership of Bond that made Lancashire such a force in both the Gillette Cup and the John Player League in recent seasons. Is it fair to either Bond or Lancashire?'

It may not have been, but the studious followers of the game were to be proved right. Though Lancashire reached the 1974 final – a poor match won by Kent by four wickets on an indifferent September Monday – and won it again in 1975, they were never again quite the irresistible force they had been in the early seventies. David Lloyd was by no means the most popular choice as captain – the team seemed to want the other Lloyd – and soon Bond's team started breaking up. Bond, now the manager, had been succeeded by captains who did not quite have his skill in extracting the best out of their various resources.

But if this was hard for Lancashire, who had grown used to success, it provided fresh opportunities for teams that had suffered at their hands. It was, perhaps, a pointer to the future that the first team to break their winning Gillette run – after fifteen successive victories since 1970 – should have been Middlesex, captained by Mike Brearley. Though Lancashire fought tenaciously, in the end Brearley's steady nerve, to quote *Wisden*, brought Middlesex victory by four wickets.

Gillette 1973, however, belonged to Gloucestershire, who had suffered so much at Lancashire hands, and won nothing since 1877, when they had captured the County Championship. Despite their South African all-rounder Mike Proctor, and the gifted Pakistani Zaheer Abbas batting at no. 3, their progress to the final owed much to Roger Knight, now captain of Surrey. In the first round his 75, and 2 for 43, earned him the Man of the Match Award and victory for his team by 34 runs; in the quarter-finals against Essex Gloucester's triumph by 30 runs rested heavily on Knight's all-round skills: 60 runs, three wickets and two excellent catches.

In the semi-final and final, though, Proctor played major parts. Worcester's biggest crowd since the visit of Bradman's 1948 Australians saw Proctor make 101 out of 243 for 8 in the semi-final; dropped before he scored, then again at 18, he went to his century in two and three-quarter hours. Even then Worcester, needing 41 from six overs with six wickets in hand, had a sporting chance until Proctor, returning for a late burst, took three wickets, including that of Turner, who made 109, effectively to win the match.

The final was against Sussex at Lord's; Sussex in their fifth final in this competition. They were without one of their main bowlers, Tony Buss, and for the superstitious lost the toss and had to field. It was a curious fact that since 1963 the side batting first had won in alternate years and history was with Gloucestershire. Perhaps more to the point Sussex had to bat in fading light during the latter part of their innings. This proved crucial when Proctor came back for his second spell, though by then Sussex were already struggling. Proctor and his captain, Brown, had earlier rescued Gloucestershire; Proctor made 94, and put on 74 with his captain, who himself went on to make 77 not out, hitting 46 out of 68 from the last eight overs. Sussex seemed to have an outside chance at 155 for 2, after forty-four overs, requiring just under 6 an over. But Greig was run out for 0, and after that Proctor and Knight were rather too much for the Sussex tail.

The first round of the 1973 Gillette had seen a minor county at last defeat a first-class county. And what a defeat! On 30 June 1973 Durham met Yorkshire at Harrogate. Conditions seemed ideal and Boycott on winning the toss batted. But the Durham opening bowlers, ironically named Wilkinson, and Alan Old, Chris Old's brother, bowled tightly. Wilkinson bowled Boycott for 14, and Brian Lander, the captain, took 5 for 15 in eleven overs and four balls (Lumb, Hampshire, Hutton, Carrick and Nicholson). Yorkshire struggled to 135 in fifty-eight overs and four balls and despite their efforts in the field could not prevent an historic Durham victory by five wickets.

It is taking nothing away from Durham to suggest that they might have been shown the way in an early season Benson & Hedges match, when at Northampton an Oxford University side containing Imran Khan and Tim Lamb had beaten Northants by two wickets. For the rest, the zonal matches in the Benson & Hedges produced predictable victories by heavy margins and the real surprise came in the quarter-finals when Essex overwhelmed Illingworth's Leicestershire by six wickets.

But Essex themselves fell by 46 runs in the semi-final to Kent, a side that two years after the traumatic defeat in the Gillette final by Lancashire now looked set to write new one-day records. Cowdrey had been succeeded by Denness as captain – soon to succeed Illingworth as England captain – and Kent seemed to have the ideal one-day side. At one stage Kent were campaigning successfully on all four fronts: the championship, John Player, Gillette and Benson

& Hedges. Their championship hopes fell away and Gillette was later lost, but in the Benson & Hedges final in mid-July they easily secured one leg of their subsequent limited-overs double. Watched by a crowd almost 2,000 larger than turned up for the Gillette final later that year, Kent defeated Worcestershire more easily than the margin of 39 runs suggests. Apart from one brief spell in the Worcestershire innings when Gifford and d'Oliveira put on 70 in twelve overs, Kent were always ahead.

Their John Player triumph was somewhat more unexpected; they had not headed the table until 24 June. But from then on they gathered fresh momentum with every match and in the end finished six points ahead of second-placed Yorkshire, a huge margin in a competition often decided by fancy mathematical calculations.

Yorkshire could argue that Kent owed much to their three overseas stars: John Shepherd, Asif Iqbal and the West Indian Bernard Julien. But credit was also due to the far-sightedness of the club and particularly Leslie Ames. After Kent had won the Gillette Cup in 1968, the committee, confident that honours would come, had boldly increased their playing staff to fifteen or sixteen. So Kent were not caught on the hop when the inevitable Test calls came.

Ames, in fact, had been the earliest of cricket managers long before it became the vogue of the eighties. As Cowdrey assumed the captaincy Ames, who had never captained Kent, became manager in 1960 and secretary-manager in 1961. He was shrewd to realize the special requirements of one-day cricket, as Dudley Moore, a veteran observer of the Kent scene, noted in the 1974 *Wisden*:

> He was quick to appreciate the peculiar demands of the new game. Always an aggressive batsman himself, he was continually calling for a positive approach – for batsmen to get on with it even if they got out. And he could well afford such an outlook with the batting talent Kent had at their command. Whatever the arguments about the merits of the one-day game versus the three-day game Ames knew that one-day cricket was here to stay and vast crowds all over Kent on Sundays backed his judgement to the hilt.

1974, in fact, saw Kent win the Gillette – but in many ways for Kent and cricket it was a poor season. Rain and poor Tests cut into attendances, many counties reported losses and the cricket that summer, except in patches, had a curiously somnolent air. The

Gillette Cup itself was sorely tried by rain, which affected nearly every round, and, as we have seen, the final for the only time in its eighteen-year history was played on a Monday.

Much of the cricket played was of poor quality. In fact the low standard of batting in the second-round match between Middlesex and Lancashire surprised even *Wisden*. There was an early shock when Lincolnshire followed Durham's 1973 example and beat a first-class county: Glamorgan by six wickets. The next day Lancashire did their usual demolition job of Gloucestershire and we knew there was to be a different winner in 1974. Yorkshire beat someone in a Gillette match for the first time since September 1969 when they had won the trophy. That someone turned out to be Hampshire, and considering that their side contained Richards, Greenidge, and Roberts, this must be classed as a surprise.

But that apart, the matches rarely caught fire. There were, of course, some fine individual performances: Clive Lloyd in the quarter-final against Yorkshire rescued Lancashire with 90; the semi-final between Kent and Somerset when, possibly, Close's run-out off the last ball before lunch turned the match for Kent to win by three wickets. But a competition like Gillette is shaped by the final and a Monday match could never reproduce the fervour and excitement of a Saturday final. Though the battle of tactical skills between Denness and David Lloyd was interesting, it was strictly for the devotees.

A note of unintentional humour had come in the quarter-final between Worcestershire and Nottinghamshire. Rain had dragged the game into a second day and Notts resumed on the second morning at 81 for 5 chasing 252, with Sobers still at the crease. The Press Association's overnight copy summing up the match for the papers headlined its story: 'Sobers Stumbling-Black.' Sobers did go on to score 84 but it was not enough of a stumbling-black, er, -block, to prevent a Worcestershire victory.

The 1974 Benson & Hedges and the John Player saw a further spreading of the cricketing titles. Leicestershire won the John Player trophy for the first time. With Illingworth free from Test calls he could, as Illy recalls:

now really concentrate on my efforts to improve my adopted county. In 1974 we had the nucleus, with McKenzie and Higgs to open the bowling and Terry Spencer proving a very good war-horse too. He cut a few yards off his run and while he could still be very lively, for the first time in his life he was not trying to knock everybody's head off, and he became a very good bowler for us. Brian Davison was just coming in and he could bowl seam-up. For spin we had Birkenshaw, myself, Balderstone and John Steele coming along, so we had a good all-round attack with most of them able to bat a bit.[21]

Leicester first led on 7 July, and though pressed hard by Kent and Somerset came home two points ahead. This time it was Kent's turn to suffer from Test calls and injuries, and they lost their early momentum. Leicester were also helped by the rain which washed away a crucial match against Somerset when a victory for the cider county might still have allowed them to catch the Midlanders.

The Benson & Hedges tournament, however, was to provide a somewhat different ending. In many ways these matches, particularly in the knock-out stages, provided some of the best one-day cricket of the year. The Midlands zonal section provided quite a tight race, with Worcestershire and Leicestershire qualifying ahead of Warwickshire only because they had a higher striking rate with the ball. All the four quarter-finals produced interesting games, with two of them reaching quite memorable heights. Surrey beat Yorkshire by 12 runs in a match where the final result was in doubt till late in the day when Jackman and Arnold finally shut out the Yorkshire tail. Lancashire struggled to beat Worcestershire by 36 runs, the margin concealing the early batting horrors they had endured. And at Leicester, a 'grand match' saw the home side win by 8 runs. When the last over began Kent needed 15 to win: Luckhurst got 5, then, needing 10 off two balls, tried to hit a six and was caught.

But it was the match at Taunton that earned the rare *Wisden* accolade of 'epic'. *Wisden* accorded it on the basis of the play; looking back we have other impressions, principally because of the subsequent history of the man who was responsible for an astonishing Somerset victory. Let his biographer, Dudley Doust, tell the story:

Botham had played in only four first-class fixtures that year and had little to show for it: an innings of 26 and a single wicket at the cost of 144 runs in fifty overs. Still, at very nearly the last minute Close named him in the side for the crucial match. Hampshire batted first and, after floundering, put up a passable total of 182 runs with Botham, a first-change bowler, taking two satisfying wickets, those of the great Barry Richards and Peter Sainsbury, yielding only 33 runs.

In reply, Somerset stumbled to 113 for 7 when young Botham came in. His partner, Cartwright, skied the next ball to deep mid-on – out – and sent the huge home crowd into gloom. Somerset: 113 for 8, with 70 runs needed off the remaining fifteen overs. Botham soon clubbed a towering six over square leg, and with Hallam Moseley pushing singles at the other end, the score climbed to 131 when the dreaded Roberts, then the scourge from Antigua, was again given the ball. An ugly lifter from Roberts, which Botham was shaping to hook, soon shattered the youngster's back teeth, dropping him like a sack of grain to the ground. 'I spat out blood and a couple of broken teeth and the lads brought me a glass of water,' Botham was later to recall, lucidly, as in a slow-motion film. 'I shook myself and felt fine. As I look back on it, hitting me in the mouth was the worst thing Andy could have done. It seemed to relax me. It made me all the keener. The next ball, he tried the obvious thing, a yorker, and I stood back and clipped it for three.' The rest is history: the last ball before the final over, which was to be bowled by Roberts, was smashed by Botham to the boundary to bring him his forty-fifth run and Somerset an astonishing triumph over Hampshire. Botham was engulfed by fans – not for the last time – and won the Gold Award. The next morning England had a new cricketing hero. A star was born. Ian has kept one of the newspaper headlines of the day. It reads simply: 'Blood, Sweat and Cheers.'[22]

Back in London, Frank Keating, sweating over an uncomfortable *Guardian* subs-desk trying to make sense of Henry Blofeld's copy, would carefully note the birth of the new hero.

After this, the semi-finals were prosaic in comparison. John Edrich, captain of Surrey, continued his good Benson & Hedges summer by playing a match-winning innings of 62 as Surrey defeated Lancashire by 36 runs. In the other semi-final between Leicestershire and Somerset, the new hero Botham was bowled by a discarded one – Illingworth – for 18, who then successfully tamed his old friend Brian Close for Leicester to win by 140 runs. Close, however, was not pleased by the quality of the pitch, and lodged a protest.

The final was a tactical triumph for John Edrich. His cautious 'seal one end up' 40 provided a measure of consistency in a Surrey batting order which was either good or bad – mostly bad. It got worse when 168 for 6 became 168 for 9 in the space of three balls from Higgs, whose hat-trick emulated the feat of his colleague McKenzie against Worcester in the same competition in 1972.

But if 171 did not seem much for Leicester to chase, they reckoned without the astuteness of Edrich in handling his bowling and fielding. In the fifty-fourth over Leicestershire were bowled out for 143: 27 short. Edrich, as much for his batting as his generalship, won the Gold Award.

Illingworth was to have his moment of glory at Lord's in the following year, but before that the cricket dream that many a cricket follower had had was to come true. We were on the threshold of the first cricket World Cup.

# 4
# The Cup from the Pru

> The Rothman World Cup, introduced for the first time and well won by England, provided three one-day matches of considerable interest.
>
> *Wisden,* 1967

> The first World Cup cricket tournament, officially called the Prudential Cup, proved an outstanding success.
>
> *Wisden,* 1975

The idea of a cricket World Cup had long fascinated most cricket followers. As long as only England and Australia mattered as Test-playing countries, a World Cup was somewhat superfluous. Even then, in 1912, there had been a triangular tournament in England between England, Australia and South Africa, with England easily running out victors by four wins to two draws. But rain interfered with the matches, few – even on an August bank holiday – watched Australia play South Africa – and, crucially, the home authorities made less than £5,000. They were, of course, two-innings three-day matches.

The rise of the West Indies in the early fifties and then the other Test-playing countries made the question more relevant: who are the world champions? It was a potent subject in the bars and clubs of the cricket world. If the West Indies beat England, they lost in Australia as happened between 1950 and 1952, if England won in Australia, they lost at home to the West Indies as they did between 1971 and 1973. Between 1971 and 1973 India could lay reasonable claim to being 'world champions' with victories over the West Indies and England away, and then England back in India. The way Test cricket was played, talk of a team as world champions could console and delight the partisan though it could never convince the sceptic. And the memories of the 1912 triangular tournament were so frightening that even sixty years later few English administrators were willing to discuss anything that resembled such a competition.

In 1966, thanks to the enterprising sponsorship of Rothmans, a 'World Cup' tournament was played at Lord's between England, the West Indies and a Rest of the World XI. Rothmans brought over a galaxy of stars for the Rest of the World XI – the West Indies were the summer tourists – and donated a handsome cup to the winners and gold medallions worth £100 apiece to each member of the winning team.

The matches, played on three successive days – 10, 11 and 12 September – saw the three sides play each other twice in matches restricted to one innings and fifty overs a side. England, capably led by Colin Cowdrey, beat the Rest of the World XI, led by Bobby Simpson, by 82 runs. Then, after the West Indians had won a narrow 18-runs victory over the Rest, England beat the West Indians by 67 runs. And a vintage England XI it was too: Cowdrey, Dexter, Titmus, Parfitt, Edrich, d'Oliveira, Snow and two wicket-keepers, Parks and Murray.

But despite the fine weather the crowds were poor: just over 13,000 for three days with a top gate of only 4,861 for the final England match. Though Rothmans again sponsored it for 1967 when the Rest of the World won the Rothmans World Cup, the authorities did not seek any further development of the World Cup idea. By the time it was revived in the mid-seventies, the shape of cricket had changed: in addition to domestic one-day cricket, England regularly played one-day internationals, and, conveniently, there was a hole in the cricket calendar. It was not without some irony that this had happened because South Africa, in some ways a pioneer of 1912, was excluded from world cricket due to its apartheid policies.

1975 had originally been earmarked for a full tour of South Africa. But after the cancellation of the 1970 South African tour, and the sporting boycott imposed on that country, there was never any possibility that the 1975 tour would take place. The TCCB began looking for something to fill the slot.

The World Cup naturally suggested itself, and during its annual meeting at Lord's on 25 and 26 June 1973, the International Cricket Conference approved the TCCB's plan for a sixty-overs-a-side World Cup to be played between eight teams – the then six Test-playing countries, and two special invitees: Sri Lanka, who had been clamouring to get into the first division for some time, and East Africa. There would be two groups of four teams playing on a league basis, with the two top teams in each group going on to the semi-finals. The final was to be at Lord's, on the normal Saturday of a Lord's Test. Two months later, as expected, the 1975 South African tour was cancelled, and Australia agreed to tour England after the World Cup – playing three Tests (in the event four Tests were played).

After the 1973 England–West Indies one-day international at Headingley a group met in the small bar below the main Leeds complex and the TCCB sounded the Pru out. Would they be interested in sponsoring a World Cup? It would make a nice move: three years of one-day internationals followed by a world one-day international. The Pru were interested and though the original TCCB price was considered to be steep, eventually the company proved willing.

It was ideal: cricket's first World Cup, followed by cricket's most established international contest: England v. Australia. And English cricket, at last learning some of the PR tricks that were the hallmark of cricket's sponsors, began to exude remarkable confidence. For the first time, after repeatedly turning down the idea, Lord's had acquired an efficient PR department. On 9 and 10 October 1974 Lord's held a seminar for the various interested parties: advertising and PR executives, television, press and county secretaries and officials.

Donald Carr, the TCCB Secretary, fairly bubbled with enthusiasm for the coming summer. 'It is the most interesting programme the country has ever known. As regards the World Cup, sponsorship and television should at least cover all the expenses of the competition. Receipts should produce a satisfactory and substantial profit to be distributed among the member countries of the International Cricket Conference.'[23] A.B. Quick, the Essex Chairman, told the somewhat surprised audience that even though not a ball had yet been bowled in the 1975 season, it was already a success: promotional income, from sponsorship and television, should be £750,000, which would leave a tidy sum in hand. Within days of the seminar the Prudential confirmed that they would sponsor the World Cup to the tune of £100,000.

There were to be only two minor hiccoughs before the Prudential Cup began on 4 June. The first concerned the draw and took place in that dreadful summer of 1974. It was announced by Billy Griffith, in a room opposite the Long Room, and known at Lord's as the

Writing Room, the traditional place for a press conference at the headquarters. I was sitting next to an Australian journalist and he could hardly contain himself as he heard the draw: Group A: England, India, New Zealand and East Africa; Group B: West Indies, Australia, Pakistan and Sri Lanka. It was, perhaps, bad luck that the draw was announced just a few days after England had bowled out India for 42 in eighty-seven minutes to win a Test by an innings and 285 runs.

Australian journalists were convinced that the draw was 'fixed' and after incessant questioning Billy Griffith, much nettled, conceded that England and Australia had been seeded. A few weeks later, when Pakistan annihilated England in the Prudential one-day internationals, Group A looked ridiculously easy; even non-Australians were beginning to suspect that Lord's, albeit clumsily, had tried to provide England with the best possible chance of qualifying for the finals, or at least the semi-finals. An England v. West Indies or Australia final was of course the dream ticket but in the process they had produced two groups so badly unbalanced that there were serious doubts about the competition.

These were dramatically increased when five days before the competition began, the second day of the County Championship match between Derbyshire and Lancashire was abandoned because of a freak snowstorm that swept the Buxton ground. Mid-winter could not have looked more desolate. However when the day of the first Prudential matches dawned, sunshine bathed the country, and it developed into a heat wave that lasted for much of the summer. It was late September before the rains returned – to the relief of some. By then the first World Cup had passed into cricket history as one of the most brilliant fortnights the game had known.

The first Saturday of the competition saw relatively easy victories for England and New Zealand in Group A and Australia and the West Indies in Group B. Though England beat India by a massive 202 runs – the biggest victory in the history of one-day internationals – the talking point was the strange batting tactics employed by Sunil Gavaskar. In near perfect weather, before a crowd of 20,000, England batted first; Amiss forced the second ball of the second over from Ghavri off his legs for four, and England were away.

The Indians, captained by their off-spinner Venkatraghavan, dropped Bedi on the grounds that his subtlety was likely to prove expensive, and played a hand of average seamers. But though Venkat was reasonably inexpensive – 41 runs in twelve overs – the

Vivien Richards, the greatest batsman of our day, hitting a six (1a) into the Tavern during the 1979 World Cup Final. His innings that day won the cup for the West Indies though later in the year he made 153 at Melbourne playing many shots like the one in 1b. That innings, which destroyed the might of Australia's bowling is still rated their greatest one-day innings ever.

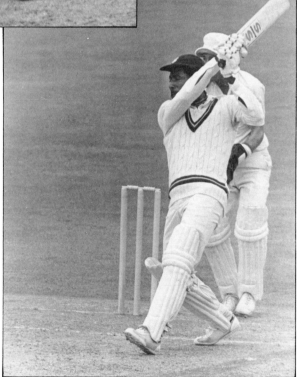

Benson & Hedges Marketing Department

Clive Lloyd has probably been the most effective and match-winning one-day player ever. Here he is seen in his two characteristic roles: hammering the ball powerfully through the covers (2a) and prowling, cat-like, in the covers (2b). Both his batting and his fielding brought Lancashire and the West Indies many a great one-day triumph.

The greatest one-day side ever? The West Indian side that won the first Prudential World Cup with such brilliance and skill and included veterans like Kanhai and Gibbs and newcomers like Vivien Richards. Possibly the only challenge to them could have been provided by the 1979 West Indian side that won the second World Cup.

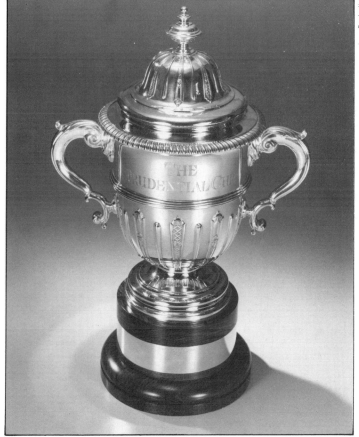

Three in a row! It will take a very good team to prevent the Prudential World Cup from going to the West Indies for the third time this summer. They won it on both previous occasions (1975 and 1979) and seem capable of completing the hat-trick.

In 1950 when the West Indies first won at Lord's, their supporters swarmed across the hallowed turf providing Lord's with their first taste of Caribbean magic. Since then such scenes, like this one after the West Indies had won the 1979 World Cup, have become very familiar.

Ian Botham plays his one-day cricket just as he plays his five-day cricket. Here he employs the reverse sweep in a 1982 Benson & Hedges Quarter Final match against Kent – a shot that has earned him runs and made him look ridiculous.

Basil D'Oliveira leg-glancing in the Benson & Hedges Cup Final at Lords in 1974 when he top-scored for Worcester. It was in a later final that, despite a pulled ham-string muscle, he was to play a brave if futile innings in support of his county.

Barry Richards, the other great cricketing Richards, although from South Africa, often played some memorable one-day innings particularly in partnership with the West Indian Gordon Greenidge – a pairing that provided both cricketing and racial contrast.

Patrick Eagar

Gordon Greenidge playing one of his characteristic shots during his record innings for Hampshire against Glamorgan at Southampton on 16 July 1975. Richards and Greenidge put on 210 and then Greenidge went on to make 177.

Two of the most influential one-day cricketers caught, momentarily, at the wrong end. John Shepherd (left) was one of the first overseas cricketers to make a mark in a one-day final, Asif Iqbal (right) played many great innings for Kent and nearly won them the 1971 Gillette Final.

What is Illingworth whispering to Dexter? Two of the most successful one-day captains – and both former England captains – at the presentation of the Benson & Hedges Cup in 1975. Illingworth has just won the trophy for Leicestershire who under his leadership in the seventies were to become a one-day power. Dexter had tasted similar success leading Sussex in the sixties.

12 Patrick Eagar

The sight that all batsmen fear. Joel Garner has probably been the single most influential bowler in Somerset's one-day successes. He is so tall that at the moment of delivery his bowling hand is over the sight-screen; he's mean and very, very accurate, with apparently an inexhaustible supply of yorkers.

Graham Gooch in the 1979 Benson & Hedges Final. His century was one of the few major innings played by English-born players on such important set-piece occasions and not only established his position, but also helped Essex win their first title in 103 years.

13 Benson & Hedges Marketing Department

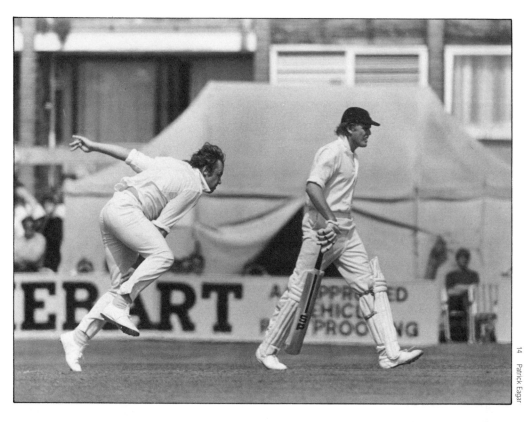

Mike Procter bowling against Hampshire in the Benson & Hedges Cup in 1977 when his hat-trick destroyed Hampshire batting. For a time he was Gloucestershire and his all-round skills and leadership won them many a famous victory.

Allan Lamb's batting and Northants's ability to score runs quickly have brought them many recent one-day successes. Here he is in the 1980 Benson & Hedges Final.

Peter Willey driving powerfully in the 1980 Benson & Hedges Final. Willey, who headed the 1969 John Player League Table, has been a greater success at one-day cricket than five-day and it was his batting in 1979/80 one-day matches in Australia that contributed to England's successes.

17

If Rip Van Winkle should suddenly awaken would he recognize the scene? This is probably the most famous tree in cricket, in the most traditional of cricket grounds: St Lawrence ground at Canterbury. Although a hit against the tree still counts for four today the tree is surrounded by adverts which few could have imagined twenty years ago.

No not a football crowd. But the scene at a Benson & Hedges semi-final in 1975. Some crowd violence is not uncommon at cricket grounds though, mercifully, it is not quite as bad as football.

When No-Score is a bad score. The scoreboard from the Worcestershire – Somerset group match in the Benson & Hedges competition in 1979 when Somerset declared their innings closed after just one over with the total on one off a no-ball. Worcestershire won, Somerset qualified for the knock-out stages but the storm their action caused led not only to Somerset being disqualified but to a change in the rules.

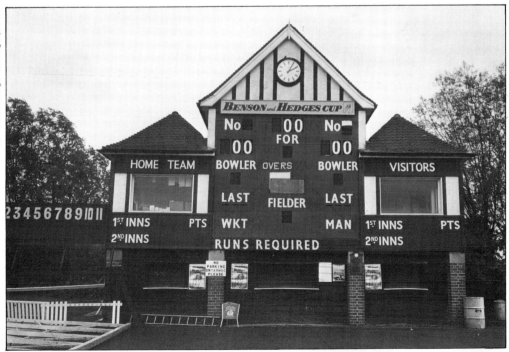

Lord's full for the 1979 Benson & Hedges Cup Final and a sight to keep many a county treasurer happy. One-day cricket came in apologetically to save the three-day game. Now, despite reservations from the traditionalists, its great occasions attract the biggest crowds outside Test matches.

The future is here and it works – at least in Australia! Packer-style night cricket showing (21a) the quite magical effect of cricket played under the Sydney lights and (21b) cricket played in clothes that look more like Marks & Spencer seconds.

The moment that fooled everybody. Lilley had apparently been caught by Kallicharran at cover. The crowd, thinking Australia were beaten, invaded the pitch to celebrate the West Indies winning the 1975 World Cup Final. But the umpire signalled a no-ball and the West Indies had to wait a few more minutes before they could savour their triumph.

seamers were mercilessly plundered. Amiss, who owed his cricket renaissance to the invaluable practice that the Indian bowlers had provided in 1972, now put on an exhilarating display: 98 at lunch in a score of 150 for 1.

He finally scored 137 off 140 balls in an innings that was technically flawless and remarkably calm. Apart from Greig, who made 4, all the English batsmen made runs; Old and Denness put on 89 in the last ten overs, 63 of these coming in the last thirty balls. By the time the sixtieth over was completed, England had reached a colossal 334 for 4, exactly the same number of runs that they had scored on the first day of the previous summer's Test against India at the same ground, when they went on to reach 629.

For all practical purposes the match was over, but India's response mattered, not only for morale but because should they finish level on points the run-rate would make a difference. But Gavaskar, it seems, had decided that the match was over – and in front of the huge crowd, many of them colourful Indian spectators, he decided to convert a match into a virtual net. In sixty overs he made 36 not out, as India crawled to 132 for 3. He disgusted his own supporters, was disowned by his captain and manager, was later reprimanded by his board – and quite confounded everyone else. To this day he has never provided any sensible explanation, though in 1982, after yet another massive one-day defeat at the hands of England, he could joke about it. The Indian manager, Raj Singh, had spoken of the six-hitting exploits of the great C.K. Nayadu, and Gavaskar responding said, 'Well, you have heard how C.K. could win matches with his batting; you know how I can lose matches by mine.' The most plausible explanation is that Gavaskar had lost form; he could neither score nor get out and suffered a sort of brainstorm – years later he would once or twice give his wicket away in Tests by playing in the most reckless one-day fashion.

The New Zealand–East Africa match produced an easy victory for the Kiwis by 80 runs, the principal feature of this being the 171 not out made by Glen Turner, a batsman who had arrived in England in the late sixties as a correct but methodical batsman and used the experience of domestic English one-day cricket to learn how to play his strokes entertainingly. The East Africans were making up numbers in the competition and it showed; they lost by ten wickets to India, and by 196 runs to England. Composed mainly of people of expatriate Indian or Pakistani stock they might have done better had they selected some of their younger, possibly better players, or even East Africans like Basharat Hassan, Owen-

Thomas and Solanky, playing in county cricket. They were probably not helped by their supporters, whose enthusiasm rather outweighed their knowledge. They seemed to be more interested in their batsmen hitting fours, though they were not always sure who was at the crease.

The West Indies' victory over Sri Lanka was just as easy. Julien took 4 for 20, Boyce 3 for 22 and Roberts 2 for 16, bowling out Sri Lanka for 86. Only three batsmen reached double figures, Tissera the highest of them with 14. By half-past three the match was over as the West Indies hit the 87 required for the loss of only Fredericks's wicket. Because of the early finish the West Indians took the field again to amuse the crowd for an exhibition twenty–overs match.

The only match that provided some contest was the Australia–Pakistan clash at Headingley. Pakistan's triumphs in the 1974 Prudential Trophy had fostered dreams of winning the cup and as the organizers shrewdly arranged the match at Leeds, the Yorkshire Pakistanis thronged Headingley. For the first time since 1966, the gates were closed with 22,000 inside. Australia with a left-hand, right-hand opening combination (the New South Wales pair Alan Turner and Rick McCosker) made a sound start. But though both the Chappell brothers made useful runs, at 128 for 4 Pakistan seemed to be in with a chance. However, Ross Edwards held Australia together and when, to everyone's surprise, at 199 for 6 Pakistan brought on their leg-spinner Wasim Raja, Australia plundered runs: 79 in the last ten overs.

An Australian total of 278 always seemed too much for Pakistan, the more so when Lillee reduced them to 27 for 2. But Majid, mixing luck with brilliance, and Asif, kept Pakistan in the chase till Majid fell to Mallett for 68. Then Lillee returned to bowl Asif for 53 and blow away the tail, finishing with 5 for 34; Australia won by 73 runs.

The second-round group matches – four days later – produced some of the most sensational cricket ever seen in the one–day game. Again all the fun was to be had in Group B, while Group A produced limp victories: England, thanks to 131 from Fletcher, defeated New Zealand by 80 runs. India got some consolation by beating East Africa by ten wickets, in front of only 720 paying spectators. Madan Lal, who had conceded 64 runs for one wicket against England, took 3 for 15 and Gavaskar in twenty-nine overs and five balls made 65, underlining the gulf between Indian and East African cricket.

On paper there should have been a similar gulf between Sri Lanka and Australia. Sri Lanka, fearful of a quick despatch, as in the West Indies match, won the toss and put the Australians in. This did not seem to do them much good, for Alan Turner started scoring freely, and Australia soon were racing away to a great score. The Sri Lankan bowling was friendly, the fielding eccentric and after sixty overs Australia reached 328 for 5; Turner 101, McCosker 73, with fifties from Greg Chappell and Doug Walters. The Oval crowd had barely begun to debate how long these amateurs would last against Thomson and Lillee when, in the words of Thomson (as told to David Frith), 'it all clicked just right'.[24]

Thomson and Lillee had smashed England during the previous winter's Ashes tour, and the pair were welcomed with that mixture of awe and faint disbelief that England reserves for fast bowlers who have destroyed the country's batting. Most of the interest centred on Thomson who seemed to be the living embodiment of the most cherished English myth, that Australia could always whistle up a champion from their unknown outbacks. In fact, before the 1974–75 tour Alec Bedser, chairman of the selectors, had expressed, albeit jocularly, just such a fear.

In the first match against Pakistan Thomson had lived up to his tag of wild and unpredictable by bowling five no-balls, including a wide that went for four. The crowd had booed him and he had given them the Harvey Smith two-finger salute. Then, at the nets preceding the Sri Lanka match, Thomson's no-ball problems had worsened, leading to much press speculation. But new, better-fitting boots eventually solved the problem.

At the Oval on that June day the Sri Lankans seemed to be making the most unexpected and spirited response to the Australians. They scored 23 runs in the first five overs, at tea, after twenty-five overs, they were 115 for 2, and by the thirty-second over, the 150 was on the board with Wettimuny past his 50 and Mendis, playing quite beautifully, on 32. Then Chappell called on Thomson again. Do something. Anything. Thomson had solved his no-ball problems and the Australians, who under Ian Chappell began to specialize in this, decided to gee him up. Thomson later described to David Frith what happened.

They knew I was keyed up and out to prove everything, that I was a hundred per cent again. Anyway, I hit this bloke Mendis on the head. They're only little fellas, so you couldn't call it a bouncer exactly. He fell down face-first, and when they brought him around, his captain's saying 'You'll be all right' or something or other. But Mendis just says, 'Oh my God! I'm going!' [Mendis vehemently denies saying this.] He went out: he wasn't coming back! They took him to hospital. But the real trouble came when I hit Wettimuny on the foot. He was waltzing round and he wanted to go too. That was enough for him. I'd already hit him on the chest. As I walked past him at the end of the over I said to him, 'Look, it's not broken, you weak bastard,' I said. 'I'll give you a tip,' I said. 'If you are down there next over, it will be!'[25]

Wettimuny had already begun to feel shivers down his spine. Thomson appeared to be swearing and grinning at the same time, and sure enough, in the next over the ball landed on the same spot and Wettimuny's instep again took the full force. Now came the infamy. Thomson recalls:

The ball had come straight back up to the pitch to me, and as I collected it, the boys are yelling out, 'Throw down the stumps, two-up, throw down the stumps!' I'm saying to myself, 'No, no, I can't do that, no,' all in a split-second. Then I thought, 'Bugger it,' and I threw the ball and knocked the stumps over. I jumped up and shouted an appeal, but no other bastards moved. They all sat or stood there with their arms folded! They'd done me stone cold on purpose.[26]

Perhaps so, but now the Oval was indignant. Whenever Thomson bowled he was booed. As it happened Wettimuny's runner was in his ground, though Wettimuny was carried from the field to hospital. However, Tissera (52) and the captain Tennekoon (48) fought on to take gallant Sri Lanka on to 276 for 4 – a defeat by 52 runs. Faced with a prospect as daunting as India's against England, they had shown what could be done with spirit and a will to try and win – whatever the odds.

The Thomson–Sri Lankan story did not end there. All the World Cup players were staying in the same Kensington hotel and next morning, as Thomson came down for breakfast, he found himself surrounded by Sri Lankans, some of them sporting bandages. But instead of a knife in the back, as Thomson expected, they just wanted to offer breakfast. Suddenly Thomson discovered he had no appetite. Frith, Thomson's biographer, reckons that Thomson might have faced charges. A policeman overheard an exchange at the hospital between one of the injured batsmen and a medical attendant:

'What happened to you?'

'I was hit playing cricket.'

'Where?'

'At the Oval.'

'Who did it?'

'Thomson!'

At this point the policeman asked, 'Do you wish to prefer charges?' but the Sri Lankans did not pursue the matter, though in the macabre humour that Ian Chappell had, he called Thomson 'Our ambassador to Sri Lanka' at a Lord's Tavern dinner.

Meanwhile, 110 miles away, at Edgbaston, there were equally exciting things going on at the match between the West Indies and Pakistan – though here the excitement had everything to do with cricket, and nothing to do with blood sports; this match would later earn the description, 'little short of a cricket miracle'. Pakistan, without their captain Asif, were captained by Majid, who set a fine example by scoring 60. Zaheer made 31, Mushtaq 55, Wasim Raja 58 and Pakistan a good 266 for 7. In fact, at various times their batsmen had played with such command that they had looked like getting considerably more. When Sarfraz took the first three West Indian wickets to make them 36 for 3, it looked like Pakistan's day. Lloyd and Kanhai engineered a partial recovery but by the time the eighth wicket fell the West Indies were only 166, 101 behind. At this point Deryck Murray, one of the few West Indians to play with the necessary discipline, found a useful partner in Holder. Even so when in the forty-sixth over Sarfraz had Holder caught by Pervez for 16, the West Indians were still 64 runs short of victory. It was seven o'clock, the 20,000-odd at the ground were thinking of wending their way homewards, when the miracle happened.

Murray found an ideal partner in Roberts and they slowly began to take the game away from the Pakistanis. With five overs left, 23 were wanted, and, crucially, Sarfraz's quota of twelve overs had been exhausted. The source of the crowd noise now told the story. The Pakistanis were becoming quieter, the West Indians, just beginning to glimpse an incredible victory, more exuberant. With three overs left, West Indies were 251 for 9: 16 wanted. With nine balls left, 10 runs were wanted, and Murray survived a possible run-out when a straight throw would have meant the end. The Pakistani fielders were getting rattled, and they had no real one-day bowlers left. With 5 runs wanted Wasim Raja, a leg-spinner, bowled the last over. It was an unlikely card to play – and it proved no trump. Roberts got two off a leg-bye, with the help of an overthrow, another two, then the final, winning, single. It had been the most memorable victory in the history of the game, the most crushing defeat.

Later, the West Indians would see this as the turning-point in their World Cup campaign. Clive Lloyd, who had earlier been very upset about an umpiring decision, now found himself celebrating:

> In all my days of playing cricket, I have never known such elation in a dressing room. Some years later, when we won a similarly close World Series Cricket match in Australia, there was great jubilation but it wasn't quite as emotional. Men with years of cricket experience were jumping up and down and hugging each other. Several were sobbing uncontrollably.[27]

It was only in the final group matches that Group A came alive. England, already home and dry, easily beat East Africa by 196 runs. If this seemed almost a practice match, the one between India and New Zealand was for real. Both sides had one victory, and this was the decider. Despite the modest bowling resources of both sides, both sets of batsmen struggled to make runs. India did not get going till Abid Ali, at no. 7, made 70 and took them to 230. A lot depended on Turner, and his 114 not out guided New Zealand to a four-wicket victory in the last over but one. It was not a very smooth win but New Zealand always seemed just ahead.

With both the West Indies and Australia having qualified for the finals, their group match meant nothing – except in psychological terms. And for all the ballyhoo before the match, the crowd of mainly West Indians with a smattering of Australian exiles from Earl's Court, did not see a great match. Australia, put into bat, lost a wicket without a run on board, and were always struggling. Their 192 owed a great deal to Edwards's 58 and Marsh's 52. The West Indian reply answered one question: what will the heirs of Weekes and Walcott do when Lillee and Thomson drop them short? Fredericks was hooking and cutting from the first ball, and Kallicharran was quite magical. In ten balls from Lillee Kallicharran hit 4, 4, 4, 4, 4, 1, 4, 6, 0, 4: 35 runs. Lillee conceded 66 runs in ten overs and by the time Kallicharran was out, he had made 78, and victory was a formality.

The West Indies easily brushed aside the New Zealanders in the semi-finals, beating them by five wickets. Apart from a brief period before lunch when they were 92 for 1, the Kiwis never looked like offering much of a challenge. The England–Australia semi-final was better balanced. For the first time in the series the pitch was grassy and the Headingley weather characteristically overcast. Australia won the toss, put England in, and while the country waited for the confrontation between Lillee–Thomson and the English batsmen, Gary Gilmour, an unconsidered all-rounder from New South Wales, stole the honours.

Bowling left-arm over the wicket he was lively, could swing both in and away from the batsman, and exploited the conditions well by keeping to a full length. With the first ball of his second over, and the score on 2, he had Amiss lbw for 2 and England were on the slide. Gilmour bowled his twelve overs in one spell and removed the first five in the order and Knott: he had taken 6 for 14, and England were 36 for 6. England did not look like reaching 50 but Denness held on to make 27, Arnold, the next highest scorer made 18 not out, and England, 52 for 8 at lunch, reached 93.

Australia seemed to be coasting at 17 for no wicket but then Arnold had Turner lbw, Snow had both the Chappells and Old took three wickets. Australia were 39 for 6 when Gilmour joined Walters. Not a man who believed in leaving things half done, Gilmour began to play his shots and with the experienced Walters to guide him, they put on 55 runs to win the match by four wickets. Both captains criticized the pitch – Denness understandably more than Ian Chappell – but that was hardly surprising given that nineteen batsmen had scored only 187, and an 120-overs match had finished after only sixty-five had been bowled.

Nothing like this marred the final which was just what the advertising executives would have ordered: brilliant sunshine, a lovely mid-summer's day, capacity crowds, and two great teams. Had England been one of them, the final would have been ideal, but by the end of this match even that seemed unimportant. It was the longest day of the year, 21 June, and a glorious one for cricket. The West Indies came to the final as the shortest of short-prized favourites. They had been made favourites even before the competition began; now with their impressive wins behind them they seemed unstoppable. Their win against Pakistan had been critical. Lloyd himself would later see that victory as the moment the West Indians were convinced they could win the cup.

In that match he felt he had been given wrongly caught behind – a decision that had so upset him that he had thrown his bat round the dressing room. When, eventually, the West Indians won, Lloyd, unable to control himself, had raced from the dressing room out into the section of the pavilion reserved for members, shouting, 'That will teach you . . . you cheats.' Later, much calmer, Lloyd would feel that, 'That was a very important win. After that I believe the team as a whole knew that it would not be stopped and would win the cup. It was the type of performance which helped erase the age-old feeling that the West Indies were no good fighting from behind.'[28]

In the final, as Lloyd walked out to bat, the West Indies once again had to fight. Chappell had won the toss, put the West Indians in and through a piece of luck (Fredericks hooked Lillee for six but in completing the stroke overbalanced on to his wicket), and good cricket reduced the West Indians to 50 for 3. Australia had done everything right and though Lloyd soon hooked Lillee for a six, on 26 he offered a catch to Ross Edwards at mid-wicket. Edwards dived but could not hold it and Lloyd was convinced that, somehow, this was going to be his day.

The pitch held nothing for the bowlers; the Australians had no spinners, just a pack of quick to medium-pacers, and Lloyd's bat – having got rid of its croak – began to trumpet some extraordinary shots. While the grey-haired Kanhai, who in his younger days himself played like this, dropped anchor – he did not score for eleven overs – Lloyd took Australia apart. In eighty-two balls he made 102 with two sixes (both off the back foot) and twelve fours. He and Kanhai had put on 149 in thirty-six overs when there was another controversial Lloyd dismissal. Lloyd chased a ball going down the leg side from Gilmour and in trying to glance it got an edge. Umpire Bird heard the snick, saw the deviation but was not sure it carried. As West Indians and Australians offered conflicting advice Bird walked towards umpire Spenser and when he confirmed it, gave Lloyd out. At 199 for 4 with Richards, Boyce, Julien and Murray to come a total in excess of 300 looked on. But Gilmour removed Richards for 5, and the patient Kanhai for 55; 209 for 6. But nos. 7, 8 and 9, Boyce, Julien, and Murray took the West Indies to 291 for 8 – not overwhelming but commanding.

Australia lost McCosker early, but Turner and Ian Chappell, driving and placing the faster bowlers with astonishing ease, soon picked up momentum. However the need to score at just under five an over began to pressurize the Australians. They went for runs that were not there, or somewhat marginal. Richards, having done nothing with the bat, figured in two run-outs, twice throwing down the stumps from side-on, running out Turner at 40, and Greg

Chappell at 15; he also made the throw that enabled Lloyd to run out Ian Chappell for 62. Then Lloyd bowled Walters for 35, and slowly Australia, losing more wickets, began to fall behind the required run-rate.

For much of the day Mike Brearley had sat at the Nursery End with Peter Walker and others, luxuriating in the cricket atmosphere that only the West Indians bring to the game: a wonderful mixture of exuberance and exhortation. Now, as Thomson came out to join Lillee at 273 for 9, Brearley went to sit by the boundary rope, confident the end was near. It had been a good final, but a twist was still to come. For Lillee was confident Australia could get the runs and Lillee and Thomson began to push the ones and twos and slowly runs came. Suddenly Lillee drove Holder in the air, neatly to Kallicharran at cover. The match was over, Brearley and his friends picked up their beer cans and scorecards, the West Indians raced on to the ground. Umpire Bird lost his white cap, the spare ball and received a sharp blow that made him feel dizzy, Thomson lost his sweater. (In the group match between these two countries Bird had another white cap stolen which he subsequently saw being worn by a London bus conductor who proudly claimed he had got it from 'Umpire Dickie Bird'.)

But nobody had noticed that Spenser had ruled Holder's delivery a no-ball, Kallicharran shied at the stumps and missed, and the ball was lost. The crowd from the Tavern, anticipating victory, advanced on to the ground. Thomson shouted to Lillee, Lillee bawled at Thomson – eventually they began running. Thomson recalls:

We ran a fair few runs but the umpire was going to give us two. I said, 'Hey, how much are you giving us for that?' and Tom Spenser says 'Two' – real abrupt. 'Pig's arse!' I shouted. 'We've been running up and down here all afternoon. Who are you kidding?' I really got into him. Then I think he changed it. [29]

Spenser awarded three runs. And still Lillee and Thomson went on picking up more. They had put on 41, just 17 short, when at 8.43 p.m. Thomson lost a ball from Holder against the background of the bricks of the pavilion. He started to run anyway, Murray got the ball and, underarm, threw down the stumps. Thomson was run out and West Indies were World Cup champions. Thomson felt 'a numb feeling, because we were not all that used to losing. I sat in the dressing room there and felt really annoyed, what a bastard: we played wrongly.'

But if he was exhausted, and hated losing, the West Indians celebrated – and with them the cricket world. It had been, as Mike Brearley was to write later, 'a miraculous day, in cricketing terms: perfect weather, perfect pitch and a superb game'. A crowd of 26,000 had watched the final – 158,000 the entire tournament – and cricket's official verdict was provided by the editor of *Wisden* who, reviewing the match, wrote in the 1976 *Wisden*:

> From 11 a.m. till 8.43 p.m. the cricketers of the Caribbean had been locked in a succession of thrills with cricketers from the Southern Cross. It might not be termed first-class cricket, but the game has never produced better entertainment in one day . . . It was the longest day of the year; the longest day in cricket history and one that those who were there and the millions who watched it on television will never forget.

Curiously, the only sour note was struck by the West Indian Board who, thinking the trophy and £4,000 should be enough, did not respond with any bonuses for the players – apart from the agreed fee of £350 a man. Clive Lloyd's wounded feelings were assuaged when the Guyanese Government flew him back home with the trophy and he was swept through the streets of Georgetown in a motorcade.

The competition, however, brought a special glow to one-day cricket and within days of the final the annual meeting of the ICC decided to hold another. Though India were keen to host, England, where summer light does allow 120 overs in a day, still seemed the best choice. And with the Prudential still keen and generous – their outlay was £250,000, and they gave the trophy and £10,000 – 1979 was designated the next World Cup year. India had originally been promised the entire summer. The World Cup, followed by four Tests, would fit the summer very nicely.

1979 saw not only a World Cup but what was quickly dubbed a mini-world cup. The idea of nominating two countries to represent the lesser cricketing countries outside the major six, did not seem adequate. Soon after the 1975 final, associate members of the International Cricket Conference began planning a preliminary competition, to be held just before the 1979 cup, with the finalists joining their big brothers.

Good as these matches were for the soul of cricket, it was evident that no sponsor would like to put any money in – or at least, not in a major way (individual matches did have limited local sponsorship).

So the associate members formed their own committee, and led by the enterprise and generosity of John Gardiner, the Englishman who represents the United States of America on the ICC, they organized the somewhat grandly named ICC Trophy matches in May 1979.

As it happened the fortnight of the competition in May produced some of the most deplorable weather, the wettest May since 1772, of even that indifferent summer: twelve of the matches were abandoned without a definite result. The worst-affected team was Papua New Guinea who saw two of their matches produce 'no result'. In a competition that was already exotic, Papua New Guinea were perhaps the most colourful team. Their first match was against the rather portly-looking East African side at Wolverhampton's pretty, if small, Tettenhall ground, which is often confused with a neighbouring cemetery. (All matches in this competition were played in the Midlands, on grounds within forty miles of Birmingham.) The Papuans, unaccustomed to the weather, suffered through a morning of mist, rain and cold. Then after they had lunched on English curry (the ladies at the Wolverhampton club, in an interesting reflection on cultural values, had decided that curry would be the most acceptable common food for the East Africans, Papuans and the English), play eventually got going.

It was clear that conditions were rather too unfamiliar for the Papuans, and the East Africans, despite their portliness, were a class higher. Even so there was scope for some of the Papuan batsmen, particularly Api Leka who made 51 not out in 161 for 8. His principal accomplice in the Papuan rescue from 43 for 6, was one Charlie Harrison whose parents had come from Coventry, but who himself had been born in Rawalpindi, and after schooling in Australia had worked in a Heineken subsidiary in Port Moresby, the Papuan capital. Rain, of course, ruined the match but it provided the essential flavour of a competition which while strong on colour and exoticism also provided good cricket.

In the end there was no schoolboy-fiction finish: one of the associate members did not win the Prudential Cup. However, there were moments of individual glory, as for John Valentine, the twenty-four-year-old French teacher from Montreal, who spear-headed Canada's bowling, and took the scalps of Majid Khan, Mike Brearley and Rick Darling.

Sri Lanka eventually beat Canada in the ICC Trophy final played at Worcester, two days before the Prudential World Cup final, by

60 runs in a match which saw 588 runs scored. If some of the prowess of the Sri Lankan batsmen were well-known, it was the resilience of the Canadian batsmen – a mixture of native-born and expatriate West Indians – that came as a surprise. It typified the mixture of exhilarating, infuriating cricket – two run-outs, one off a no-ball – that seems to characterize this tournament. The final also introduced us to 'Percy', self-appointed Sri Lankan cheer-leader, whose brand of encouragement and exuberance found full expression in the World Cup match in which the Sri Lankans beat India by 47 runs.

Wider political issues had touched the ICC Trophy matches. Sri Lanka's Government forced its cricketers to withdraw from their group match against Israel, who, as a result, won their one and only match by a forfeiture. But by the time the 1979 World Cup proper had begun, cricket appeared to have sorted out its own internal political problems. Ever since 1977 the cricket world had been divided between those who supported traditional cricket, run by representative national bodies, and those who had signed up for a very different type of cricket pioneered by Kerry Packer, an Australian TV magnate. We shall examine the Packer phenomenon and its legacy in a subsequent chapter. Here it is worth noting that in the months prior to the World Cup there were anguished debates about the participation of Packer's World Series cricketers in the World Cup.

The West Indies, Australia and Pakistan were the teams worst affected, as Packer had lured most of their best cricketers away for his rival circuit. Would the respective national bodies choose their Packer cricketers? If they did, would the other cricketers play, particularly the English, who were vehemently opposed to Packer? Fortunately, in the weeks just prior to the tournament the Australian Board – the one most affected by Packer's cricket – announced that peace had returned to cricket. If the reconciliation did not allow the Australians to select their own Packer players – in effect, their 'B' team played – the West Indians and Pakistani Packer players happily meshed in with colleagues who had stuck to traditional cricket. For the first time in two years, the atmosphere in cricket was without the rancour and deep suspicion that had characterized the game ever since Packer appeared.

But if cricket's storms had passed, the summer weather was not quite as brilliant as that which marked the 1975 World Cup. The first group matches dawned overcast and the only cheerful note was that it did not rain and the cold was not as severe as it had been a few days previously. This time the seedings, and the draw, had been done with more finesse. England were in the apparently tougher Group B facing Pakistan, Australia and Canada, while the holders, West Indies, were in Group A with India, New Zealand and Sri Lanka.

The West Indies easily won their opening match against India by nine wickets. Gavaskar hit the first ball for four, then, shaping to hook Roberts, found the ball a bit quicker than expected and provided Holding a high but not difficult catch. The only other resistance came from Gavaskar's brother-in-law, Viswanath, who, as he did so often for India, matched immaculate defence with some of the most delightful wrist-work. But finally he was unable to keep an express Holding ball out – after making 75 – and by then the Indian innings was ready to be buried. Their score of 191 was never much of a target, especially when Greenidge, after a slow start, began to open up. Of more interest at this stage was the friendly banter, and contrast of styles, provided by the rival West Indian and Indian supporters. The latter favoured flags, the former small hand-held bells – and soon these were ringing happily all over Edgbaston.

The West Indies had more than just an easy victory to celebrate. The match unveiled the fast bowling attack that has, in recent years, made the West Indians such a feared side: Roberts, Holding, Garner and Croft. Roberts had played in the 1975 cup, and was well established; the Oval Test of 1976 had seen the rise of Holding; but Garner and Croft were, relatively speaking, newcomers to the West Indian side. English cricket had been much surprised when the West Indians left out Wayne Daniel, the Black Diamond of Middlesex, but such was the success of this quartet that by the end of the cup it seemed to make no difference.

The other outstanding match, at least on paper, was the clash at Lord's between England and Australia. For the England team, under Mike Brearley, this match began as if England were continuing the immensely successful 1978–79 tour of Australia. Most of the players had been on that tour and the Australians, under Kim Hughes, showed the same flashes of sudden madness which undid much good, if not brilliant, cricket. The Australians, though badly beaten in the previous winter's Tests had, in their turn, won the one-day series quite comfortably. As any meeting between these sides is an occasion, Lord's was packed. Australia, put in by Brearley, began well: 97 for 1 at lunch. Brearley had caused some surprise by giving Boycott an over before lunch, but he made the breakthrough just after lunch and four subsequent run-outs caused an Australian collapse: the last nine wickets falling for the addition of 62 runs. England, despite a genuinely quick spell by Hogg, made the runs with six wickets in hand. If this match heralded the arrival of Boycott the bowler (Boycott the batsman made 1, falling to his old nemesis Hogg) the English conclusion that he and Gooch could between them provide the fifth bowler in a match of this kind would have serious consequences later.

The second-round matches were drowned by the full force of the rain that had been ever threatening. The West Indians and Sri Lankans hung about the Oval for three days, playing cards and watching the ducks paddle about on the rain-drenched ground. Not a ball was bowled and both teams took two points.

England and New Zealand, on the other hand, booked their semi-final places. The English victory over Canada was delayed by a day due to rain and in the manner of nearly all rain-affected one-day matches the game was played in indifferent weather in front of a pitiful crowd. England won by eight wickets, though the Canadians, having been bowled out for 45, salvaged some pride by removing Brearley for 0 and Randall for 5, before Gooch and Boycott did their stuff.

New Zealand, who always seemed to be playing India to decide a semi-final World Cup place, won by an identical margin. India, put in to bat under overcast skies on a Leeds wicket that provided traditional help to the seamers, never really looked like making a big score. A dogged 55 by Gavaskar with some help from Patel and Kapil Dev enabled them to reach 182, which set a target for the Kiwis of just over 3 an over. Edgar, the opening batsman, made 84 not out and, despite a wobble in the middle, a New Zealand victory was never in doubt.

Pakistan, who had easily accounted for Canada in the first-group match, similarly despatched Australia. Hughes's side was weakened by an injury to Hogg, and this so unbalanced the attack that Australia had to use fairly irregular bowlers like Cosier, Border and Yallop to bowl twenty-four out of the sixty overs. They cost 148 runs and after a slow start – 125 for 2 in thirty-five overs – Asif Iqbal, the captain, and Javed Miandad hit 87 in fourteen overs, followed by Asif, Wasim Raja and Imran who scored 47 in the last five overs. End-of-innings runs are often crucial both in setting the target and the psychological effect they have, and Australia never got going in response. Hilditch made 72, but that was largely a lone effort as Pakistan won by 89 runs.

This left the final-group matches looking a bit limp; England,

Pakistan, New Zealand had qualified. There was some very slight doubt about the West Indies who, to make absolutely sure, needed to beat New Zealand.

The match showed, yet again, how well Lloyd had moulded his side.

Put into bat – the West Indians are happiest when chasing runs – they never quite mastered the New Zealand attack which was a clutch of medium-pacers, all bowling the same stuff, supporting their one genuine quick bowler Richard Hadlee. The New Zealand tactics were readily to concede 3 or 4 runs an over when these bowlers were on, but aim to cut off the boundaries and try the patience of the stroke-makers. Another West Indian side might have lost their heads. Lloyd's, led by the captain himself, did not and finished on 244 with Lloyd 73 not out, Greenidge 65 and Kallicharran 39, providing the necessary efficient support.

Even that target against such a tight West Indian attack would have been difficult to make. New Zealand were already without one of their leading batsmen, Howarth, and at 27 Edgar was run out for 12. Though most of the major batsmen reached double figures, they never looked like getting 245, and lost by 25 runs.

Both Pakistan and England were, of course, through to the finals but their match was a nerve-tingling affair, not least because the victorious side knew it would avoid the West Indies in the semi-finals. Pakistan won the toss and exploiting the Headingley conditions well soon had Brearley and Randall out with only 4 scored. Worse was to follow, for the gentle medium pace of Majid Khan took 3 for 27 (Boycott, Gower and Botham). At 118 for 8, the large Pakistani contingent could feel more than satisfied. But, as so often, the English tail wagged profitably: Willis, 24 not out, and Taylor, 20, put on 43 runs. A target of 165, however, did not look big enough and the ease with which Willis and Taylor had batted suggested the wicket was now going to present few problems to the Muslim country's brilliant stroke-makers.

This prediction was turned on its head by Mike Hendrick – a bowler who often beats the bat, or makes the chance that does not stick, but rarely has the figures his bowling deserves. That day Hendrick tore through the top half of the Pakistani batting, finishing with 4 for 15 (four of the first five in the order), and, at 34 for 6, Pakistan seemed beyond repair. Asif and Wasim Raja took the score to 86 but even after they had gone Pakistan had some hope as long as Imran Khan was there.

It was then that Mike Brearley played his master-stroke. He

brought on Boycott, who had already taken 2 for 15 in eight overs against Australia, and 1 for 12 in nine overs against Canada. Headingley had seen many a great Boycott innings, now they were to see this most enigmatic of cricketers bowling gentle seamers with his cap on to such effect that in five overs he gave away only 14 runs and took the crucial wickets of Wasim Bari and Sikander Bakht. England had won an important battle by 14 runs.

Two days later Sri Lanka won an even more important battle, though this had no bearing on the cup. They defeated sad India by 47 runs, providing the most convincing of arguments for their admission as a full Test-playing country.

The semi-finals played in weather of the excellent 1975 vintage reproduced much of that year's thrilling cricket as fortunes fluctuated. This was particularly true of the Old Trafford clash between England and New Zealand. Boycott had proved so effective as the fifth bowler that England played an extra batsman – Wayne Larkins – and this worked splendidly. Despite a very Brearleyish 53, and a belligerent 71 by Gooch, England were 145 for 5 when Randall came in to bat. He had been having a lean time but showing uncharacteristic good sense he so perked the tail that another 76 was added while he was there, of which Randall made 42 not out.

A target of 3.7 an over for a good batting side like New Zealand was not impossible, and at various stages in their innings – when the openers were together, or when Wright and Turner looked inseparable – they seemed capable of doing it. But all the breaks went England's way: Boycott had the dangerous Howarth lbw with a full toss bowled round the wicket and Randall ran out two of their batsmen, Wright and the captain, Burgess. England suffered a few agonies when Cairns and Lees hit huge sixes but, in the end, too much was expected of the New Zealand tail and they failed by 9 runs.

The other semi-final between the West Indies and Pakistan at the Oval epitomized the sort of match that everybody expected of the World Cup. At a sun-drenched Oval, one great side battled with another that, on its day, looked capable of beating anybody. The West Indies, put in to bat, made 132 for the first wicket and the way in which Greenidge and Haynes mastered the early attack suggested a record score. But the Pakistani fill-in bowlers Majid and Asif first applied the brake, then Asif took the wicket of Greenidge for 73. However, Richards, Lloyd, and King all made useful runs and 293 for 6 was a big score.

It looked still bigger when Sadiq was out for 2, with the score on 10. Then Majid was dropped on 10, and he and Zaheer put on 156 more runs. Until then the lack of variety in the West Indian attack seemed to have made little difference, but with these two Pakistanis looking in such command Lloyd had to turn to Richards. Though he conceded 12 in his first over, the change from brutish pace to gentle off-spinners probably unsettled the batsmen. In his next overs Croft, returning to the attack, dismissed Zaheer, Majid and Miandad in twelve balls for 4 runs. Richards, too, left his mark as a bowler with the wickets of Mudassar, Asif and Imran. Pakistan's glory dreams were once again extinguished.

We were left with the dream final that all England wanted: the home country versus the mighty West Indians, acknowledged champions in this class of cricket. Not even the most partisan Englishman could pretend that England were as gifted but they had immense experience of one-day cricket, had often beaten superior sides, and in Brearley probably had the most outstanding captain the game had known for some time. Though this did not appear significant at the time, England chose to go into the match with an extra batsman, confident that Boycott, Gooch and Larkins could work the fifth-bowler fiddle. They were also without Willis.

Brearley won the toss, put in the West Indies and after a slow start Lord's exploded – not with West Indian cheers but unexpected English happiness. Greenidge was splendidly run out by Randall, Haynes edged Old to Hendrick, Lloyd was caught and bowled by Old – after some heart-stopping juggling – and Kallicharran bowled by Hendrick. West Indies were 99 for 4, and might have been in a worse mess had Richards been adjudged lbw second ball. Richards, however, soon settled in and at lunch West Indies reached 125 for 4 after thirty-four overs.

When play resumed after lunch Brearley faced a crucial decision. Should he use his main bowlers and try and bowl out the West Indians, or should he try the Boycott–Gooch–Larkins fiddle, leaving his main bowlers for the final ten overs or so. He went for the fiddle – and it failed. Boycott, Gooch and Larkins were hit for 86 runs, at more than 7 an over (the main bowlers kept the run-rate down to about 4 an over). This was always a possibility, and Brearley himself would advance this as the principal reason for defeat. But the surprising thing about the assault was that it was carried out not by Richards, already secure as the world's best batsman, but by Collis King, who had been turned down by Glamorgan and done nothing till then to suggest he was capable of such mayhem. In what was effectively eleven overs, King hooked, pulled and drove with such awesome power that he made 86. By the time Edmonds had had him caught by Randall at square leg, he and Richards had put on 139 in twenty-one overs, and taken the match out of England's hands.

Richards, now at his majestic best, began to conjure up strokes of such breathtaking audacity that despite Brearley's best fielding plans, the runs came. The tail provided him with little support (the last four batsmen made ducks) but Richards could go it alone. He put the seal on his 138 not out, in only 156 balls, by hitting the last ball that Hendrick bowled – a good length, perfectly respectable delivery – for six between square and fine legs. The *World of Cricket 1980* would describe it aptly as 'a front-foot straight drive executed at right angles'.

So England set out to score 287 at the rate of just under 5 an over. The sun shone brilliantly and Boycott and Brearley made hay, but slowly: 79 runs at tea. This would have been wonderful in a Test, but in the World Cup they had used up twenty-five overs and the run-rate had risen remorselessly to 8 an over. Brearley's personal inclination was to have a 'go', aiming for 6 runs an over after tea. But, much to his later regret, he was 'talked out of this in favour of a more modest target'. In fact, Boycott and Brearley scored 50 from the next thirteen overs, reducing the required rate to 7 an over. But, crucially, they had allowed Richards – the West Indian fifth fiddle bowler – to bowl ten overs for a mere 35 runs and as they tried to accelerate they came up against the fearsome pace quartet.

Even then England were in with a chance as Gooch and Randall, taking over after Boycott and Brearley had gone, at last provided the much-needed acceleration. But it could not last – and it didn't. They had put on 48 in forty-three balls, when Randall, going down the wicket, was bowled by Croft for 15. Now Garner came back at the Nursery End and England collapsed.

The forty-eighth over had begun with England 183 for 3, Gooch 32. It ended with England 186 for 6, Gooch bowled Garner 32, Gower bowled Garner 0, Larkins bowled Garner 0, Gower and Larkins going in successive balls. Botham was caught by his old friend Richards in front of the Tavern boundary, and Garner again got two legs of a hat-trick: Old and Taylor. In all he had taken five wickets for 4 runs in eleven balls and the English batsmen seemed unable to pick up either the line or the length. This was not surprising since he stands six foot nine inches, and bowling from the Nursery End, he often delivered the ball from a height of well over seven feet and above the sight-screens, making it almost impossible to pick up. When Croft bowled Hendrick to seal the English defeat by 92 runs, Lord's – as in 1975 – gave itself over to the West Indians.

The use of a stop-gap fifth bowler, the absence of Willis, the cautious Test-style opening of Boycott and Brearley (why were they opening in a one-day match?) were all quoted as factors in England's defeat; but in the end England had simply been beaten by the best side in the world. As Mike Brearley wrote afterwards, 'There have probably been better Test teams than this West Indies one, for they lack high-quality spinners. But I cannot imagine that in the history of the game, there has been a side better equipped for one-day cricket. In fact their closest rivals were probably the winners of the 1975 World Cup.'[30]

# 5
# Something for Everybody

Ability can sometimes be held in check by using the right tactics in the one–day game; that's why matches can be won or lost if only one or two players get decent scores. As far as bowling in limited–overs matches is concerned, it's not absolutely vital to have the best or fastest bowlers at your disposal; after attacking with the new ball what bowlers have to do is to bowl to their field, maintain a good line and length and let the batsmen make mistakes. That's the name of the game. The one–day game isn't necessarily dominated by simple ability alone.

Geoffrey Boycott reflecting on the one–day game
after an experience of Packer-style cricket
in the 1979–80 series in Australia[31]

At the beginning of the 1975 season, only nine counties had won a limited–overs competition. Lancashire and Kent had won five competitions: the northern county three Gillette Cups and two John Player trophies, Kent two Gillette, two John Player and a Benson & Hedges Cup. Sussex, Warwickshire and Yorkshire had each twice won the Gillette, Gloucestershire had won the Gillette once, Surrey the Benson & Hedges once, Leicestershire the Benson & Hedges twice and John Player once, while Worcestershire had won the John Player once. Eight counties had little to show for their twelve years of limited–over competition but the first season of World Cup cricket not only brought good weather but also provided cheer for the have-nots of the cricket world: both for those who had never won anything and those who had forgotten what it was like to win. However, the most immediate impact of the World Cup was on the crowds.

The first World Cup, followed as it was by a series with Australia on home turf back-to-back with one in which England had been crushingly defeated would, in any event, have been of great interest. But it was the impact on English domestic one-day cricket that is interesting. The best yardstick for this is often the league, with its accent on family entertainment. For some years John Player League attendances had been fluctuating: up one year, down the next. They had risen to 341,406 in 1971 but then gone down, up, down to a low of 281,621 in 1974. The World Cup in 1975 boosted it to 374,299, a peak it has never again attained. (The 1979 World Cup did not quite have the same impact and after some years of falling attendances the 1982 season saw the attendances reach a new low of just 189,900.)

The sun played a part, but some of the crowds in 1975 did come to acclaim a new Sunday champion: Hampshire. It was to prove the culmination of a good year for Hampshire: the semi-final of the Benson & Hedges (losing to the eventual winner Leicestershire), quarter-finals of the Gillette and winners of the Fenner Trophy – beating Yorkshire on their home ground. In the Sunday League they lost their first match to Worcestershire but were head of the table by 15 June, and, though defeats against the old rival Lancashire and, surprisingly, Warwickshire – by eight wickets – lost them the leadership, they were back at the top on 24 August and eventually beat Worcestershire to the title by two points.

The surprising thing was not their victory but that Hampshire in those days did not win more often. For at various times they appeared to have the team that could take over from Lancashire or Kent as the kings of one-day cricket. In fact, apart from a John Player title in 1978, Hampshire have won nothing else in limited-overs cricket and went without victory for two years in the Benson & Hedges competition before they surprised everybody, including perhaps themselves, by beating Middlesex in May 1981.

In the mid-seventies their opening pair of the West Indian Gordon Greenidge and the South African Barry Richards was probably the best seen in county cricket for years; both Turner and Jesty were, at that stage, potential England players and their bowling offered the fire-power of Roberts supplemented by the guile of Sainsbury and the containing steadiness of Rice. Greenidge, who in retrospect always seemed to be scoring double-century opening stands with Richards, believes that Hampshire did not succeed more often partly because his partnerships with Richards were not quite as prolific as nostalgia would have us believe. In ten years as opening partners they put on 100 on twenty-four occasions, and in limited-overs cricket they had eleven century partnerships. One of these came in the 1975 John Player match against Gloucestershire when the pair put on 138 inside twenty overs, the runs coming in only sixty-two minutes as Richards made 57 and Greenidge 72.

The classical Richards–Greenidge partnership – the one memory insists they played all the time – came in that season's second-round Gillette match against Glamorgan at Southampton. The previous week Glamorgan had beaten Hampshire in the championship, one of the five defeats responsible for the county's failure to win the title. In the Gillette on 16 July, Richards and Greenidge put on 210 for the first wicket with Richards, in his languid style, scoring a century before lunch, hitting two sixes and twenty-two fours, and Greenidge, demonstrating the brutal power that marks his best form, going on to make 177, his last 104 runs, after Richards's fall, coming in twenty overs. Eventually he fell to Malcolm Nash, who had once been hit for six sixes in an over by Sobers. After Greenidge hit yet another six – he hit seven in all – Nash took a white handkerchief from his pocket and waved in mock surrender. Hampshire's 371 for 4 is the highest total ever made in limited overs in this country and Greenidge's 177 was only bettered by Gooch's 198 in 1982 in the Benson & Hedges. In fact Greenidge's nearest challenge has been from himself in a 1979 John Player match against Warwickshire that Hampshire won by one run, after Greenidge had made 163 not out in a total of 250 for 5.

Greenidge was to hit another century – 111 – against Leicester-shire in the Benson & Hedges semi-final but on that occasion Richards failed, bowled by McKenzie for 2 off the sixth ball of the match, and led by Balderstone's 101, Leicestershire won easily to enter their third final in four years.

This was, perhaps, the most complete of Leicestershire's Benson & Hedges triumphs – they have not won the competition since – for apart from one, unexpectedly heavy, group defeat against Warwickshire, Leicestershire were rarely in trouble that year.

Their closest match was against Lancashire in the quarter-finals. Faced with the accuracy of McKenzie and Higgs, and the spin of Illingworth and Steele, Lancashire struggled to make 180 and might not have even made that had Hayes, who made 67, not been dropped. But then Leicestershire were themselves 132 for 7, with Tolchard alone of the main batsmen left. However, Tolchard added 38 runs for the eighth wicket with McVicker and Leicestershire went through with nine balls to spare.

The final with Middlesex promised much. Middlesex, so long in the shadows, under Brearley had begun to suggest that they might be a power in the land. Their erratic play in group and earlier knock-out matches had made their fans Valium addicts, yet it suggested both resilience and luck. The Benson & Hedges zonal system had again been rearranged and Middlesex, now restored to the South Zone, began poorly by losing to Essex by 82 runs. But they improved on what was generally considered an inept performance by playing their part in an extraordinary match with Kent. Kent having been 53 for 8, reached 137; Middlesex having been 9 for 3, reached 97 for 3 before collapsing to 135 for 8 and losing by 2 runs. Middlesex had an awful fright against Minor Counties (South) but qualified on the mathematics: they had a better striking rate with the ball than Sussex. Middlesex could thank Graham Barlow for qualifying; it was his run-out of Yeabsley, the Minor Counties' last man, that gave the Middlesex striking rate the essential lift.

Middlesex kept the druggists busy as they made their way to Lord's. In the Benson & Hedges quarter-final they beat Yorkshire by four wickets, but with only five balls in hand; in the semi-finals they won against Warwickshire by 3 runs, largely through Price's three wickets in his last two overs. After all this the final against Leicestershire was intensely disappointing. Brearley – still far from the complete captain he was to become – won the toss and batted. On a day of mixed weather both he and his batsmen struggled. They made 146, 83 of them from Mike Smith. Leicestershire were never in any real trouble and made the runs with only five wickets down.

Home advantage, the first time this had been a factor since Middlesex had never qualified for a knock-out final, had counted for nothing in the final. It was to count for little later in the summer too when Brearley's team faced Lancashire in the Gillette final.

Lancashire had advanced to the final with a sure touch. They had beaten Northants at home by nine wickets, Hampshire by six wickets, and then Gloucestershire by three wickets in the semi-finals. Clive Lloyd had contributed little so far to these victories and was due for a big innings. It came, appropriately enough, in the final, which was just as well as it rescued what was a drab, lacklustre occasion. David Lloyd won the toss and defying tradition put Middlesex in (according to the Gillette records, it was the turn of the side batting first to win). Middlesex made 180 and with the exception of Gomes who made 44, all their batsmen struggled on a damp pitch that became slower as the day wore on. Lancashire too struggled and might have done much worse if Clive Lloyd had been held by Smith when he drove Titmus waist-high to the fielder at mid-on. Just as Lloyd's reprieve from a similar shot to the Australian Edwards in the World Cup final earlier that season had convinced Lloyd it was his day, now he began to play with that awesome sureness that has been a hallmark of his cricket – a repeat almost of his World Cup innings. Lloyd's 73 not out easily earned him the Man of the Match Award and won Lancashire the match.

Just as the one-day competitions had heralded Lancashire's revival in the early seventies, so Middlesex's success in reaching two limited-overs finals was to lead to better things: they won the championship outright in 1976 – for the first time since 1947 – and later enjoyed more one-day success. 1976 was also to see the first of the Cinderella counties get some reward for their persistence and patience. Northants had never won anything since their admission to the championship in 1905, but in 1976, with Mushtaq Mohammed as captain, they finished second in the championship and won the Gillette. Though they had reached the semi-final in the inaugural year of the competition, and four quarter-finals between 1964 and 1968, they had not progressed beyond the second round since 1969. And in 1976 they nearly came a cropper in their second-round match – their first outing in that year's competition – against their old enemy Nottinghamshire.

Willey, Cook, Steele and Mushtaq all made runs as Northants totalled 275 for 5 in their sixty overs. Though Notts began badly, Smedley, 72, and Randall, 73, kept them in the chase. But when they went, the county fell behind and began the last over with an impossible 17 wanted. In the quarter-finals Northants met Hertfordshire who had in the previous round beaten Essex by 33 runs. The victory, on probably a poor wicket, owed much to the bowling of Johns, whose spin bowling had won him an Oxford blue in 1970 and Dilip Doshi, then playing in the shadow of the mighty Bishen Singh Bedi. The quarter-final did not give a chance of comparing the methods of these two left-armers, for Bedi did not play. Hertfordshire were destroyed by Sarfraz and Dye and could only muster a pitiful 69 in forty-four overs.

Bedi did play in the semi-finals against Hampshire and, curiously, took his county to the finals with his bat, scoring a four off the fifth ball of the final over to clinch a win by two wickets. Such heroics had not looked necessary when Hampshire without Greenidge (on tour with the 1976 West Indians) struggled to 215 for 7. Richards made only 19 and Turner alone impressed with 86. Northants, now strengthened by the Somerset exile Virgin, reached 180 for 3, when suddenly a panic induced by the prospect of a Lord's final set in. Virgin was run out, five wickets fell for 31 runs and at 211 for 8, only Bedi, Sarfraz and Dye stood between Hampshire and an improbable victory. Bedi hit the four and Northants were through.

The final was just as close-run an affair, though at one stage it seemed that Mushtaq had made a monumental blunder by letting Bedi bowl the last over. Lancashire had had a fairly easy ride to the finals: their victory against Middlesex in the second round – by three wickets with eight balls to spare – was probably the toughest match en route. Neither Gloucestershire in the quarter-finals, or Warwickshire in the semi-finals, had really extended them. But without a run being scored Dye's inswinging yorker bowled Engineer, and after Wood had made 14 he was struck on the hand by a ball from Dye and retired from the match, not only affecting the team batting but also depriving Lancashire of an effective one-day bowler. This time there was no Clive Lloyd to wave his magical bat and when the last over began Lancashire were 169 for 7. Mushtaq, who seemed to have plenty of economical, tried, one-day bowlers at his disposal, called on Bedi.

The idea of such a delicate, subtle and quintessentially three-day bowler bowling in a one-day final may seem odd – and so it did to many even at that stage. But Bedi, once he had got into his stride, had figured quite prominently in the Northants attack that season – and not merely in the County Championship. He had taken 1 for 12 in twelve overs in the second-round Notts match and in the semi-finals against Hampshire bowled his full quota of twelve overs, five of which were maidens, with 31 runs scored off the remaining seven. In the final he had, till the last over began, taken 3 for 26; the wickets of David Lloyd, Abrahams, and Ratcliffe. Mushtaq did have in hand five overs from Dye – his best bowler, perhaps, in the circumstances, and six from Hodgson, who in his previous six had taken 1 for 10. But Bedi seemed the man of the hour and he bowled to Hughes.

It is the sort of thing that can happen in fiction but rarely in life. Hughes, who had made 13 not very spectacular runs until that stage, cover-drove the first ball for four. Bedi loped in again, varied his trajectory and angle a bit, and Hughes picked him over mid-wicket for six. If Hughes, whose season's average was 16.38, did not feel it the crowd began to sense it: this was a repeat of the 1971 Mortimore treatment. They buzzed as Bedi bowled, Hughes swung hard, the ball fled to various corners of the field but the next two balls yielded just two each. Bedi was now bowling noticeably flatter, the famous loop was no longer quite so evident, but Hughes still wafted the fifth ball over long-on for six. Bedi tried to push the last ball quickly through but Hughes had anticipated and it went sailing over mid-wicket for another six. The Bedi treatment had, in some ways, been more spectacular than the Mortimore one: 26, compared to 24 five years ago.

Not only had Hughes seen Lancashire to a respectable 195 but he seemed to have provided them with a psychological advantage. That fillip, however, soon disappeared thanks to an opening partnership of 103 between Willey and Virgin. With Wood absent the Lancashire attack was a bowler short, and though the others did their best, in the end Bedi's 26-run final over did not cost Northants as much as had looked likely. As Jack Simmons ran up to bowl the first ball of the fifty-ninth over George Sharp, the old trusted wicket-keeper swung it for four and Northants at last won a trophy.

1976 was, of course, Kent's year. For the second time in four years they did a limited-overs double; winning the Benson & Hedges in commanding style and the John Player League in a photo-finish. In both competitions Kent had shown the most unchampion-like form. They lost their opening Benson & Hedges zonal match by nine wickets to Yorkshire for whom Old took wickets and Boycott and Lumb made runs. Then in the John Player League they lost five of their first nine games but won six of the next seven to take the title in a climax that had the BBC television producers scratching their heads and everyone waiting for the final ball of the summer to be delivered by Malcolm Nash. That final day had begun with Somerset and Sussex at the top of the table with forty points each and Essex, Kent and Leicestershire all four points behind. Kent, Essex and Leicestershire won, Sussex lost and as Glamorgan's Nash came in to bowl the final ball of the match between Glamorgan and Somerset, Somerset needed 3 to tie and 4 to win, but a tie would have been sufficient for them to take the title.

The match had been gripping all along. Thousands of Somerset supporters had arrived in Cardiff so early that they managed to get into the ground and car park free of charge. Close won the toss and put Glamorgan in, a decision he was later to regret. After he dropped Alan Jones early in his innings (he had actually made the catch then dropped it) and a fielding mix-up allowed Nash to escape a run-out, Glamorgan totalled 191 for 6. Somerset were always struggling but some superb batting by Burgess took them tantalizingly near the target. There had been the usual chapter of run–outs, misunderstandings, and general chaos before Nash ran in to bowl to Burgess. He hit Nash over his head but as the batsman went for the third run Dredge hesitated just a fraction and failed to beat the throw by inches. Glamorgan had won by one run. Kent and Essex finished on the same number of points: forty; had the same number of away wins – five, but Kent had 0.42 of a better run-rate than Essex.

It was the Northants victory, however, that set the trend in limited–overs competitions in the next few seasons. For suddenly the have–nots became the haves. Between 1977 and 1982 Somerset and Essex won their first-ever titles, Northants won a Benson & Hedges Trophy and then in 1981 Derbyshire won the first Nat West Trophy.

But first, in 1977, as *Wisden* said, the soubriquet Proctorshire took on a new meaning. For several years it had been a convenient and expressive term to describe the effect Proctor was having on Grace's old county. In 1977 he took them to third place in the championship and victory in the Benson & Hedges – quite against the odds. The omens seemed right when Gloucestershire qualified for the knock-out stage, just pipping Lancashire in the process; they won their group match at Old Trafford on higher scoring rate in a rain-ruined match.

It was in the quarter-finals that Proctor began to stamp his immense abilities on that year's competition. In the quarter-final Gloucestershire met Middlesex at Bristol and faced with a characteristic opening burst from Daniel were soon 23 for 3. Zaheer and Shepherd mended matters but 194 did not seem a winning total when Mike Smith and Clive Radley took Middlesex to 104 for 2. But Proctor, who had made 0, timed his return with the ball to perfection. Middlesex required 23 off the last five overs when Proctor removed Smith – caught by Foat for 41 – Selvey and Daniel in quick succession to earn a Gloucestershire victory by 18 runs.

Often in cricket an ordinary, all–too–forgettable match is redeemed by an individual's brilliance. The semi-final not only produced a good match but also a great individual performance. Gloucestershire and Hampshire had met in indifferent May weather in Bristol, and Hampshire, powered by some short and furious Roberts bowling and a Greenidge century, had won the match by eight wickets: Proctor doing his best but not quite enough: 46 and none for 28. Now in glorious June before a packed Southampton crowd, Gloucestershire began well. Stovold and Sadiq put on 106 for the first wicket, but the other batsmen failed to build on this and the last seven wickets went down for 18 runs in a mad ineffectual scramble typical of this cricket.

A target of 180, frankly, did not seem difficult for a side whose openers Richards and Greenidge had often made that many on their own. Though Proctor opened with great fire, Richards and Greenidge played the first four overs in their familiar style and one waited for the strokes to follow. Instead we got a Proctor sensation.

With the fifth ball of his third over Proctor bowled Greenidge for 9. The last ball was safely dealt with by Turner. The following over – from Brain – produced 5 runs. Then off the first ball of his fourth over Proctor produced a ball of such pace that Richards, shaping up to play defensively, was beaten: lbw for 3. As often happens, the bowler seems in such situations to be ten times faster than he is, though Proctor was indeed bowling very quickly. This was Jesty's thought, for the next ball beat Jesty just as comprehensively and he, too, went lbw. Many bowlers have got two legs of a hat-trick, then ruined it by either trying too hard or attempting to be too clever. But Proctor kept to the lines he knew could not fail: fast and straight, and Rice was clean-bowled: the most satisfying way to complete a hat-trick. Hampshire, having collapsed from 13 for none to 18 for 4, seemed doomed. Turner and Cowley in their dogged style pulled the county round by putting on 109. But Shackleton bowled Cowley, Brain bowled Turner and then Proctor returned to have Taylor caught and Stephenson bowled to finish with 6 for 13, quite the best bowling ever seen in this sort of competition. But even that may be demeaning it – for this was good bowling by any standards and the Gloucester victory by just 7 runs emphasized how crucial it had been.

As it happened Northants and Kent were fighting an equally close match. It would have been apposite and historically convenient had Northants won, instead of losing by 5 runs, a match that Asif Iqbal, captaining Kent for the first season, recalls as his best one-day match. His choice as captain had been the subject of much criticism. A Pakistani leading one of the most traditional of English counties was controversial in itself but here was a Pakistani who had proved himself a mercenary by signing with Packer. There had been resignations from the Kent committee over the employment of Packer players and Asif's captaincy of Kent would always provoke criticisms and doubt in the hop county. This match, in fact, saw a battle between two men who were both to captain Pakistan. Mushtaq, captain of Northants, had recently taken over as captain of his country, while Asif was to succeed him a few years later. Traditional county enmity spiced by Pakistani rivalry produced a marvellous match that was not decided till the final over.

Asif rates this as an even better one-day match than the 1971 Gillette final against Lancashire. His own and Woolmer's batting – 65 not out and 51 run out respectively – helped Kent reach 211 for 6 wickets. But what Asif recalls with particular pleasure is that in the last over of the Kent innings he hit the last two balls for fours. That was to have an important bearing on the match. Though three of the first four batsmen in the Northants order did not make runs, hard hitting from Steele, Larkins and Sarfraz left Northants requiring 7 runs off the last four balls. But as first Sarfraz, then Steele tried to hit a six off the third and fourth balls, they were both caught and Asif was left reflecting on what might have happened if he had not hit those two fours. Of such stuff are memories made.

Kent went into the final strong favourites. By then they had won one-day competitions six times and appeared to have the ideally equipped side. At Lord's though they were faced with a different facet of Proctor's cricket: his captaincy and his ability to inspire a team. Great captains, unless their influence is immediately evident, as was Mike Brearley's, are hard to define. In this case the *Wisden* editor, Norman Preston, was in no doubt that Gloucestershire's 64-run victory was 'a superb team effort inspired by their splendid captain Proctor'. At every critical stage he did the right thing.

The South African won the toss – admittedly a matter of luck but good captains seem to be blessed with it – and in the first two overs from Jarvis the Gloucester opening pair of Sadiq and Stovold made 19. Though Proctor himself made only 25, the rest of his batting mustered 237. It left Kent to average just over 4 runs an over. Proctor and Brain immediately removed Clinton and Rowe with only 5 on the board. Asif might have turned the tide but he managed only 5, and despite 64 by Woolmer and 55 by Shepherd, Kent never seemed to get on top of the Gloucester attack. Proctor always seemed to have the right bowler on for the right batsmen, Stovold followed up his 71 with a marvellous catch of Ealham, and long before the end a Gloucestershire victory looked secure.

It was this certainty, perhaps, that made their supporters celebrate even before the match was formally over. In the closing minutes play was often held up while fans invaded the pitch and when the presentations were going on in front of the pavilion, the fans had to be forced back by squads of police in a scene more common on football terraces: helmets went flying and a number of police and fans were injured. Jack Bailey, the MCC Secretary, had no doubts that the Gloucester fans were responsible and made the sort of statement that in the past had become the staple of many football administrators: 'I thought the behaviour was disgraceful, but it's a problem endemic to society. How can you control a crowd that size? The only way is with fences and it would be a sad day for cricket if fences ever went up to cage supporters in. The police did well but did not have a chance.'

Not everybody was surprised, for crowds at one-day matches, even Lord's finals, had begun to exhibit Wembley behaviour. But after this the authorities did decide that one of the Wembley trappings had to go. In 1963, when Gillette had started, Gordon Ross, keen to import a bit of the Wembley cup atmosphere, had designed a platform in front of the pavilion that would resemble the famous Wembley steps. Now these steps were discarded and cricket returned to the presentation format more common to the game: in front of a balcony of the pavilion with the crowds below: a bit like the Royal Family doing their stuff from the windows of Buckingham Palace.

The other one-day matches in 1977 were not particularly memorable. Leicestershire won the John Player for the second time, and if their winning margin of just two points over Essex was close, these two were well ahead of the rest of the pack. The Gillette saw Middlesex saunter home in dreadful weather against surprise finalists Glamorgan. It was a poor affair, brought alive only when Mike Llewellyn hit a 4, 6, 4 off Gatting, then hoisted a ball from Emburey over mid-on and into the guttering beside the broadcasting box near the top tier of the pavilion; not as far as Albert Trott's great hit but almost equal to the one that Keith Miller had made in the famous 1945 Dominions match.

Otherwise the only talking-point of the year was raised by Kent: that Gillette rules may have helped Middlesex share the championship title with them. The semi-finals of the Gillette produced some appalling weather. Not a ball could be bowled in the three days set aside for the semi-final between Middlesex and Somerset. A County Championship match was postponed to try and fit in the match and eventually on the Friday a fifteen-overs-a-side match took place. In the sort of farce such circumstances inevitably produce, Middlesex won by six wickets. But, more importantly, the postponed championship match was eventually played at Chelmsford and Middlesex secured seven points from it. Had the postponement not occurred the match would undoubtedly have been washed out, since a fifteen–overs–a–side thrash is unimaginable in a championship match, and Middlesex would not have secured any points. Then Kent would have won the title outright. The rules were subsequently changed and it now stands that if a sixty–overs match is not finished in time then it is decided by the toss of a coin.

Many in Somerset felt badly done by; fifteen overs was hardly a fair or reasonable way of deciding such an important cricket match. And this feeling that luck was against them produced a certain streak in Somerset cricket that manifested itself in the now infamous 1979 Benson & Hedges match.

Somerset, founded in 1875, had long been one of those counties that evoked kindly thoughts; a team full of the characters cricket cherishes but never a serious contender for honours either in the three-day game or in limited overs. In the early years of the Gillette they had developed the knack of losing to the eventual winners, and in 1972 had been beaten by the all–conquering Lancashire side by only 9 runs. They had been in the 1967 final and once or twice had successful runs in the John Player League which suggested something glorious was possible. But it was not until Brian Close had moved to Somerset and started moulding the side that the county began to entertain serious hopes of winning honours. In 1974 they finished two points behind eventual champions Leicestershire in the John Player League and might have won had rain not played havoc with their match against Illingworth's side.

But it was in 1978, the first season of Brian Rose's captaincy, that everything seemed to come right for the county. Luck was with them in the early group matches of the Benson & Hedges. They won three of their four matches – one against Hampshire was rained off without a ball being bowled – but they could easily have lost to Glamorgan and Worcestershire. Glamorgan, in fact, presented Somerset with victory when with 4 runs required off the last nine deliveries and four wickets in hand, a sudden panic set in: there were two run–outs and the scores were tied with a single off the last ball. Somerset won because they had lost fewer wickets. The match with Worcestershire was just as close. Somerset, after trailing for much of the match, finally made the 180 required with two balls and two wickets to spare.

The relatively easy 102–runs victory over Sussex in the quarter-finals suggested that this could indeed be their year in the Benson & Hedges, but in the semi-finals they came up against Kent. Both Richards and Botham failed, Garner did not play and, despite the efforts of the others, Somerset lost by 41 runs.

The Gillette, however, seemed to bring out the best from the county, or at least Vivian Richards. In the first round they met Warwickshire, and the Midlands county with steady contributions from their leading batsmen made 292 for 5 in their sixty overs. Rose fell lbw to Brown with the score on 17, but then Richards took over. The light was often poor, and the Warwickshire bowlers sensed a quick kill but Richards was in one of those imperious moods that brooks no opposition. He went on to play what has been described by many, including Bill Edrich, as one of the greatest innings ever seen.

Yet Richards had begun the season in bad form and with Packer comfortably in the background, his early form had been so disappointing that he had discussed his technique with the Somerset coach Peter Robinson. Robinson reckoned that Richards was not quite getting to the pitch of the ball; he was only half there when the ball arrived with his feet in a tangle. He had just about begun to get back into form when the Warwickshire match took place. With the target 5 an over Richards could not afford to take too many risks and for most of the innings he grafted with one eye on the scoreboard while his mind worked out the mathematics. He believes he has never worked harder during an innings and was helped by Denning – 60 in a partnership of 137 in twenty-four overs – and Roebuck – 45 and a partnership of 96 in seventeen overs. In the end Richards could almost decide how he wanted the match to end, finishing it with a fifth six that landed on the roof of the pavilion.

Somerset had relatively easy victories: over Glamorgan in the second round, Denning masterminding their batting this time; and Kent in the quarter-finals. They met Essex in the semi-finals at Taunton. On a fresh pitch Somerset were soon in trouble against John Lever. It could have been worse for both Richards on 22 and Rose were dropped at slip. These two went on to add 84 in twenty-three overs and after Rose had fallen to Pont for 24, Richards, just as he had done against Warwickshire, took control of the innings in a partnership with Roebuck. Roebuck was not in his best form and during the first 40 runs of his partnership he did not get a single run. But Richards kept him going with little chats and eventually the two put on 103. In forty-five overs Richards made 116 with one six, one five and fourteen fours. After he was out Marks and Breakwell put on 79 runs in the last ten overs.

If Somerset had benefited from dropped catches, then Essex too had their luck: Gooch was dropped and went on to make 61, and

Richards thought he had run out Fletcher before he had scored; Fletcher went on to make 67.

At one stage Essex required 122 from eighteen overs. Fletcher and Pont put on 80 in twelve overs and when the last five began the target was down to 42. Suddenly Botham, who had done nothing (7, bowled East) ran out Pont and in the very next over, caught and bowled Fletcher. The last over arrived with 12 wanted. Smith hit a single, East edged a boundary before being bowled by Dredge. Then, to the horror of Somerset supporters, Dredge bowled a no–ball. The ball itself was hit and with Somerset suddenly acquiring several fielding captains an overthrow led to 3 runs in all. Finally as the eight-minute over drew to an end Lever needed to score 3 off the last ball to win; Essex had got 2 when Rose's throw beat Smith. The two counties were tied on scores but Somerset went through because they had lost fewer wickets. It was to lead to the most momentous week in their cricket history.

The Gillette success had been paralleled by John Player triumphs. Somerset had begun their John Player games rather indifferently. Rain washed out their opening match against Hampshire and by early June they had lost two of the three matches played. But then they picked up momentum in remarkable style, beating many of the teams that at the end of the season were to figure in the top half of the table, with something to spare. In fact apart from a 16-run triumph over Yorkshire which looked closer than it was they had had few struggles. As they entered the final week of the 1978 English cricket season they led Hampshire and Leicestershire – whom they had beaten by four wickets – by four points. On the Sunday after the Gillette final all they had to do was to tie with Essex at Taunton and a cricket title would at last be theirs.

But if the morning of Saturday, 2 September dawned with Somerset anticipating all sorts of glorious possibilities, by the evening of Sunday, 3 September such hopes had been crushed with a finality that affected even those for whom Somerset cricket meant little more than a scorecard in a newspaper. Yet it began so wonderfully well. Arnold Long, the Sussex captain, won the toss and put Somerset in. This seemed a bad error when Imran's very first over went for 14 runs – all to Rose. But Arnold was soon bowling in his most menacing and economical style and gave away 7 runs in six overs. Long was proving to be an astute leader. He had gone into the match with a left-arm spinner and an off-spinner – normally considered rare luxuries in this type of cricket. But both of them bowled well: Cheatle took 2 for 50, Barclay 2 for 21 including the wicket of Richards for a moderate 44, and Somerset were restricted to 207 for 7. They feared it would not be enough and so it proved. Sussex had a good start, and though Garner and Botham broke through the middle – and might, just might, have crashed through the crucial Parker–Phillipson partnership when they were taken off – in the end the Sussex victory was comfortable enough: five wickets with six overs and five balls to spare. The Somerset supporters sang and hoisted their banner 'Richards walks on scrumpy' but in the dressing room it was all despair as Richards squeezed his loser's medal and flung it away. Eventually the players stirred themselves and left for Taunton with Botham characteristically trying to lift them with a promise of victory on the morrow. The visitors happened to be Essex.

The two counties had similar cricketing flair. Bitter rivals, as Peter Roebuck noted, but both possessed 'a strange, unpredictable genius'. Somerset may have made a tactical mistake at the start of the match by including Hallam Moseley in preference to Joel Garner. In retrospect, the decision sounds amazing but that season Moseley had been bowling well in the Sunday matches and Rose felt he deserved a chance to win a medal. The decision seemed vindicated as Moseley bowled a superb opening spell and reduced Essex to 29 for 3. But Fletcher, dropped at slip off his first ball, soon hit out with such abandon that he made 76 not out, and with the late-order batsman helping out and Somerset collapsing in the field, Essex totalled 190 – a very good John Player total. The crowd, though, were not worried; if anything they were confident. They had Richards and surely this time Viv would do it. Richards seemed to be fully aware of his role and sent his first five scoring strokes all for fours. Then suddenly, having decided to swing Gooch off his pads for another lofted four, he changed his mind and tried to play safe for a single. He only succeeded in edging it to Hardie. He had made only 26. Botham, as in the Gillette final, tried to fill the breach with a bold 45 but Somerset still needed 11 when the final over began.

The tension had become so unbearable that Roebuck, who does not much care for this type of cricket, could hardly bear watching. Soon after he was out he changed from his cricket clothes and went walkabout round Taunton.

It was beautifully tranquil in the streets, with scarcely anyone about at all. A few swans wandered down the Tone, undisturbed by the muffled roars from a few hundred years away. Ducks paddled about. A few families pottered around on their Sunday outing, blissfully unaware of events at the County ground. It was a lovely day. I'd not noticed before. I bumped into an old friend. Why wasn't he at the cricket? Took the family, couldn't bear it, how do you players manage? We don't, I smiled, we just keep going, hoping for the best. We can't cope really, who could?[32]

Roebuck returned to watch the death throes. Seven came from the first five balls but as Moseley went for a non-existent third off the last ball he was run out. Somerset had lost by 2 runs.

They had the same number of points as Hampshire (forty-eight) and had won the same number of matches (eleven), lost the same number (three) and won the same number of away matches, but they had achieved a run-rate of 4.580 against Hampshire's 5.355. So Hampshire were 1978 John Player winners by a run-rate margin of 0.775. For all the loving sympathy of the Taunton crowd that evening the Somerset players were inconsolable and as the crowds called out the names of their favourites, Richards seized his jumbo bat and broke it against the stone floor of the dressing-room shower. Later he would tell a friend that that weekend had been like experiencing a death in the family.

Out of the sadness though also grew a bitterness that would quite astound the cricket world almost nine months later. The 1979 season had begun with rain and moderate matches. Somerset were in Group A with Worcestershire, Glamorgan, Gloucestershire and Minor Counties (South). By the time they met Worcestershire in the final match of the group they had beaten the other three. But unless they beat Worcestershire they could not be sure of qualifying, except on a technicality. They had been beaten for the John Player by a marginally superior run-rate so why not make sure they could win by just such a margin?

The mathematicians in the team worked out that if Somerset scored a run then declared they would finish with a better run-rate and a sure place in the quarter-finals, whatever happened to their rivals. The Somerset players considered the argument of their mathematicians, took a vote and with only two abstentions, agreed to the plan. Rose telephoned Donald Carr at Lord's to enquire whether this was permissible. Carr answered that the rules did not prevent it but he appears also to have warned of the consequences. However, they were not clearly understood and the plan was put into operation.

Somerset's openers Rose and Denning faced one over from Holder, during which he conceded a run through a no-ball. Then to the utter amazement of everybody, Somerset declared their innings closed. Worcestershire took ten balls to score the two required – all to Turner – and the match was over after just sixteen balls had been bowled. It had lasted in all twenty minutes, ten of them the statutory time between innings. Worcestershire were so furious that they refunded the admission money of the hundred paying spectators and their chairman commented, 'It is a great pity when the supreme game of cricket is brought down to this level.'

The storm that broke over the action raged for some time and eventually the TCCB met and disqualified Somerset from the competition, for bringing the game into disrepute. They also out-lawed such declarations. Their place was taken by Glamorgan who during that period had spent a frustrating three days at Watford watching the rain wash away their match against Minor Counties (South).

The day the TCCB announced their decision – 1 June – Essex went to the top of the Schweppes championship and established them-selves as such strong favourites that Ladbrokes would only quote 13 to 8 on Keith Fletcher's side winning the title. By 21 August they had won the championship. If their victory in the 1978 John Player League match had played a part in Somerset's declaration at Worcester, then they were quite unwittingly the beneficiaries of Somerset's disqualification. For as the Benson & Hedges knock-out draw panned out, it became reasonable to speculate that had Somerset qualified they might have met Essex in the final. Glamorgan, who substituted them, lost to Derbyshire, who in turn lost to Surrey in the semi-finals. Ironically Essex had lost to Surrey in the qualifying group by just 7 runs with two balls to spare. But in the final they met a Surrey side that was without their principal bowler, Sylvester Clarke. Jackman also was not quite fit. This, though, does not detract from the achievements of Essex, or obscure the fact that, unusual in recent one-day finals, we saw an English batsman take centre stage.

These finals had often provided the stage for an overseas player to display his brilliance. Clive Lloyd, Asif Iqbal and earlier in the same 1979 season Vivian Richards had all done so. Now Gooch, who had suggested that he might go the way of many a recent English batsman – all promises and no fulfilment – seized the chance to play a great innings. He had scored explosive half-centuries in the Prudential World Cup and in the Benson & Hedges matches leading up to the final, had scored 133 against the Combined Universities in a competition first-wicket record stand of 223 with Alan Lilley, then quite butchered the Warwickshire attack for 138 in the quarter-finals. But at Lord's there was a power and majesty that had everybody in raptures. It began with a square cover drive, included a lofted six off Knight and in the end reduced the Surrey attack to such a state that even the experienced Pocock conceded 73 runs in eleven overs. Gooch was finally bowled, swinging cross-batted, by Wilson, Surrey's most successful bowler. He made 121 in 203 minutes off 141 balls, including three sixes and eleven fours. *Wisden* could hardly contain itself. As it named Gooch one of the cricketers of the year, it said, 'It was his masterpiece at Lord's against Surrey which lifted him above the ranks of the ordinary; which convinced everyone of his star status.'

Gooch had been well supported by McEwan. In fact the South African had for a time overshadowed him as he made a stylish 72 off ninety-nine balls and Essex's closing 290 for 5 left Surrey a mountain to climb. A total like that often produces a sad response from the chasing side, but Surrey, ably led by Howarth and Knight, and well supported by Smith and Roope, kept in the hunt for a while. In the end, however, the margin of 35 runs and three overs and two balls told the story of Essex's superiority.

It had been a marvellous day of high summer, the pitch was near-perfect and, as Christopher Martin-Jenkins had observed, this was the day that the Benson & Hedges finally made its mark. There might have been better finals, but the final of 1979 seemed to bring together everything essential to a memorable match: hot weather, a great crowd, a team finally earning reward for its years of persistence and a wonderful innings from a potentially great batsman. Gooch had made history both for Essex and the Benson & Hedges.

Somerset may have averted their eyes from the final, but they recovered from their self-inflicted wounds splendidly. Rose had made some unwise statements the day after the infamous declaration when, as his house was besieged by reporters, he steadfastly defended the decision, claiming that outsiders who were not there could not judge their action. Some Somerset players had thought of seeking legal redress for their disqualification but saner counsel had prevailed and, eventually, Richards, Botham and Garner sought and obtained cricketing redress. Once again in the last days of the cricket season of 1979 Somerset were chasing two titles.

As luck would have it, Somerset had met Derbyshire in the second round of the Gillette, a team they would have met in the quarter-finals of the Benson & Hedges had things worked out correctly. They annihilated Derbyshire by eight wickets and there seemed to be something quite ruthless about the side now. In the quarter-finals against Kent, Joel Garner took 5 for 11, the first four wickets in six overs, and Kent were bowled out for 60 – beaten by 130 runs.

Then, in the semi-final, Middlesex were overwhelmed by seven wickets. For a change Burgess dealt with the top of the batting, Garner the tail and Denning made the runs. The final was against Northants, back for their second Gillette in three years. Northants were somewhat surprise finalists. Apart from Sarfraz, their bowling was hardly county standard and they owed their day at Lord's to the fact that the first five in their order: Cook, Larkins, Williams, Lamb and Willey often made runs both copiously and at great speed.

By now a Somerset script for these matches was becoming familiar. If they fielded then Garner would appear at the Nursery End and bowl with economy and deadly accuracy. If they were batting the only really relevant question was: will Richards do his thing? In between there would be something from Botham, though he never seemed to fulfil the expectations he aroused.

Richards had made 73, 44 and 32 in the matches leading up to the final – and though these had contained the usual Richards repertoire a Lord's final called for something special. Many remembered the innings that had, effectively, won the West Indies the Prudential World Cup a few weeks previously, and when Rose and Denning provided the ideal platform with the help of some wayward Northants bowling the stage seemed set for the Antiguan. He did not disappoint. It was an innings in many ways very different from the 138 not out of the Prudential World Cup. This time there was no Collis King to tear into the attack at the other end (Botham did a mini-King making 27 from seventeen balls with five fours) and Richards had to shepherd the entire innings. He performed so well that he did not lift a ball until after lunch and was there until the last over, making 117 in a Somerset total of 261.

Now the other principal actor in these Somerset one-day productions took his turn. In Garner's first spell he removed Larkins and Williams, he came back to remove Willey and ended with 6 for 29. Although Alan Lamb made 78, Garner never really gave the Northants batsmen the chance to accumulate or accelerate. When Garner finally bowled Griffiths, Northants were still 45 runs behind.

Somerset players still remembered the weekend of the previous summer and the double they had lost. Now they had won one leg of an even more improbable double. The next day they travelled to Nottingham for their final John Player League match. For much of the season Somerset had been just behind Kent and when the final matches began that Sunday Kent were firm favourites. They had a two-point lead and all they needed was to beat Middlesex in Canterbury. Twelve thousand packed the St Laurence ground and this match soon began to develop a symbiotic relationship with the Somerset match. When Middlesex faltered, as in the early part of the innings, so did Somerset. Botham with two huge sixes put on 33 in two overs with Roebuck, while in Canterbury Barlow was rescuing Middlesex. So it went on. Somerset seemingly played with one ear cocked to events at Canterbury, their supporters in the stands listening to the transistor and shouting encouragement or groaning at the situation. Eventually Botham took the last Notts wicket and even as he ripped up the stumps as souvenirs, a roar from the supporters confirmed the news: Kent had lost. Somerset had done the double.

The seasons since then: 1980, 1981 and 1982 have seen new champions in the various one-day competitions. Warwickshire's triumph in the John Player League in 1980 proved that the county had at last learnt the basics of this rather special type of cricket. When the competition had begun in the late sixties the Warwickshire side seemed well equipped for it. Yet they lost their way so completely that for the first few years they found it difficult to beat anyone in the Sunday League. Their triumph in 1980 was all the more remarkable as they had finished 1979 bottom of the table with only two wins. A great deal was owed to Bob Willis's leadership and the principles they followed: better fielding and more thought on the tactical requirements of the game. But most interesting was the vital part played in their success by the Indian left-arm spinner Dilip Doshi. The bespectacled bowler, rather moodily philosophical even by Indian standards, had struggled to make the Indian Test side – and only did so after Bedi had left the scene. He had joined the county in 1980 from Notts after none too successful a season with them. His forte was the County Championship; he became the first Warwickshire bowler to take 100 wickets since Lance Gibbs in 1971. Few had expected him to play much of a part in the limited-overs competition, least of all in the roughest of them all: the John Player forty-overs thrash.

But in the very first match against Hampshire in Southampton he bowled eight overs taking 3 for 42; Turner, Jesty and Pocock went in a spell of 3 for 9 that set up Warwickshire's impressive eight-wicket victory. After that he was almost a regular participant in the Sunday matches, invariably chipping in with useful wickets. Left-arm spinners had occasionally prospered in this competition before but rarely a player so cast in the old-fashioned mould. Warwickshire could have gained nothing from his batting – he rarely had to display the technique that has earned him the nick-name Sir Gary (after you know who) in the Indian Test team – and though a safe fielder, Doshi's lack of speed is such that most batsmen would find it comfortable to contemplate two runs even if the ball was hit straight to him.

The other surprise of 1980 was that Middlesex did not win even more titles than they did. Mike Brearley's team had come a long way since 1975 when they lost two successive finals by fairly wide margins. In 1979 they had finished in fourteenth place in the championship and done nothing in the limited-overs competitions. Though the amazing Ashes series of 1981 was to crown Mike Brearley's career in a unique fashion, at the beginning of the 1980 season there were quite a few critics of both his style and his captaincy. The winter tour of 1979–80 had been hard, and despite England's successes in the one-day competitions, Brearley's hand-ling of the Test series (lost 3–0 to Australia) had lost him much support. Brearley himself returned to the country feeling jaded and in need of a rest. The Middlesex cricket sub-committee was sufficiently concerned to ask him how he planned to rectify the 1979 deficiency and whether he was sufficiently committed to the cricket job. When Brearley confirmed that he was, and that he intended to be more forthcoming with advice and suggestions to players about how they should tackle the game (a sore point during the winter's Australian tour), they reconfirmed him in the job.

Brearley clearly felt this 'slight sting to my pride' but what further charged Middlesex batteries was the arrival of Vincent van der Bijl – a tall South African who brought the ball down from nine feet, making it both swing and lift, and who had a way with sixes, particularly in the one-day matches. He proved, in Brearley's words, 'the biggest single factor behind our successes'. He had originally been signed up because Middlesex were worried about the effect the expected loss of Daniel to the 1980 West Indian side would have on their bowling resources. In the event the West Indians did not select Daniel and Middlesex suddenly found them-selves equipped with one of the most dangerous attacks a county had ever had. Brearley's nucleus of Butcher, Barlow, Emburey, Gatting and Edmonds, now found their task made much easier by a lethal spearhead.

Their two most memorable matches were in the Benson & Hedges, before they lost a close semi-final to Northants by 11 runs. The first against Somerset in the group competition was one of the most gripping ever seen. Middlesex, recovering from a bad start – 45 for 3 – reached 282 through 93 from Barlow and 95 from Gatting – the two putting on 163 in thirty overs. A score of 282 for 6 in fifty-five overs was a tremendous total and seemed beyond Somerset for whom Gavaskar was playing as a star substitute for Richards – absent with the 1980 West Indians. In the previous match against Kent the Indian had shown that when he made up his mind he too could play this game. Set 243 to win he and Rose had put on 241 in forty-four overs with Gavaskar making 90. Now, without Rose, he led the Somerset reply and made 123 with three sixes and twelve fours. But after he had been stumped, Somerset lost their momentum and the ninth-wicket pair found the task of scoring 10 from the last five balls just a bit beyond them.

The other Benson & Hedges match involving Middlesex that excited great interest was against Sussex in the quarter-finals. The counties have always been traditional rivals but that season there seemed to be a special edge to their meetings, spiced inevitably by personal factors. The flashpoint in the Benson & Hedges quarter-final was the bowling of Daniel. The day of the quarter-final produced characteristic swinging Lord's weather and Imran Khan swung the ball so extravagantly that he bowled eight wides in his first five overs and eleven of the nineteen that Sussex bowled altogether. Sussex, in fact, conceded 38 extras which was 9 more than the margin of Middlesex's victory. The rest of the Middlesex score was made up of bits and pieces in the best limited–overs tradition. Middlesex finished on 195 and once Sussex began their reply Daniel was in the centre of things. He produced a lifter that broke Wessels's hand but it was when he was brought back in late evening to deal with Imran and the Sussex tail that we had the sort of explosion the day had been building up to.

At that stage with six wickets down and over 160 on the board Sussex were still in with a chance. Daniel now produced a series of bouncers and Pigott was hit on the arm. Imran, the non-striker, complained to the umpire about the number of bouncers Daniel was bowling. As Imran was to recall later, 'When I bowl bumpers at tail-enders, I am warned; Daniel bowled five, so I objected.' But

Brearley, who was fielding at mid-off and had not been at all amused by Imran's attempt to bowl bouncers, was so incensed by his objections to the Daniel ones that he decided to broadcast his views. He told Imran, 'They weren't bouncers, they were below shoulder-level. And anyway, you tried to get up but couldn't.'

Imran's retort was forceful and abusive and the two men had begun to eye each other much in the fashion footballers do when they are about to do something silly. Just then Gatting rushed in and pinioned Brearley's arms and umpire van Geloven playing the referee to perfection then stood between the players and directed them back to their proper places. Brearley was so upset about Gatting's action that he fairly blasted him and has since written that Gatting must have been watching too many football matches (his brother is a football player) to produce a reaction that Brearley thought was both extravagant and unnecessary. Brearley had no intention of assaulting a Pathan armed with helmet, bat and gloves. Brearley's attempts to make the incident look more innocent than it appeared were not accepted by the umpire who in his report stated that he had never heard such bad language, on or off the field, as Imran had used. The TCCB held an inquiry, Sussex reprimanded Imran and Middlesex expressed regret about Brearley's action.

The clashes between the two counties continued for the rest of the season. In the Gillette semi-final later that summer Daniel took 6 for 15 as Sussex, chasing 179, were routed for 60, the last five wickets collapsing for 18 runs.

Sussex could be said to have had some compensation in the championship match at Hove when after being made to follow on a double century by Wessels saw them to 550 for 9 in their second innings. By tea it was clear that Sussex had saved the game and prevented Middlesex from winning the championship at Hove (they were to win a week later at Cardiff). But Barclay refused to declare till just a few minutes of the match were left. Anticipating a Middlesex victory I had been sent down to interview Brearley, and after the match as I waited in some trepidation for him, the glee of the young Sussex supporters at thus thwarting the former England captain was plainly evident. 'Don't bother to ask Brearley; if you want to know the facts go ask Imran what he thinks of Brearley,' with the clear inference that while Imran was a he-man, Brearley was something less than one.

Brearley has since explained that in 1980, freed from the cares of the England captaincy – more a coconut than a crown, as his colleague Mike Smith called it – he felt 'less inhibited', and allowed a little aggression to 'come out in my play'. Maybe, but it also showed how even English cricket had been affected by the actions and deeds – at least in one-day cricket – that over the years had been the preserve of the Australian game. This was hardly surprising for the one-day form had now acquired a completely new persona.

# 6
# From Flannels to Pyjamas

> You are not going to watch a boring cricket match where twenty-
> two people stand around for six hours doing virtually nothing.
> You are going along to watch an event.
>
> Tony Skelton, general manager
> of Kerry Packer's promotion and marketing company

> It [one-day cricket] is not the game of cricket as I know it. It is an
> Americanization. It is ridiculous to call it cricket. It should be
> known as 'kickit', or 'snickit' or 'cashit'. People who watch it are
> spending their money the way they want to. But the damage is
> being done in referring to it as international cricket . . . this is big
> business. It is a strong desire to make money.
>
> Bill O'Reilly, one of the all-time greats of Australian cricket[33]

It was perhaps appropriate that the biggest change in the game of
cricket since W.G. Grace, who made the modern game, should
have originated with a man who was the straight guy for the
Australian comedy star Paul Hogan. Sometime in November 1976
John Cornell – the straight guy – met an old journalistic colleague
Austin Robertson and started talking about ways of making more
money for cricketers. A series of televised one-day matches featuring the top Australian players seemed the best idea, and Cornell
soon put the idea to a certain Kerry Packer. His Australian TV
station – Channel Nine – had recently started showing the Hogan
shows and it seemed a natural enough thing. As it happened Kerry
Packer, then little-known outside Australian broadcasting circles,
had just been turned down, yet again, by the Australian Board in his
bid to win exclusive television coverage of the Tests in the country.

Packer, who had once told the officials of the Australian Board, 'There is a little bit of the whore in all of us, gentlemen; what is your price?', was determined to get his own back, and soon plans were set afoot to promote World Series Cricket that would rival the game as organized and presented by the cricket authorities of the Test-playing countries. On 9 May 1977, during a now-forgotten John Player League match between Sussex and Yorkshire at Hove, the news broke that Kerry Packer had signed thirty-five of the world's leading players – representing all the Test-playing countries barring India and New Zealand – to promote a series of matches in the Australian winter of 1977–78.

The revelation created a storm that tore cricket in half and did not abate till the cricket authorities and Packer signed their peace terms – very much Packer's terms – in the summer of 1979 and normal cricket service resumed. Since then the marketing of Australian cricket has revealed the deep influences Packer has had on the game. Packer, always a cricket buff, had become interested in the commercial possibilities of big-time cricket when a marketing analysis for his Channel Nine had shown that the most exciting potential lay with sports programmes. But Channel Nine had to get exclusive coverage and market it properly. So right from the start of World Series Cricket, it was marketed in a way more associated with sports in America than in the countries influenced by the British.

Yet interestingly, perhaps because Packer wanted his cricket to rival the Tests, World Series Super-Tests were initially not much different in form from the traditional game. The players were paid a lot more money (the most attractive feature of Packer cricket), the games were often played on grounds that had never before seen cricket, such as the VFL Park at Waverley in Melbourne, a stadium built to house the Australian Rules Victorian Football League (specially prepared turf pitches had to be laid) and some of the psyching and ra-ra familiar to American sportsmen were used. But even on the first day of the game between Australia and the Rest of the World, the differences from the traditional game were slight. Henry Blofeld, a committed critic of Packer, watching that first Packer match felt that the absence of crowds was due to the lack of tradition, the fact that the Australians were wearing 'caps of screeching gold' rather than the historic baggy dark green caps.

It is the people who wear those green caps who bring the Hill at Sydney screaming to its feet. Instead of that the public were being asked to believe that the figures in the shining gold caps represented Australia – and they were anonymous enough to make me look twice when Australia were in the field to see if that really was Greg Chappell at second slip.

It was in the one-day matches that Packer introduced the changes that now characterize that type of abridged cricket. In the first Packer year his players were involved in the International Cup Series featuring Australia, the Rest of the World and the West Indian XIs in Tests and one-day matches. In addition to this, there were International Country Championship matches of two and three days between the three sides but played mostly in the Australian outback. It was in this competition, which generally included the lesser stars of Packer cricket, that the first radical changes were introduced. In the middle of the pitch a circle with a thirty-metre radius was drawn round each set of stumps. For the first ten overs of a limited-overs innings, nine fielders including the bowler and the wicket-keeper had to be inside the circle. After ten overs six of the eleven fielders had to remain within the magic area. The idea had been borrowed from South African one-day cricket where it had been introduced to increase scoring opportunities.

The early Packer matches, despite the publicity, were not a great success, and crowds only started coming in when Packer introduced night cricket. Then crowds, which had averaged less than 3,000 for the daytime matches, swelled to several thousand and 24,000 turned up for the second night match in Perth. Tony Cozier, the West Indian cricket writer working for Packer, felt that Packer's best chance of success lay in one-day cricket, and at the end of the first season of Packer cricket it became clear that his greatest success had been with one-day night cricket. In the first season, the only change made to accommodate this type of cricket – apart from the floodlights – was the use of the white ball, and helmets by players.

Night cricket really took off on 27 November 1978 when just after 7 p.m. the police outside the Sydney cricket ground had the gates closed with more than 44,000 inside to watch the opening game of the World Series International Cup between Australia and the West Indies. Before the match even the most optimistic Packer promoter had predicted no more than 10,000, or possibly 20,000. The crowds had been so unexpected that Packer himself intervened to get the gates opened and admit many more free of charge, though so few policemen were present that there was crowd trouble of the type soon to become common in Australian cricket.

In this match the original Packer idea was to get both the Australians and the West Indians to discard the cherished flannels for coloured clothing, but the Packer people had run up against certain problems. The clothes were meant to be coloured, not so much as a gimmick, but because the white ball used in these night matches could be seen more clearly against coloured clothing. But the West Indians had objected to the pink colour selected for their team. In the Caribbean pink is the colour worn by acknowledged homosexuals and Clive Lloyd's West Indians, aggressively hetero-sexual, did not want to bear that tag when they returned home. (They did, though, wear it the first year, changing to maroon later.) January 1979 saw the West Indies emerge wearing coral pink with the Australians in wattle yellow; pads, gloves and boots were suitably dyed and the most enduring symbol of cricket, the twelfth man, normally laden with drinks, towels, etc., had now been replaced by a red and white motorized trolley, quickly nicknamed the buggy.

Though wolf-whistles greeted the appearance of Clive Lloyd and Ian Chappell for the toss, the impact made on the Australian public was enormous. Four days before the match just 2,000 had watched the official England and Australian sides play a one-day inter-national. Mr Bob Parish, Chairman of the Australian Board, had explained this away by saying that he thought the public had too much cricket. Yet this Packer match created a horrendous traffic jam round the stadium hours before the match, roads were blocked and eventually 45,000 people packed into the ground – Packer's highest ever official crowd till that date.

It demonstrated that Packer had found the key to unlock the vast public interest that had never cared for, or even acknowledged, traditional cricket.

In marketing cricket, at least in Australia, Packer broke through the sort of insularity that the game has always cherished. There is a story told about a Hungarian refugee arriving in England in the late summer of 1938 at the height of the Munich crisis. He sees a newspaper headline in an evening paper: England in danger. He rushes to buy the paper only to discover that it refers to an England collapse against Australia in a Lord's Test match.

The Hungarian refugee was George Mikes, who has since made a good living writing about the joys of life as a naturalized English-man. He also later learned to love cricket, much to the dismay of his friend, the cartoonist Vicky. Yet the story is in the great cricket tradition of the foreigner trying and failing to understand the

English national game, illustrated as much by the quite nonsensical verses that seek to explain cricket to a foreigner (in fact they are only funny if you know cricket) as by the persistent surprise that the French, for instance, have never learnt the game. In 1963 during the final moments of that summer's Lord's Test – one of the finest Tests in the history of the game – Peter Wilson, covering Wimbledon, could not keep away from the television broadcasts of the match. As he did so a French writer came up to him and said, 'Please to tell me why ees zat black man throwing zat ball at zat white man?' A reasonable enquiry at Wimbledon, though to Wilson and many others just another hilarious indication of the foreigner's inability to understand cricket.

The very complexity of the game, of course, has always meant that its appeal, though intense, must to an extent be specialized. Yet cricket through perverse decisions has often turned its face against proselytizing. Till the early years of this century American cricket was, arguably, as strong as any cricket in any other part of the world. The Philadelphians had J.B. King, who in 1908 headed the English bowling averages by taking eighty-seven wickets at an average of 11.01. King was one of the early swervers, a trick which cricket probably owed to baseball (C.B. Fry always referred to Frank Lever, the first Australian bowler to master this difficult cricket art as 'a baseball swerver'). But suddenly American cricket withered away, partly because of the formation in 1909 of the Imperial Cricket Conference. The very word Imperial, with its connotations of Empire, excluded the Americans and they took to other sports. It is possible that even otherwise they might have preferred baseball and tennis but certainly the growth of cricket as an Empire game enshrining certain very English virtues did play a part in alienating them. Packer's innovations, though a simplification, succeeded in broadening the game, attracting new spectators. It was ironical, but in some ways inevitable, that this should have happened in Australia, which before Packer had never really cared for one-day cricket. In the post-war years as Australia opened its gates to immigrants from southern Europe the idea that cricket might become popular with the sons of Greeks, Italians or Yugoslavs had always excited interest. One Yugoslav did make it in the seventies, even if he felt it necessary to change his name to Len Pascoe from the very good Yugoslav one of Durtanovich. Almost every England tour of Australia in the fifties and early sixties ended with the discovery of some south European-sounding name playing Australian grade cricket, and the ritual hope that in time these 'new' Australians would come to love the mother country's game. It never happened.

Packer's marketing men were the first to realize that if they did not play, they might at least come and watch. And the game was given mass appeal by the use of techniques the Americans had used in popularizing baseball to their immigrants. Thus, when Mike Brearley and Dudley Doust went to their first day–night game in Sydney, 'the sudden explosion of whistles and cheers reminded him [Dudley] of a crowd at an American baseball game'. Packer's men never concealed their deeply felt conviction that traditional cricket as a game for flannelled fools and hot lazy summers had no future. As Tony Skelton, his then general manager, told me in the winter of 1979–80, when cricket was reunited Packer's men would run the marketing of it: 'We are not interested in the traditional cricket lover. If we had to concern ourselves only with cricket lovers, then the game has a diminishing future. It will die.'

For Skelton, and others like him in the Packer entourage, cricket was to be marketed like any other commodity. Market research had shown that people remembered cricket matches in terms of feats: the time when Bradman scored his 100th hundred, or when Lindwall took his 200th wicket. So the commercial promoting the game plugged the line: 'Give your kids something to tell their kids about': perhaps the first time a bowler would break the hundred-mile-an-hour barrier, or a slip-fielder take more catches than any other fielder in the history of the game. Hence Tony Skelton's maxim that, 'You are not going to watch a boring cricket match where twenty-two people stand around for six hours doing virtually nothing. You are going along to watch an event.' And in order to make it an event, particularly in the night matches, Packer's men filled every available hour with something. During the interval between the innings, a whole rock band complete with amplifiers was wheeled on to the ground in an enormous lorry to perform while the cricketers and the public ate their lunch (or more often in the night matches, their dinner).

Packer's commercialism also appealed to the twin sentiments of Australian life: a certain boorish nationalism and a compulsive desire to be champions. Australians like to stress their nationalism. In recent years a popular advert on the commercial stations has been the one about the colours of Australia: the colour of the Pacific, the colours of its sunset, of its children, of its animals, and so forth.

In the two seasons of World Series Cricket when Packer was at war with the established cricket authorities, this commercialism was meant to convince the Australian public that Packer's men represented the real Australia and provided the real Tests, not weak, watery imitations like those put out by the established cricket authorities. T-shirts emblazoned 'Big Boys play at night' summed up the feeling about those promotions.

In 1979–80, after cricket had been reunited but with Packer's company running the promotional side of the game the commercial ads unashamedly stressed the country's nationalism. The most popular one retold the great legends of Australian cricket: the Don and bodyline, then proudly declared that Australia now had the greatest side ever; it ended with the enduring Packer jingle 'C'mon Aussie', that is now as much part of the Australian scene as, say, the Sydney Harbour Bridge.

Packer's market-research methods – whatever we may think of them – worked, and the second, and as it proved last, year of Packer's cricket was undoubtedly a success. In 1979–80, after rock concerts were introduced during the intervals, the number of under-fifteens jumped from 22 to 42 per cent. As many as 75 per cent of one Melbourne crowd confessed they had never been to cricket before but had been attracted by the fare served up by Packer. And there was the new audience of women: young Australian females flocking to a game they had discovered was no longer for the fuddy-duddies. All the more interesting since in these recessionary times this crowd was not affected by the unemployment situation. The research showed that a good many women had come to Packer matches because they wanted to see the thighs of Imran Khan.

The effect of these changes was to give rise to speculation that in time two types of cricket would develop: a Packer-type cricket, simple, full of well researched marketing gimmicks, running alongside the more traditional game. Even at the end of the first year of the Packer series there had been speculation that the Packer game was ideally suited for export to countries like the United States. And in the second year a match was played at New York's Shea stadium in front of a fairly respectable crowd. The city's 2½ million West Indians were considered particularly vulnerable to the charms of this type of cricket. Since the demise of Packer's cricket not much has been heard about this, though it must remain a possibility. What cannot be denied are the changes in the way cricket is marketed, at least in Australia.

When in April 1979 the Australian Board and Kerry Packer settled their differences, the Board's Chairman, Bob Parish, issued a statement in which Packer's company was allowed to 'promote', and arrange 'the televising and merchandising' of a revised series of Tests and one-day matches to be played every season in Australia. For that first season a proposed tour of India and England was replaced by one in which England and the West Indies would play Tests against Australia, and one-day matches with Australia.

For these one-day matches the Board 'agreed to consider favourably the introduction of the thirty-yard circle in limited-overs matches, day–night matches and, on an experimental basis, the use of coloured clothing in Benson & Hedges World Series one-day limited-overs international matches'.

England, rushed into these matches and none too happy about them, refused to play for the Ashes in the Tests and haggled over the conditions for the one-day internationals. Eventually they agreed to day–night cricket and the use of white ball and dark blue pads. But they did not wear any coloured clothing and understandably objected to the thirty-yard fielding rules. At that time it was confidently predicted that these changes would never be permitted. In fact, within a year the thirty-yard rule had come to English limited-overs cricket, and in the summer of 1980 night cricket was played in England, though after a somewhat more extensive trial in 1981 quickly abandoned. In the winter triangular one-day series between England, Australia and New Zealand, England had been playing in what John Woodcock described as Coventry City blue, while the Australians played in Norwich City yellow and the New Zealanders in mauve. They looked like pyjamas but these marketing ideas were now part of cricket.

There can be little denying their impact. After the first match in last winter's Benson & Hedges World Cup series, John Woodcock wrote in *The Times*:

Of the many day–night matches I have seen in Sydney this, more than all the others, had about it the lust and passion of the bull ring. Half an hour before the start, which was at 2.30, the gates had been closed leaving several thousand people outside. The police had reduced the capacity of the ground to 45,000 though the attendance return was only 42,050. *Of these I was assured that anything up to 30,000 could have been adherents only of the one-day game. By 8.30 any resemblance between what was happening and any normal game of cricket was coincidental. The sound and the fury, the beating of the boards and the booing of the English batsmen were orgiastic. This was not so much sport as jingoism. But there it was.*

*Australia bowled very well, swept along on this fiercely patriotic tide.*

Woodcock had found the scenes of mass hysteria 'discordant and unattractive' but the Australian crowds loved it. A few weeks later more than 84,000 packed Melbourne to see a thirty-seven-overs-a-side match between England and Australia, and twenty years after Gillette had first begun the pyjama game had become a national institution.

Not all these changes, of course, will come to English limited-overs cricket, although since Packer the English cricket authorities have been quick to seize every new idea and see whether it will work. Six months after England had played in day–night cricket, Surrey, under their astute manager, Micky Stewart, were pioneering a night match at Chelsea's Stamford Bridge ground between themselves and the West Indians. In the sort of spectacle that would have horrified most people in 1977 but seemed very natural that August night, a specially prepared pitch was laid on the Stamford Bridge ground and marketing men imported some of the atmosphere that is now normal in Sydney's day–night matches. In the event other limited–overs commitments prevented Surrey from playing and Essex took their place but most people came away thinking it could work. The next year Lambert and Butler, in fact, sponsored a proper night-cricket competition and though this did not work, Surrey's interest stayed firm. As Bernie Coleman, a prominent member of Surrey and the TCCB said at the time, English cricket would always be prepared to look at any idea that seems worthwhile and market it themselves, rather than allow freelance people, like Packer or Bagenal Harvey, to corner the show.

It seemed a philosophy for the age and one that cricket, whatever the purists may think, was willing to adopt. We must give the public what they want, said one great Hollywood impresario and cricket, twenty years after the first sponsors had offered to insure a competition against rain, at last seemed to be realizing the need for such pragmatism.

Cricket has always been a very special kind of theatre, under-stood only by the cognoscenti. Once initiated, you're hooked for life – but few are actually drawn to it because the complexity and the rituals are often so forbidding. The Americans were the first to realize the need to combine sport as theatre with sport as spectacle. Though American football is complicated, the spectacle it presents with all the razzamatazz is often so enticing that strangers who know nothing about the game, and even less of America, are drawn to it. This is being proved by the popularity of Channel 4's screening of American football games.

Kerry Packer, who has recently been honoured in Australia for services to the media, was the first to introduce into cricket this American concept of showbiz theatre. His cricket is aggressively marketed and splendidly presented, and it can rival any of the great productions of our time. If cricket can realize that this may not be an entirely unwelcome development then the one-day game could claim a position almost as unique as the five-day Tests. Cricket need not go the way of rugby and split up into rugby union and rugby league. But for that English cricket has to appreciate that the one-day animal, though different, is just as valid. And even more valid since it is different.

# Rules

## Natwest Bank Trophy Rules

The playing conditions for first-class matches in the United Kingdom will apply except where specified below.

### I  DURATION OF MATCHES

The matches will consist of one innings per side and each innings will be limited to sixty overs. The matches are intended to be completed in one day, but three days (four days, if Sunday play is scheduled) will be allocated in case of weather interference.

Matches scheduled to start on Saturday, but not completed on that day, may be continued or, if necessary, started on the Sunday during the hours of 2 p.m. to 7 p.m. Umpires may order extra time until 7.30 p.m. on the Sunday if, in their opinion, a finish can be obtained that day.

*Cup Final only*:

In the event of the match starting not less than half an hour nor more than one and a half hours late, owing to weather or the state of the ground, each innings shall be limited to fifty overs. If, however, the start of play is delayed for more than one and a half hours, the sixty-over limit shall apply.

### II  HOURS OF PLAY

Normal hours will be: 10.30 a.m. – 7.30 p.m.

The umpires may order extra time if, in their opinion, a finish can be obtained on any day or in order to give the team batting second an opportunity to complete twenty overs.

The captains of the two teams in the final, will be warned that heavy shadows may move across the pitch towards the end of the day and that no appeal against the light will be considered in such circumstances.

## III  INTERVALS

*Lunch:*            12.30 p.m.–1.10 p.m. (if start of play 10.00 a.m.)

                      12.45 p.m.–1.25 p.m. (if start of play 10.30 a.m.)

These timings may be varied if, owing to the weather or state of the ground, an alteration has been agreed upon by the captains or ordered by the umpires.

*Between innings:*   ten minutes

*Tea:*             twenty minutes

(a)  In an uninterrupted match, the tea interval will be taken at 4.15 p.m. or after twenty-five overs of the innings of the side batting second, whichever is the later. (In the event of a wicket falling during the twenty-fifth over of the side batting second, the tea interval will be taken immediately.)

(b)  In a match where the start is delayed or play is suspended for such a length of time as to make it impracticable to adopt (a) above, owing to the unlikelihood of completing the match on that day, the tea interval will be taken at 4.00 p.m., except in the following circumstances.

   (i)  If nine wickets are then down or no more than six overs of an innings remain to be bowled, the tea interval will be taken at the end of the innings, or after thirty minutes play, whichever is the earlier.

   (ii)  If, between the hours of 3.15 p.m. and 4.00 p.m., play is suspended (this includes a suspension which may be in progress at 3.15 p.m.), the tea interval of twenty minutes will then be taken.

*Note:* The timing of any interval may be delayed for a maximum of fifteen minutes on the second or third day of a match, if the umpires consider that a finish can be obtained within that time.

## IV  LIMITATION OF OVERS BY ANY ONE BOWLER

In a sixty-over match no bowler may bowl more than twelve overs in an innings. In a match where the start is delayed and the innings of both teams is restricted from the start to less than sixty overs, no bowler may bowl more than one-fifth of the total overs allowed, except that where the total overs is not divisible by five, an additional over shall be allowed to the minimum number of bowlers necessary to make up the balance – e.g. in a thirty-three-over match, three bowlers may bowl a maximum of seven overs and no other bowler more than six overs. In the event of a bowler breaking down and being unable to complete an over, the remaining balls will be bowled by another bowler. Such part of an over will count as a full over only in so far as each bowler's limit is concerned.

The number of overs bowled by each individual bowler shall be indicated on the scoreboard, from the commencement of an innings.

## V RESTRICTION ON PLACEMENT OF FIELDSMEN
At the instant of delivery a minimum of four fieldsmen (plus the bowler and wicket-keeper) must be within an area bounded by two semi-circles centred on each middle stump (each with a radius of thirty yards) and joined by a parallel line on each side of the pitch. In the event of an infringement, the square-leg umpire shall call 'No Ball'.

## VI LAW 14 – DECLARATIONS
Law 14 will not apply in this competition. The captain of the batting side may not declare his innings closed at any time during the course of a match.

## VII LAW 24.1 – NO BALL – MODE OF DELIVERY
Law 24.1 will apply in this competition, except that no bowler may deliver the ball underarm.

## VIII LAW 25.1 – WIDE BALL – JUDGING A WIDE
Umpires are instructed to apply a very strict and consistent interpretation in regard to this law in order to prevent negative bowling wide of the wicket or over the batsman's head.

The following criteria should be adopted as a guide to umpires:
(a) If the ball passed either side of the wicket sufficiently wide to make it virtually impossible for the striker to play a 'normal cricket stroke' both from where he is standing and from where he should normally be standing at the crease, the umpire should call and signal 'Wide'.

*(b)* If the ball passes over head-height of the striker standing upright at the crease, the umpire should call and signal 'Wide'.

*Note:* The above provisions do not apply if the striker makes contact with the ball, or if it passes below head-height between the striker and the wicket.

## IX THE RESULT

### *(a) A Tie*

In the event of a tie, the following will apply:

*(i)* The side losing the lesser number of wickets shall be the winner.

*(ii)* If both sides are all out, the side with the higher overall scoring-rate shall be the winner.

*(iii)* If the result cannot be decided by *(i)* or *(ii)*, the winner shall be the side with the higher score: 1. after thirty overs, or if still equal: 2. after twenty overs, or if still equal: 3. after ten overs.

### *(b) Unfinished Match*

If a match remains unfinished after three days, (four days, if Sunday play is scheduled) the winner will be the side which has scored the faster in runs per over throughout the innings, provided that at least twenty overs have been bowled at the side batting second. If the scoring-rate is the same, the side losing the lesser number of wickets in the first twenty overs of each innings will be the winner.

If, however, at any time on the third day, (fourth day if Sunday play is scheduled) the umpires are satisfied that there is insufficient time remaining to achieve a definite result or where applicable, for the team batting second to complete its sixty overs, they shall order a new match to be started, allowing an equal number of overs per side (minimum ten overs each side) bearing in mind the time remaining for play until scheduled close of play.

In the event of no result being obtained within this rule, the captains are unable to reach agreement on an alternative method of achieving a result to the match, it shall be decided by the toss of a coin.

# Benson & Hedges Cup Rules

The playing conditions for first-class matches in the United Kingdom will apply, with the following exceptions:

# I DURATION

The matches will consist of one innings per side, each innings being limited to fifty-five overs.

All matches will be completed in one day, if possible, but two days will be allocated for zonal league matches and three days for knock-out matches in case of weather interference.

Matches scheduled to start on Saturday, but not completed on that day, may only be continued on the Sunday, with the approval of the Board.

# II HOURS OF PLAY

Normal hours will be 11 a.m. to 7.30 p.m. (start at 2 p.m. on Sundays). The umpires may order extra time if they consider a finish can be obtained on any day, or in order to give the team batting second an opportunity to complete twenty overs.

# III INTERVALS

*Lunch:* 1.15 p.m. – 1.55 p.m.
*Between innings:* ten minutes
*Tea:* twenty minutes

(a) In an uninterrupted match, or a match where, in spite of interruptions the umpires consider that the match can be completed on that day, the tea interval will be taken at 4.30 p.m. or after twenty-five overs of the innings of the team batting second, whichever is the later. (If a wicket falls in the twenty-fifth over of the team batting second, tea will be taken immediately.)

(b) In a match where the start is delayed or play is suspended to such an extent that it is impracticable to adopt (a) above, owing to the unlikelihood of completing the match on that day, the tea interval will be taken at 4.30 p.m.

*Notes:* (i) Adjustments may be made to times of intervals by agreement between the captains, umpires and the ground authority.

(ii) The timing of any interval may be delayed for a maximum of fifteen minutes on the second or third day of a match, if the umpires consider that a finish can be obtained within that time.

# IV LIMITATION OF OVERS BY ANY ONE BOWLER

In a fifty-five-over match no bowler may bowl more than eleven overs in an innings.

In a match where the start is delayed and the innings of both teams is restricted from the start to less than fifty-five overs, no bowler may bowl more than one fifth of the total overs allowed, except that where the total overs is not divisible by five, an additional over shall be allowed to the minimum number of bowlers necessary to make up the balance – e.g. in a thirty-three-over match, three bowlers may bowl a maximum of seven overs and no other bowler more than six overs.

In the event of a bowler breaking down and being unable to complete an over, the remaining balls will be bowled by another bowler. Such part of an over will count as a full over only in so far as each bowler's limit is concerned.

The number of overs bowled by each individual bowler shall be indicated on the scoreboard, from the commencement of an innings.

## V RESTRICTION ON PLACEMENT OF FIELDSMEN

At the instant of delivery a minimum of four fieldsmen (plus the bowler and wicket-keeper) must be within an area bounded by two semi-circles centred on each middle stump (each with a radius of thirty yards) and joined by a parallel line on each side of the pitch. In the event of an infringement, the square-leg umpire shall call 'No Ball'.

## VI LAW 14 – DECLARATIONS

Law 14 will not apply in this competition, the captain of the batting side may not declare his innings closed at any time during the course of a match.

## VII LAW 24.1 – NO BALL – MODE OF DELIVERY

Law 24.1 will apply in this competition, except that no bowler may deliver the ball underarm.

## VIII LAW 25.1 – WIDE BALL – JUDGING A WIDE

Umpires are instructed to apply a very strict and consistent inter-pretation in regard to this law in order to prevent negative bowling wide of the wicket or over the batsman's head.

The following criteria should be adopted as a guide to umpires:

(a) If the ball passes either side of the wicket sufficiently wide to make it virtually impossible for the striker to play a 'normal cricket stroke' both from where he is standing and from where he should normally be standing at the crease, the umpire should call and signal 'Wide'.

(b) If the ball passes over head-height of the striker standing

upright at the crease, the umpire should call and signal 'Wide'.
*Note:* The above provisions do not apply if the striker makes contact
with the ball, or if it passes below head-height between the striker
and the wicket.

## IX  THE RESULT
### (a)  Unfinished Match
If a match remains unfinished after the last scheduled day for play,
the winner will be the side which has scored the faster in runs per
over throughout the innings, provided that at least twenty overs
have been bowled at the side batting second. If the scoring-rate is
the same, the side losing the lesser number of wickets in the first
twenty overs of each innings will be the winner. If, however, at any
time on the last day the umpires are satisfied that there is insufficient
time remaining to achieve a definite result or, where applicable, for
the team batting second to complete its fifty-five overs, they shall
order a new match to be started, allowing an equal number of overs
per side (minimum ten overs each side) bearing in mind the time
remaining for play until 7.30 p.m. In this event the team-selection
for the new match will be restricted to the eleven players and twelfth
man originally chosen unless authorized otherwise in advance by
the Secretary of the Board.

If it is impossible to achieve a result in a zonal league match, it
shall be declared 'No Result'.

In the event of no result being obtained within this rule in a
knock-out match, and the captains are unable to reach agreement on
an alternative method of achieving a result to the match it shall be
decided by the toss of a coin.

### (b)  A Tie
In the event of a tie, the following shall apply:
(i)   The side taking the greater number of wickets shall be the
      winner.
(ii)  If both sides are all out, the side with the higher overall scoring-
      rate shall be the winner.
(iii) If the result cannot be decided by (i) or (ii), the winner shall be
      the side with the higher score (a) after thirty overs, or if still equal
      (b) after twenty overs, or if still equal (c) after ten overs.

## X  POINTS SCORING-SYSTEM FOR
## ZONAL LEAGUE MATCHES
(a)  The team winning the match to score two points.

(b) In a 'No result' match, each team to score one point.

(c) In the event of two or more teams in any zone having an equal number of points, the positions in the table shall be based on the faster rate of taking wickets in all zonal league matches (to be calculated by total balls bowled, divided by wickets taken).

# John Player League Rules

The playing conditions for first-class matches in the United Kingdom will apply except where specified below.

## I HOURS OF PLAY
All matches shall commence at 2 p.m., (except on 11 July, when play will commence at 1.30 p.m. and all timings will be brought forward by half an hour), with a tea interval of fifteen minutes at 4.15 p.m., or between innings, whichever is the earlier. The duration and time of the tea interval can be varied in the case of an interrupted match. Close of play shall normally be at 6.40 p.m., but play may continue after that time if, in the opinion of the umpires, the overs remaining to be bowled can be completed by 7 p.m.

## II LENGTH OF INNINGS
(i) In an uninterrupted match:

(a) Each team shall bat for forty overs unless all out earlier.

(b) In the possible event of the team fielding first failing to bowl forty overs by 4.10 p.m., the over in progress shall be completed and the innings of the team batting second shall be limited to the same number of overs as the innings of the team batting first. See *Note 1*.

(c) If the team batting first is all out and its last wicket falls within two minutes of the scheduled time for the tea interval, the innings of the side batting second shall be limited to the same number of overs as the innings of the team batting first (the over in which the last wicket falls to count as a complete over).

(ii) In matches where the start is delayed or play is suspended:

(a) the object shall always be to rearrange the number of overs so that both teams have the opportunity of batting for the same number of overs (minimum ten overs each team). The calculation of the numbers of overs to be bowled shall be based on an average rate of eighteen overs per hour (one over per three and a half minutes or part thereof) in the time remaining before close of play at 6.40 p.m. See *Note 2*.

(b) If the start is delayed by not more than one hour and the innings of both teams is thereby reduced to not less than thirty overs per team, the time of close of the first innings (and start of the tea interval) shall be fixed allowing three and a half minutes for each over to be bowled. If the team fielding first fails to bowl the revised number of overs by the agreed time for the close of innings, the principles set out in Rules II *(i)(b)* and *(c)* will apply. If the number of overs of the side batting first is reduced in any other circumstances, no fixed time will be specified for the close of their innings.

(c) If, owing to a suspension of play during the innings of the team batting second, it is not possible for that team to have the opportunity of batting for the same number of overs as the team batting first, they will bat for a number of overs to be calculated as in *(ii)(a)*.

(d) In the event of suspension occurring in the middle of an over, the full number of overs to be bowled in the time remaining will be calculated as in *(ii)(a)*, any balls remaining to be bowled in the over during which play was suspended, being added.

(e) The team batting second shall not bat for a greater number of overs than the first team, unless the later has been all out in less than the agreed number of overs.

*Note 1*

All teams are normally required to bowl at an average rate of twenty overs per hour. It is appreciated, however, that in certain exceptional circumstances it may not be possible to attain this average, and a short additional period for each innings is allowed in the hours of play. If, at 6.40 p.m. more than three overs remain to be bowled, play may continue as in Rule I above, but the matter will be referred to the Discipline Committee.

If the umpires report that a team fielding first has failed to bowl its full quota of overs on account of unnecessary 'time-wasting', the matter will also be referred to the Discipline Committee.

*Note 2*

Umpires will notify the home authority of the time of resumption of play, following any delay or suspension immediately they have reached a decision. The home authority will provide a representative who will be responsible for assisting umpires in calculating the revised number of overs to be played in the match and for notifying the decision of the umpires immediately to all concerned.

## III THE RESULT

*(i)* A result can be achieved only if both teams have batted for at least ten overs, unless one team has been all out in less than ten overs or unless the team batting second scores enough runs to win in less than ten overs. All other matches in which one or both teams have not had an opportunity of batting for a minimum of ten overs shall be declared 'No Result' matches.

*(ii)* In matches in which both teams have had an opportunity of batting for the agreed number of overs (i.e. forty overs each, in an uninterrupted match, or a lesser number of overs in an inter-rupted match – see Playing Condition B *(ii)*, the team scoring the higher number of runs shall be the winner. If the scores are equal, the result shall be a 'Tie' and no account shall be taken of the number of wickets which have fallen.

*(iii)* If, due to suspension of play, the number of overs in the innings of the side batting second has to be revised to a lesser number than that allotted to the side batting first, their target score, which they must exceed to win the match, shall be calcu-lated by multiplying the revised number of overs by the average runs per over scored by the side batting first. If the target score involves a fraction of a run, the final scores cannot be equal and the result cannot be a 'Tie'.

*(iv)* If a match is abandoned before the side batting second has received its allotted number of overs and it has neither been all out, nor passed its opponent's score, the result shall be decided on the average run-rate throughout both innings.

*(v)* In the event of the team batting first being all out in less than their full quota of overs, the calculation of their average run-rate shall be based on the full quota of overs to which they would have been entitled and not on the number of overs in which they were dismissed.

## IV NUMBER OF OVERS PER BOWLER

If a match starts as a forty-over match, no bowler may bowl more than eight overs in an innings and this allowance shall not be reduced even though the total overs may subsequently be restricted owing to weather interference. If, however, the start of a match is delayed and the overs of both teams are restricted to less than forty overs, no bowler may bowl more than one-fifth of the total overs allowed except that where the total overs is not divisible by five, an additional over shall be allowed to the minimum number of bowlers necessary to make up the balance – e.g. in a thirty-three-over match, three bowlers may bowl a maximum of seven overs and no other bowler more than six overs. In a match where the innings of either or both teams is reduced after the start of the match, the maximum number of overs allowed per bowler shall remain as at the start of the match.

In the event of a bowler breaking down and being unable to complete an over, the remaining balls will be bowled by another bowler. Such part of an over will count as a full over only in so far as each bowler's limit is concerned.

The number of overs bowled by each individual bowler shall be indicated on the scoreboard, from the commencement of the innings.

## V LIMITATION OF THE BOWLER'S RUN-UP
The bowler's run-up, including his preliminary approach, shall be limited to fifteen yards, to be measured from the wicket. A white line will mark the maximum distance allowed.

## VI RESTRICTION ON PLACEMENT OF FIELDSMEN
At the instant of delivery a minimum of four fieldsmen (plus the bowler and wicket-keeper) must be within an area bounded by two semi-circles centred on each middle stump (each with a radius of thirty yards) and joined by a parallel line on each side of the pitch. In the event of an infringement, the square-leg umpire shall call 'No Ball'.

## VII LAW 14 – DECLARATIONS
Law 14 will not apply in this competition. The captain of the batting side may not declare his innings closed at any time during the course of a match.

## VIII LAW 24.1 – NO BALL – MODE OF DELIVERY
Law 24.1 will apply in this competition, except that no bowler may deliver the ball underarm.

## IX LAW 25.1 – WIDE BALL – JUDGING A WIDE
Umpires are instructed to apply a very strict and consistent interpretation in regard to this law in order to prevent negative bowling wide of the wicket or over the batsman's head.

154

The following criteria should be adopted as a guide to umpires:

*(i)* If the ball passes either side of the wicket sufficiently wide to make it virtually impossible for the striker to play a 'normal cricket stroke' both from where he is standing and from where he should normally be standing at the crease, the umpire should call and signal 'Wide'.

*(ii)* If the ball passes over head-height of the striker standing upright at the crease, the umpire should call and signal 'Wide'.

*Note:* The above provisions do not apply if the striker makes contact with the ball, or if it passes below head-height between the striker and the wicket.

## X SCORING OF POINTS

*(i)* The team winning the match to score four points.

*(ii)* In the event of a 'Tie', each team to score two points.

*(iii)* In a 'No Result' match, each team to score two points.

*(iv)* In the event of two or more teams finishing with an equal number of points for any of the first three places, their final positions will be decided by:

*(a)* The most wins or, if still equal,

*(b)* The most away wins or, if still equal,

*(c)* The higher run-rate throughout the season.

# Select Bibliography

Various books played their part in the making of this book and the most useful of these were:

*Barclays World of Cricket*, edited by E.W. Swanton and John Woodcock (London, 1980)
*Benson & Hedges Cup Book of Cricket Records 1972–1981*
*The Best Loved Game* by Geoffrey Moorhurst (London, 1979)
*Beyond a Boundary* by C. L. R. James (London, 1963)
*The Complete Who's Who of Cricketers* by Christopher Martin-Jenkins (London, 1980)
*The Cricket Addict's Archives* by Benny Green (London, 1977)
*The Cricketer's Companion* edited by Alan Ross (London, 1979)
*The Cricket Rebel* by John Snow (London, 1976)
*Cricket – A History of its Growth and Development Throughout the World* by Rowland Bowen (London, 1970)
*Cue Frank!* by Frank Bough (London, 1980)
*Fast Men* by David Frith (London, 1982)
*The Gillette Book of Cricket Records 1963–1980*
*The Gillette Cup 1963–1980* by Gordon Ross (London, 1981)
*The Gloves of Irony* by Rodney Marsh (London, 1982)
*Great One-Day Cricket Matches* by David Lemmon (London, 1982)
*History of Cricket* by Trevor Bailey (London, 1979)
*History of Cricket* by Gordon Ross (London, 1972)
*Ian Botham* by Dudley Doust (London, 1980)
*I Declare* by Mike Denness (London, 1977)
*I Don't Bruise Easily* by Brian Close (London, 1979)
*It's Been a Lot of Fun* by Brian Johnston (London, 1974)
*The Limited Overs Cricket Information Group*
*A Man in the Middle* by Gordon Greenidge (with Patrick Symes) (London, 1980)
*Not Out* by Dickie Bird (London, 1980)
*One-Day Cricket* by Jim Laker (London, 1977)
*A Pitch in Both Camps* by Alan Lee (London, 1979)

*Phoenix from the Ashes* by Mike Brearley (London, 1982)
*The Packer Affair* by Henry Blofeld (London, 1978)
*Put to the Test* by Geoffrey Boycott (London, 1979)
*Slices of Cricket* by Peter Roebuck (London, 1982)
*A Spinner's Turn* by Patrick Murphy (London, 1982)
*Thommo* by David Frith (London, 1980)
*Time to Declare* by Basil D'Oliveira (London, 1980)
*Village Cricket* by Gerald Howat (London, 1980)
*Viv Richards* with David Foot (London, 1982)
*Wisden Anthology 1864–1900* edited by Benny Green (London, 1979)
*Wisden Anthology 1900–1940* edited by Benny Green (London, 1980)
*Yorkshire and Back* by Ray Illingworth (London, 1980)

# References

Unless otherwise noted, all quotations are from interviews conducted by the author.

1. *Wisden* (Queen Anne Press, 1982) p. 112
2. Jim Laker, *One-Day Cricket* (Batsford, 1977) p. 15
3. Gordon Ross, *The Gillette Cup 1963–1980* (Queen Anne Press, 1981) pp. 9–10
4. *Ibid.*
5. Brian Close, *I Don't Bruise Easily* (Futura, 1979) p. 96
6. John Snow, *Cricket Rebel: An Autobiography* (Hamlyn, 1976) p. 0
7. Brian Close, *Op. cit.* p. 138
8. Frank Bough, 'The Sunday League', *Playfair Cricket Monthly*, November 1969, pp. 6–14
9. Peter Roebuck, *Slices of Cricket* (George Allen and Unwin) pp. 105–7
10. 'Analysis', *The Cricketer*, May 20 1966, p. 3
11. Frank Bough, *Cue Frank!* (Queen Anne Press, 1980) pp. 121–22
12. Brian Johnston, *It's Been a Lot of Fun* (W.H. Allen, 1974) p. 233
13. Brian Johnston, 'International Cavaliers – In or Out?', *Playfair Cricket Monthly*, August 1968, pp. 14, 29
14. Clive Lloyd, *Living for Cricket* (Stanley Paul, 1980) pp. 32–3
15. Jim Laker, *Op. cit.* p. 9
16. Gordon Ross, *Op. cit.* p. 78
17. Jim Laker, *Op. cit.* p. 9
18. 'The "Splosh" game': Letter from Mr Drake to *Playfair Cricket Monthly*, September 1971, pp. 22–3
19. Jack Bond, 'The Captain's Column', *Playfair Cricket Monthly*, March 1971, p. 12
20. Ray Illingworth and Don Mosey, *Yorkshire and Back: The Autobiography of Raymond Illingworth* (Macdonald and Jane, 1980) p. 2
21. *Ibid.*
22. Ian Botham (Dudley Doust), *The Great All-Rounder* (Cassell, 1980) p. 14
23. Carr seminar in *Wisden* (Queen Anne Press, 1975) p. 113

24. David Frith, *Thommo: Story of Jeff Thomson* (Angus and Robertson, 1980) pp. 56–8
25. *Ibid.*
26. *Ibid.*
27. Clive Lloyd, *Op. cit.* (Stanley Paul, 1980) p. 66
28. *Ibid.* p. 66
29. David Frith, *Loc.cit.*
30. E.W. Swanton (ed.), *Barclays World of Cricket* (Collins, 1980) p. 462
31. Geoffrey Boycott, *Opening Up* (Arthur Barker, 1980) p. 162
32. Peter Roebuck, *Op.cit.* p.71
33. 'Bill O'Reilly Speaks his Mind'. Bill O'Reilly interview in *Cathedral's End* (Australia), Winter, 1982

# Statistics

It is a reflection of the value placed on one–day cricket that the traditional cricket authorities find no place for limited–over figures in their records. Roger D'Ornellas has remarked that the present method of giving limited-over results is unsatisfactory especially when a team batting second wins by a number of wickets. Robert Brooke, doyen of cricket statisticians, accepts that to give equal billing to a win by four wickets with twenty overs remaining does not quite give the most accurate picture. He has suggested that a ten–wicket win with ten overs remaining by Warwickshire over Middlesex could be recorded 'Warwickshire beat Middlesex by 10 and 10', or a three–wicket win in the thirty-eighth over by Worcestershire over Yorkshire could be written as 3 and 14. Maybe, in time, this will come but for the moment we have the problem of even collecting limited-over statistics.

The Limited Overs Information Group formed in 1977 has done much work in collecting these statistics and I am indebted to them for their help and co-operation. The statistics that follow are derived mainly from their work although Robert Brooke has updated and codified the figures in the way appropriate to this book. The summary of international matches is the work of John Stockwell, who is an authority on the subject, and the attendance figures have been compiled with the help of the TCCB's Marketing and Public Relations Department.

## International Limited–Over Cricket 1971 to 1982*

These playing records are complete to the end of the 1982 English season. They are compiled from all international matches played between Test-playing members of the ICC plus Purdential World Cup Matches involving Associate members of ICC. Other internationals played by Sri Lanka prior to their achieving full membership of ICC in 1981 have been excluded.

# ALL COMPETITIONS

*Table of Results*

| Team | P | W | L | NR |
|------|---|---|---|-----|
| England | 68 | 38 | 26 | 4 |
| Australia | 69 | 34 | 33 | 2 |
| West Indies | 49 | 36 | 13 | — |
| New Zealand | 40 | 18 | 18 | 4 |
| Pakistan | 38 | 14 | 24 | — |
| India | 30 | 7 | 23 | — |
| Sri Lanka | 10 | 3 | 7 | — |
| East Africa | 3 | 0 | 3 | — |
| Canada | 3 | 0 | 3 | — |

*Highest Totals*

| | | | |
|---|---|---|---|
| England | 334–4 | (60 overs) | v. India at Lord's 1975 |
| Australia | 328–5 | (60 overs) | v. Sri Lanka at Nottingham 1975 |
| West Indies | 313–9 | (50 overs) | v. Australia at St John's Antigua 1977/8 |
| New Zealand | 309–5 | (60 overs) | v. East Africa at Birmingham 1975 |
| Pakistan | 330–6 | (60 overs) | v. Sri Lanka at Nottingham 1975 |
| India | 265 | (53.5 overs) | v. England at Leeds 1974 |
| Sri Lanka | 276–4 | (60 overs) | v. Australia at the Oval 1975 |

*Lowest Totals*

| | | | |
|---|---|---|---|
| England | 81–9 | (35 overs) | v. Pakistan at Birmingham 1974 (reduced–over match) |
| | 93 | (36.2 overs) | v. Australia at Leeds 1975 |
| Australia | 70 | (25.2 overs) | v. England at Birmingham 1977 |
| West Indies | 127 | (47.2 overs) | v. England at St Vincent 1980/81 |
| New Zealand | 74 | (29 overs) | v. Australia at Wellington 1981/2 |
| Pakistan | 85 | (47 overs) | v. England at Manchester 1978 |
| India | 63 | (25.5 overs) | v. Australia at Sydney 1980/81 |
| Sri Lanka | 86 | (37.2 overs) | v. West Indies at Manchester 1975 |

*Highest Individual Scores*

| | | | |
|---|---|---|---|
| England | 137 | D.L. Amiss | v. India at Lord's 1975 |
| Australia | 138* | G.S. Chappell | v. New Zealand at Sydney 1980/81 |
| West Indies | 153* | I.V.A. Richards | v. Australia at Melbourne 1979/80 |
| New Zealand | 171* | G.M. Turner | v. East Africa at Birmingham 1975 |
| Pakistan | 123 | Zaheer Abbas | v. Sri Lanka at Lahore 1981/2 |
| India | 88* | D.B. Vengsarkar | v. England at Jullundur 1981/2 |
| Sri Lanka | 86* | S. Wettimuny | v. England at Colombo 1981/2 |

Thirty-six hundreds have been scored in international matches. D.L. Amiss has scored the most (four).

*Best Bowling Performances*

| | | | |
|---|---|---|---|
| England | 5–31 | M. Hendrick | v. Australia at the Oval 1980 |
| Australia | 6–14 | G.J. Gilmour | v. England at Leeds 1975 |
| West Indies | 6–15 | C.E.H. Croft | v. England at St Vincent 1980/81 |
| New Zealand | 5–22 | R.O. Collinge | v. India at Christchurch 1975/6 |
| Pakistan | 4–44 | Sarfraz Nawaz | v. West Indies at Birmingham 1975 |
| India | 4–30 | D.R. Doshi | v. New Zealand at Brisbane 1980/81 |
| Sri Lanka | 3–29 | D.S. de Silva | v. India at Manchester 1979 |

*Biggest Victory*

| | |
|---|---|
| 202 runs | England beat India at Lord's 1975 |

*Smallest Victories*

| | |
|---|---|
| 1 run | New Zealand beat Pakistan at Sialkot 1976/7 |
| 1 run | New Zealand beat Australia at Sydney 1980/81 |

## THE PRUDENTIAL WORLD CUP

*Table of Results*

| Team | P | W | L | NR |
|---|---|---|---|---|
| West Indies | 10 | 9 | – | 1 |
| England | 9 | 7 | 2 | – |
| New Zealand | 8 | 4 | 4 | – |
| Australia | 8 | 4 | 4 | – |
| Pakistan | 7 | 3 | 4 | – |
| India | 6 | 1 | 5 | – |
| Sri Lanka | 6 | 1 | 4 | 1 |
| Canada | 3 | – | 3 | – |
| East Africa | 3 | – | 3 | – |

*Highest Totals*

| | | |
|---|---|---|
| 334–4 | England | v. India, Lord's 1975 |
| 330–6 | Pakistan | v. Sri Lanka, Trent Bridge 1975 |

*Lowest Totals – Completed Innings*

| | | |
|---|---|---|
| 45 | Canada | v. England, Old Trafford 1979 |
| 86 | Sri Lanka | v. West Indies, Old Trafford 1975 |

*Highest Losing Score*

| | | |
|---|---|---|
| 276–4 | Sri Lanka | v. Australia, The Oval 1975 |

## Lowest Winning Score
46–2    England    v. Canada, Old Trafford 1979

## Biggest Victories
202 runs:  England   (334–4) over India    (132–3) at Lord's 1975
10 wkts:   India     (123–0) over East Africa (120)  at Leeds 1975

## Narrow Victory
1 wkt:    West Indies (267–9) over Pakistan   (266–7) Edgbaston 1975

## Highest Individual Innings

| | | | |
|---|---|---|---|
| 171* | G.M. Turner | New Zealand | v. India, Old Trafford 1975 |
| 138* | I.V.A. Richards | West Indies | v. England, Lord's 1979 |
| 137 | D.L. Amiss | England | v. India, Lord's 1975 |
| 131 | K.W.R. Fletcher | England | v. New Zealand, Trent Bridge 1975 |

## Best Bowling Performances – 5 or more wkts in match

| | | | |
|---|---|---|---|
| 12.6.14.6 | G.J. Gilmour | Australia | v. England, Leeds 1975 |
| 10.3.21.5 | A.G. Hurst | Australia | v. Canada, Edgbaston 1979 |
| 12.2.34.5 | D.K. Lillee | Australia | v. Pakistan, Leeds 1975 |
| 11.0.38.5 | J. Garner | West Indies | v. England, Lord's 1979 |
| 12.2.48.5 | G.J. Gilmour | Australia | v. West Indies, Lord's 1975 |

## Highest Partnerships for Each Wicket

| | | | | |
|---|---|---|---|---|
| 1st | 182 | R.B. McCosker, A. Turner | Australia | v. Sri Lanka, The Oval 1975 |
| 2nd | 176 | D.L. Amiss, K.W.R. Fletcher | England | v. India, Lord's 1975 |
| 3rd | 149 | G.M. Turner, J.M. Parker | New Zealand | v. East Africa, Edgbaston 1975 |
| 4th | 149 | R. Kanhai, C.H. Lloyd | West Indies | v. Australia, Lord's 1975 |
| 5th | 139 | V. Richards, C.L. King | West Indies | v. England, Lord's 1979 |
| 6th | 99 | R. Edwards, R.W. Marsh | Australia | v. West Indies, The Oval 1975 |
| 7th | 55 | Abid Ali, Madan Lal | India | v. New Zealand, Old Trafford 1975 |
| 8th | 48 | B.J. McKechnie, D.R. Hadlee | New Zealand | v. England, Trent Bridge 1975 |
| 9th | 60 | Abid Ali, S. Venkataraghavan | India | v. New Zealand, Old Trafford 1975 |
| 10th | 64* | D.L. Murray, A.M.E. Roberts | West Indies | v. Pakistan, Edgbaston 1975 |

## Batsmen with 200 runs or more:

| Player | | Mtch | Inns | no | Runs | HS | Av'ge | 100s |
|---|---|---|---|---|---|---|---|---|
| G.M. Turner | N.Z. | 8 | 8 | 4 | 509 | 171* | 127.25 | 2 |
| Majid Khan | Pak. | 7 | 7 | 0 | 359 | 85 | 51.29 | – |
| C.G. Greenidge | W.I. | 8 | 8 | 1 | 341 | 106* | 48.72 | 1 |
| Zaheer Abbas | Pak. | 7 | 7 | 0 | 284 | 97 | 40.57 | – |
| C.H. Lloyd | W.I. | 9 | 6 | 1 | 281 | 102 | 56.20 | 1 |

*Batsmen with 200 runs or more, Prudential World Cup (continued)*

| Player | | Mtch | Inns | no | Runs | HS | Av'ge | 100s |
|---|---|---|---|---|---|---|---|---|
| I.V.A. Richards | W.I. | 9 | 8 | 3 | 255 | 138* | 51.00 | 1 |
| A.I. Kallicharran | W.I. | 9 | 8 | 1 | 251 | 78 | 35.86 | – |
| D.L. Amiss | Eng. | 4 | 4 | 0 | 243 | 137 | 60.75 | 1 |
| G.A. Gooch | Eng. | 5 | 5 | 1 | 210 | 71 | 52.50 | – |
| K.W.R. Fletcher | Eng. | 4 | 3 | 0 | 207 | 131 | 69.00 | 1 |
| S.M. Gavaskar | Ind. | 6 | 6 | 2 | 202 | 65* | 50.50 | – |
| A. Turner | Aust. | 5 | 5 | 0 | 201 | 101 | 40.20 | 1 |

*Bowlers with 10 wickets or more:*

| Player | | Mtch | Overs | Runs | Wts | Av'ge | B/B | 4inn | RPO |
|---|---|---|---|---|---|---|---|---|---|
| C.M. Old | Eng. | 9 | 90.3 | 243 | 16 | 15.19 | 4/8 | 1 | 2.69 |
| A.M.E. Roberts | W.I. | 9 | 96.1 | 314 | 15 | 20.93 | 3/39 | – | 3.27 |
| G.J. Gilmour | Aust. | 2 | 24 | 62 | 11 | 5.64 | 6/14 | 2 | 2.58 |
| M. Hendrick | Eng. | 5 | 56 | 149 | 10 | 14.90 | 4/15 | 1 | 2.66 |
| B.D. Julien | W.I. | 5 | 60 | 177 | 10 | 17.70 | 4/20 | 2 | 2.95 |
| Imran Khan | Pak. | 6 | 59.2 | 182 | 10 | 18.20 | 3/15 | – | 3.07 |
| K.D. Boyce | W.I. | 5 | 52 | 185 | 10 | 18.50 | 4/50 | 1 | 3.56 |
| Asif Iqbal | Pak. | 5 | 59 | 215 | 10 | 21.50 | 4/56 | 1 | 3.64 |

## THE PRUDENTIAL TROPHY

*Table of Results*

| Teams | | P | W | L | NR | Series Results |
|---|---|---|---|---|---|---|
| England | v. Australia | 11 | 7 | 4 | – | 3–1 |
| England | v. West Indies | 7 | 2 | 5 | – | 0–3 |
| England | v. New Zealand | 4 | 3 | – | 1 | 2–0 |
| England | v. New Zealand | 4 | 3 | – | 1 | 2–0 |
| England | v. Pakistan | 6 | 4 | 2 | – | 2–1 |
| England | v. India | 4 | 4 | – | – | 2–0 |
| | | 32 | 20 | 11 | 1 | 9–5 |

*Highest Totals*

| 320–8 | England | v. Australia, Edgbaston 1980 |
|---|---|---|
| 295–8 | England | v. Pakistan, Old Trafford 1982 |

*Lowest Totals – Completed Innings (55 overs or all out)*

| 70 | Australia | v. England, Edgbaston 1977 |
|---|---|---|
| 85 | Pakistan | v. England, Old Trafford 1978 |

## Highest Losing Score
273–5     Australia   v. England, Edgbaston 1980

## Lowest Winning Score (full overs available)
159–3     England   v. New Zealand, Swansea 1973

## Biggest Victories
132 runs:   England   v. Pakistan, Old Trafford 1978
126 runs:   England   v. New Zealand, Old Trafford 1978

## Narrow Victories
1 wkt:     England   v. West Indies, Leeds 1973
2 runs:    Australia   v. England, Edgbaston 1981

## Highest Individual Innings
| 125* | G.S. Chappell | Australia | v. England, The Oval 1977 |
|------|---------------|-----------|---------------------------|
| 119* | I.V.A. Richards | West Indies | v. England, Scarborough 1976 |
| 118 | A.J. Lamb | England | v. Pakistan, Trent Bridge 1982 |
| 117* | C.T. Radley | England | v. New Zealand, Old Trafford 1978 |
| 116* | D. Lloyd | England | v. Pakistan, Trent Bridge 1974 |
| 114* | D.I. Gower | England | v. Pakistan, The Oval 1978 |

## Best Bowling Performances – 5 or more wkts in a match
| 8.3.18.5 | G.J. Cozier | Australia | v. England, Edgbaston 1977 |
|----------|-------------|-----------|----------------------------|
| 11.5.20.5 | G.S. Chappell | Australia | v. England, Edgbaston 1977 |
| 11.3.28.5 | B.L.Cairns | New Zealand | v. England, Scarborough 1978 |
| 11.3.31.5 | M. Hendrick | England | v. Australia, The Oval 1980 |
| 10.0.50.5 | V.A. Holder | West Indies | v. England, Edgbaston 1976 |

## Highest Partnerships for Each Wicket
| 1st | 161 | J.M. Brearley, D.L. Amiss | England | v. Australia, The Oval 1977 |
|-----|-----|---------------------------|---------|-----------------------------|
| 2nd | 148 | R.D. Robinson, G.S. Chappell | Australia | v. England, The Oval 1977 |
| 3rd | 159 | A.J. Lamb, D.I. Gower | England | v. India, The Oval 1982 |
| 4th | 105 | D.I. Gower, G.R.J. Roope | England | v. Pakistan, The Oval 1978 |
| 5th | 74 | A.R. Border, M.F. Kent | Australia | v. England, Lord's 1981 |
| 6th | 86 | K.J. Hughes, R.W. Marsh | Australia | v. England, The Oval 1980 |
| 7th | 77 | A.W. Greig, A.P.E. Knott | England | v. Australia, Lord's 1972 |
| 8th | 68 | B.E. Congdon, B.L. Cairns | New Zealand | v. England, Scarborough 1978 |
| 9th | 40 | R.W. Taylor, D.L. Underwood | England | v. Pakistan, Edgbaston 1974 |
| 10th | 24 | C.J. Tavare, J.K. Lever | England | v. West Indies, Leeds 1980 |
| | 24 | Sikander Bakht, Liagat Ali | Pakistan | v. England, Old Trafford 1978 |

*Batsmen with 200 Runs or More, Prudential Trophy (continued)*

| Player | | Mtch | Inns | no | Runs | HS | Av'ge | 100s | |
|---|---|---|---|---|---|---|---|---|---|
| D.L. Amiss | Eng. | 12 | 12 | 0 | 566 | 108 | 47.17 | 3 | 1972–77 |
| G. Boycott | Eng. | 14 | 14 | 1 | 457 | 99 | 34.25 | – | 1972–81 |
| G.A. Gooch | Eng. | 12 | 12 | 0 | 411 | 108 | 34.25 | 1 | 1976–81 |
| D.I. Gower | Eng. | 13 | 12 | 1 | 405 | 114★ | 36.8 | 1 | 1978–82 |
| K.W.R. Fletcher | Eng. | 11 | 10 | 2 | 316 | 63 | 39.50 | – | 1972–74 |
| G.S. Chappell | Aust. | 8 | 7 | 1 | 311 | 125★ | 51.83 | 1 | 1972–80 |
| A.J. Lamb | Eng. | 4 | 4 | 1 | 279 | 118 | 93.00 | 1 | 1982 |
| I.T. Botham | Eng. | 17 | 16 | 3 | 273 | 49 | 21.00 | – | 1976–82 |
| M.W. Gatting | Eng. | 7 | 7 | 2 | 260 | 96 | 52.00 | – | 1980–82 |
| I.V.A. Richards | W.I. | 5 | 5 | 1 | 249 | 119★ | 62.25 | 1 | 1976–80 |
| C.T. Radley | Eng. | 4 | 4 | 1 | 250 | 117★ | 83.33 | 1 | 1978 |
| C.J. Tavare | Eng. | 6 | 6 | 1 | 244 | 82★ | 48.80 | – | 1980–82 |
| A.W. Greig | Eng. | 16 | 14 | 3 | 237 | 48 | 21.55 | – | 1972–77 |
| D. Lloyd | Eng. | 7 | 7 | 1 | 236 | 116★ | 39.33 | 1 | 1973–80 |
| D.W. Randall | Eng. | 10 | 8 | 0 | 223 | 88 | 27.88 | – | 1976–82 |
| K.J. Hughes | Aust. | 7 | 7 | 1 | 222 | 98 | 37.00 | – | 1977–81 |
| C.G. Greenidge | W.I. | 5 | 5 | 0 | 215 | 78 | 43.00 | – | 1976–80 |

## Bowlers with 10 Wickets or More

| Player | | Mtch | Overs | Runs | Wts | Av'ge | B/B | 4inn | RPO | |
|---|---|---|---|---|---|---|---|---|---|---|
| R.G.D. Willis | Eng. | 18 | 175.2 | 574 | 25 | 22.96 | 4/15 | 1 | 3.27 | 1973–82 |
| I.T. Botham | Eng. | 17 | 157.4 | 662 | 24 | 27.58 | 4/56 | 1 | 4.20 | 1976–82 |
| C.M. Old | Eng. | 15 | 144.4 | 539 | 20 | 26.95 | 3/36 | – | 3.73 | 1973–80 |
| M. Hendrick | Eng. | 10 | 104 | 348 | 18 | 19.33 | 5/31 | 1 | 3.35 | 1973–81 |
| D.L. Underwood | Eng. | 12 | 95 | 309 | 16 | 19.31 | 3/27 | – | 3.25 | 1973–77 |
| D.K. Lillee | Aust. | 8 | 83.5 | 304 | 15 | 20.27 | 4/35 | 1 | 3.63 | 1972–81 |
| J.K. Lever | Eng. | 10 | 93 | 341 | 11 | 31.00 | 4/29 | 1 | 3.67 | 1976–80 |
| A.W. Greig | Eng. | 16 | 104.5 | 448 | 11 | 40.73 | 2/11 | – | 4.27 | 1972–77 |
| A.M.E. Roberts | W.I. | 5 | 46 | 140 | 10 | 14.00 | 4/27 | 2 | 3.04 | 1976–80 |
| V.A. Holder | W.I. | 5 | 53 | 189 | 10 | 18.90 | 5/50 | 1 | 3.57 | 1973–76 |

# The First–Class Counties
## in the three major domestic limited–overs competitions

### ALL COMPETITIONS

| Table of Results | | | | | | Winners: | | | |
| --- | --- | --- | --- | --- | --- | --- | --- | --- | --- |
| | P | W | L | T | NR | GC/NWT | B&H | JPL | Total |
| Derbyshire | 310 | 135 | 152 | – | 23 | 1 | – | – | 1 |
| Essex | 315 | 171 | 129 | – | 15 | – | 1 | 1 | 2 |
| Glamorgan | 307 | 111 | 173 | 1 | 22 | – | – | – | 0 |
| Gloucestershire | 308 | 113 | 164 | 2 | 29 | 1 | 1 | – | 2 |
| Hampshire | 319 | 168 | 129 | 3 | 19 | – | – | 1 | 1 |
| Kent | 324 | 192 | 115 | 3 | 14 | 2 | 3 | 3 | 8 |
| Lancashire | 336 | 185 | 128 | 4 | 19 | 4 | – | 2 | 6 |
| Leicestershire | 317 | 176 | 120 | 1 | 20 | – | 2 | 2 | 4 |
| Middlesex | 329 | 164 | 140 | 1 | 24 | 2 | – | – | 2 |
| Northants | 315 | 127 | 168 | 1 | 19 | 1 | 1 | – | 2 |
| Nottinghamshire | 311 | 132 | 158 | 2 | 19 | – | – | – | 0 |
| Somerset | 325 | 179 | 127 | 1 | 18 | 1 | 2 | 1 | 4 |
| Surrey | 326 | 155 | 147 | 2 | 22 | 1 | 1 | – | 2 |
| Sussex | 328 | 162 | 140 | 1 | 25 | 3 | – | 1 | 4 |
| Warwickshire | 326 | 154 | 148 | 1 | 23 | 2 | – | 1 | 3 |
| Worcestershire | 316 | 151 | 145 | 2 | 18 | – | – | 1 | 1 |
| Yorkshire | 314 | 141 | 142 | 1 | 30 | 2 | – | – | 2 |

### Highest Totals

| | | | | |
| --- | --- | --- | --- | --- |
| G.C./Nat West | 371–4 | (60 overs) | Hants | v. Glamorgan, Southampton 1975 |
| B. & H. | 350–3 | (55 overs) | Essex | v. Universities, Chelmsford 1979 |
| J.P.L. | 307–4 | (38 overs) | Worcs | v. Derby, Worcester 1975 |

### Lowest Totals – Completed Innings, Full Overs Available

| | | | | |
| --- | --- | --- | --- | --- |
| G.C./Nat West | 41 | (19.4 overs) | Middx | v. Essex, Westcliff 1972 |
| B. & H. | 56 | (55 overs) | Leics | v. Minor Counties, Telford 1982 |
| J.P.L. | 36 | (25.4 overs) | Leics | v. Sussex, Leicester 1973 |

### Highest Individual Innings

| | | | |
| --- | --- | --- | --- |
| C.G./Nat West | 177 | C.G. Greenidge | Hants v. Glamorgan, Southampton 1975 |
| B. & H. | 198* | G.A. Gooch | Essex v. Sussex, Hove 1982 |
| J.P.L. | 163* | C.G. Greenidge | Hants v. Warwicks, Edgbaston 1979 |

## Best Bowling Performances

| G.C./Nat West | 12.7.15.7 | A.L. Dixon | Kent | v. Surrey, The Oval 1967 |
| B. & H. | 11.5.12.7 | W.W. Daniel | Middx | v. Minor Cos East, Ipswich 1978 |
| J.P.L. | 7.4.0.26.8 | K.D. Boyce | Essex | v. Lancs, Old Trafford 1971 |

## Best Partnerships for Each Wicket

| 1st | G.C./N.W. | 227 | R.E. Marshall, B.L. Reed | Hants | v. Beds, Goldington 1968 |
| | B. & H. | 241 | S.M. Gavaskar, B.C. Rose | Somerset | v. Kent, Canterbury 1980 |
| | J.P.L. | 224 | J.A. Ormrod, D.N. Patel | Worcs | v. Hants, Southampton 1982 |
| 2nd | G.C./N.W. | 223 | M.J. Smith, C.T. Radley | Middx | v. Hants, Lord's 1977 |
| | B. & H. | 285★ | C.G. Greenidge, D.R. Turner | Hants | v. M. Cos. Sth, Amersham 1973 |
| | J.P.L. | 179 | B.W. Luckhurst, M.H. Denness | Kent | v. Somerset, Canterbury 1973 |
| 3rd | G.C./N.W. | 160 | B. Wood, F.C. Hayes | Lancs | v. Warwicks, Edgbaston 1976 |
| | B. & H. | 268★ | G.A. Gooch, K.W.R. Fletcher | Essex | v. Sussex, Hove 1982 |
| | J.P.L. | 215 | W. Larkins, R.G. Williams | Northants | v. Worcs, Luton 1982 |
| 4th | G.C./N.W. | 234★ | D. Lloyd, C.H. Lloyd | Lancs | v. Gloucs, Old Trafford 1978 |
| | B. & H. | 184★ | D. Lloyd, B.W. Reidy | Lancs | v. M. Cos. Nth, Old Trafford 1973 |
| | J.P.L. | 175★ | M.J.K. Smith, D.L. Amiss | Warwicks | v. Yorks, Edgbaston 1970 |
| 5th | G.C./N.W. | 148 | I.T. Botham, V.J. Marks | Somerset | v. Warwicks, Taunton 1982 |
| | B. & H. | 131 | J.N. Parker, T.J. Yardley | Worcs | v. Leics, Worcester 1975 |

*(N.B. the 134 added by M. Maslin & D.N.F. Slade for M. Cos. East v. Notts at Trent Bridge in 1976 is ignored in this instance, having been achieved for a non-first-class side)*

| | J.P.L. | 179 | I.T. Botham, I.V.A. Richards | Somerset | v. Hants, Taunton 1981 |
| 6th | G.C./N.W. | 105 | G.S. Sobers, R.A. White | Notts | v. Worcs, Worcester 1974 |
| | B. & H. | 114 | Majid Khan, G.P. Ellis | Glam | v. Gloucs, Bristol 1975 |
| | J.P.L. | 121 | C.P. Wilkins, A.J. Borrington | Derbys | v. Warwicks, Chesterfield 1972 |
| 7th | G.C./N.W. | 107 | D.R. Shepherd, D.A. Graveney | Gloucs | v. Surrey, Bristol 1973 |
| | B. & H. | 149★ | J.D. Love, C.M. Old | Yorks | v. Scot, Bradford 1981 |
| | J.P.L. | 101 | S.J. Windaybank, D.A. Graveney | Gloucs | v. Notts, Trent Bridge 1981 |
| 8th | G.C./N.W. | 69 | S.J. Rouse, D.J. Brown | Warwicks | v. Middlesex, Lord's 1977 |
| | B. & H. | 109 | R.E. East, N. Smith | Essex | v. Northants, Chelmsford 1977 |
| | J.P.L. | 95★ | D. Breakwell, K.F. Jennings | Somerset | v. Notts, Trent Bridge 1976 |
| 9th | G.C./N.W. | 87 | M.A. Nash, A.E. Cordle | Glam | v. Lincs, Swansea 1974 |
| | B. & H. | 81 | J.N. Shepherd, D.L. Underwood | Kent | v. Middlesex, Lord's 1975 |
| | J.P.L. | 88 | S.N. Hartley, A. Ramage | Yorks | v. Middlesex, Lord's 1982 |
| 10th | G.C./N.W. | 81 | S. Turner, R.E. East | Essex | v. Yorkshire, Leeds 1982 |
| | B. & H. | 80★ | D.L. Bairstow, M. Johnson | Yorks | v. Derbys, Derby 1981 |
| | J.P.L. | 57 | D.A. Graveney, J.B. Mortimore | Gloucs | v. Lancs, Tewkesbury 1973 |

*Batsmen with 7000 Runs or More*

| Player | | Mtch | Inns | no | Runs | HS | Av'ge | 100s |
|---|---|---|---|---|---|---|---|---|
| G.M. Turner | N.Z./Worcs | 256 | 252 | 19 | 9006 | 171* | 38.65 | 12 |
| D.L. Amiss | Eng/Warwicks | 282 | 277 | 23 | 8830 | 137 | 34.76 | 11 |
| G. Boycott | Eng/Yorks | 234 | 226 | 35 | 7886 | 146 | 41.29 | 5 |
| C.T. Radley | Eng/Middx | 297 | 290 | 29 | 7876 | 133* | 30.18 | 7 |
| D. Lloyd | Eng/Lancs | 276 | 263 | 38 | 7490 | 121* | 33.29 | 7 |
| Younis Ahmed | Sy/Worcs | 274 | 265 | 29 | 7300 | 115 | 30.93 | 4 |
| C.G. Greenidge | W.I./Hants | 218 | 217 | 9 | 7254 | 177 | 34.88 | 12 |
| K.W.R. Fletcher | Eng/Essex | 290 | 270 | 33 | 7239 | 131 | 30.54 | 2 |
| C.H. Lloyd | W.I./Lancs | 229 | 216 | 43 | 7073 | 134* | 40.88 | 10 |

*Bowlers with 350 Wickets or More*

| Player | | Mtch | Overs | Runs | Wts | Av'ge | RPO | 5inn |
|---|---|---|---|---|---|---|---|---|
| J.K. Lever | Eng/Essex | 297 | 2355.5 | 7690 | 438 | 17.56 | 3.26 | 23 |
| D.L. Underwood | Eng/Kent | 287 | 2300.5 | 7513 | 414 | 18.15 | 3.27 | 24 |
| R.D. Jackman | Eng/Surrey | 268 | 2240.1 | 8577 | 406 | 21.13 | 3.83 | 17 |
| S. Turner | Essex | 286 | 2281.1 | 8018 | 376 | 21.33 | 3.52 | 13 |
| J.N. Shepherd | Kent/Gloucs | 267 | 2125.4 | 7358 | 356 | 20.67 | 3.46 | 11 |
| K. Higgs | Lancs/Leics | 245 | 2002.5 | 6722 | 355 | 18.94 | 3.36 | 13 |

*All-rounders with More than 4000 Runs and 300 Wickets*

| Player | | Mtch | Runs | Av'ge | Wkts | Av'ge |
|---|---|---|---|---|---|---|
| B. Wood | Eng/Lancs/Derby | 271 | 5692 | 29.19 | 309 | 20.87 |
| T.E. Jesty | Hants | 265 | 5553 | 26.44 | 308 | 23.13 |

Other players who may pass this milestone in 1983 are:

| S. Turner | (Essex) | Current record 3886 runs, 376 wickets |
|---|---|---|
| J.N. Shepherd | (Gloucs) | Current record 3807 runs, 356 wickets |
| R.D.V.Knight | (Surrey) | Current record 6164 runs, 258 wickets |

# GILLETTE CUP/NAT WEST TROPHY
*(Competition became Nat West Trophy in 1981)*

*Finals, 1963–82*

| 1963 | Sussex | beat | Worcs | by 14 runs |
|---|---|---|---|---|
| 1964 | Sussex | beat | Warwicks | by 8 wkts |
| 1965 | Yorks | beat | Surrey | by 175 runs |
| 1966 | Warwicks | beat | Worcs | by 5 wkts |
| 1967 | Kent | beat | Somerset | by 32 runs |

| 1968 | Warwicks | *beat* | Sussex | *by 4 wkts* |
|------|----------|--------|--------|-------------|
| 1969 | Yorks | *beat* | Derby | *by 69 runs* |
| 1970 | Lancs | *beat* | Sussex | *by 6 wkts* |
| 1971 | Lancs | *beat* | Kent | *by 24 runs* |
| 1972 | Lancs | *beat* | Warwicks | *by 4 wkts* |
| 1973 | Gloucs | *beat* | Sussex | *by 40 runs* |
| 1974 | Kent | *beat* | Lancs | *by 4 wkts* |
| 1975 | Lancs | *beat* | Middlesex | *by 7 wkts* |
| 1976 | Northants | *beat* | Lancs | *by 4 wkts* |
| 1977 | Middlesex | *beat* | Glamorgan | *by 5 wkts* |
| 1978 | Sussex | *beat* | Somerset | *by 5 wkts* |
| 1979 | Somerset | *beat* | Northants | *by 45 runs* |
| 1980 | Middlesex | *beat* | Surrey | *by 7 wkts* |
| 1981 | Derby | *beat* | Northants | *fewer wkts lost, scores level* |
| 1982 | Surrey | *beat* | Warwicks | *by 9 wkts* |

## *Table of Results*

| County | P | W | L | Cup Winners | Losing Finalists |
|--------|---|---|---|-------------|------------------|
| Derbyshire | 36 | 17 | 19 | 1 | 1 |
| Essex | 37 | 17 | 20 | – | – |
| Glamorgan | 34 | 14 | 20 | – | 1 |
| Gloucestershire | 35 | 16 | 19 | 1 | – |
| Hampshire | 45 | 25 | 20 | – | – |
| Kent | 40 | 22 | 18 | 2 | 1 |
| Lancashire | 58 | 42 | 16 | 4 | 2 |
| Leicestershire | 35 | 15 | 20 | – | – |
| Middlesex | 51 | 33 | 18 | 2 | 1 |
| Northants | 42 | 23 | 19 | 1 | 2 |
| Nottinghamshire | 35 | 15 | 20 | – | – |
| Somerset | 46 | 27 | 19 | 1 | 2 |
| Surrey | 46 | 27 | 19 | 1 | 2 |
| Sussex | 53 | 36 | 17 | 3 | 3 |
| Warwickshire | 47 | 29 | 18 | 2 | 3 |
| Worcestershire | 38 | 18 | 20 | – | 2 |
| Yorkshire | 38 | 20 | 18 | 2 | – |

## Batsmen with 800 Runs or More

| Player | | Mtch | Inns | no | Runs | HS | Av'ge | 100s | |
|---|---|---|---|---|---|---|---|---|---|
| C.H. Lloyd | Lancs | 34 | 33 | 5 | 1629 | 126 | 58.18 | 3 | 1969–82 |
| D.L. Amiss | Warwicks | 42 | 41 | 4 | 1532 | 135 | 41.41 | 2 | 1963–82 |
| B. Wood | Lancs/Derby | 44 | 44 | 7 | 1354 | 116 | 36.59 | 2 | 1967–82 |
| B.W. Luckhurst | Kent | 28 | 28 | 3 | 1247 | 129* | 49.88 | 3 | 1963–75 |
| J.H. Edrich | Surrey | 33 | 33 | 3 | 1216 | 96 | 40.53 | – | 1963–78 |
| D. Lloyd | Lancs | 41 | 41 | 7 | 1204 | 121* | 35.41 | I | 1966–82 |
| G. Boycott | Yorks | 34 | 33 | 3 | 1172 | 146 | 39.07 | I | 1963–82 |
| C.T. Radley | Middlesex | 42 | 41 | 3 | 1086 | 105* | 28.58 | I | 1965–82 |
| A. Jones | Glamorgan | 34 | 34 | 2 | 1048 | 124* | 32.75 | I | 1963–82 |
| J.M. Brearley | Middlesex | 35 | 35 | 4 | 1007 | 124* | 32.48 | I | 1965–82 |
| B.A. Richards | Hants | 21 | 21 | 4 | 970 | 129 | 57.05 | 3 | 1968–78 |
| M.H. Denness | Kent/Essex | 37 | 35 | 0 | 962 | 85 | 27.48 | – | 1963–80 |
| D.S. Steele | Northants/Derby | 31 | 30 | 3 | 911 | 109 | 33.74 | I | 1965–82 |
| J.M. Parks | Sussex/Somerset | 30 | 29 | 5 | 895 | 102* | 37.29 | I | 1963–74 |
| J.H. Hampshire | Yorks/Derby | 33 | 32 | 5 | 895 | 110 | 33.15 | I | 1963–82 |
| G.M. Turner | Worcs | 23 | 22 | 2 | 894 | 117* | 44.70 | 5 | 1969–82 |
| C.G. Greenidge | Hants | 22 | 22 | I | 889 | 177 | 42.33 | 3 | 1971–82 |
| G. Cook | Northants | 23 | 23 | I | 883 | 114* | 40.14 | 2 | 1972–82 |
| B.F. Davison | Leics | 25 | 24 | 3 | 882 | 99 | 42.00 | – | 1971–82 |
| P.W. Denning | Somerset | 26 | 24 | I | 882 | 145 | 38.35 | 2 | 1970–82 |
| R.T. Virgin | Somerset/Northants | 31 | 30 | 2 | 870 | 105* | 31.07 | 2 | 1963–77 |
| I.V.A. Richards | Somerset | 21 | 21 | I | 843 | 139* | 42.15 | 3 | 1974–82 |
| K.W.R. Fletcher | Essex | 35 | 34 | 3 | 838 | 97 | 27.03 | – | 1963–82 |
| R.E. Marshall | Hants | 23 | 23 | I | 832 | 140 | 37.81 | 2 | 1963–72 |
| M.J. Smith | Middlesex | 31 | 31 | 0 | 828 | 123 | 26.70 | I | 1965–79 |
| M.J. Kitchen | Somerset | 28 | 27 | I | 815 | 116 | 31.34 | I | 1963–77 |

## Bowlers with 40 Wickets or More

| Player | | Matches | Overs | Runs | Wts | Av'ge | B/B | 4inn | RPO | |
|---|---|---|---|---|---|---|---|---|---|---|
| G.G. Arnold | Surrey/Sussex | 42 | 457.5 | 1203 | 81 | 14.85 | 5/9 | 8 | 2.63 | 1963–82 |
| P. Lever | Lancs | 41 | 469 | 1336 | 78 | 17.13 | 5/30 | 5 | 2.85 | 1963–76 |
| R.D. Jackman | Surrey | 28 | 302.5 | 846 | 62 | 13.65 | 7/33 | 5 | 2.79 | 1968–82 |
| A. Buss | Sussex | 31 | 357.4 | 1006 | 56 | 17.96 | 4/22 | 5 | 2.81 | 1963–74 |
| J. Simmons | Lancs | 41 | 387.5 | 1321 | 56 | 23.59 | 5/49 | I | 3.41 | 1970–82 |
| J.K. Lever | Essex | 29 | 298.4 | 778 | 53 | 15.62 | 5/8 | 5 | 2.61 | 1968–82 |
| K. Higgs | Lancs/Leics | 34 | 365.4 | 1055 | 52 | 20.30 | 6/20 | 3 | 2.89 | 1963–82 |
| J.N. Shepherd | Kent/Gloucs | 35 | 384.4 | 1157 | 52 | 22.25 | 4/23 | 4 | 3.01 | 1967–82 |
| J.S.E. Price | Middlesex | 26 | 295.5 | 937 | 51 | 18.37 | 6/34 | 2 | 3.17 | 1963–75 |
| B. Wood | Lancs/Derby | 44 | 399 | 1066 | 51 | 20.90 | 4/17 | 2 | 2.67 | 1967–82 |
| D.J. Brown | Warwicks | 32 | 344 | 1066 | 51 | 20.90 | 5/18 | 2 | 3.10 | 1964–79 |

## Bowlers with 40 Wickets or More, GC/NWT (continued)

| Player | | Matches | Overs | Runs | Wts | Av'ge | B/B | 4inn | RPO | |
|---|---|---|---|---|---|---|---|---|---|---|
| R.G.D. Willis | Surrey/Warwicks | 28 | 299.2 | 876 | 50 | 17.52 | 6/49 | 3 | 2.93 | 1970–82 |
| D.L. Underwood | Kent | 40 | 415.5 | 1311 | 48 | 27.31 | 4/57 | 1 | 3.15 | 1963–82 |
| F.E. Rumsey | Somerset/Derby | 23 | 262.3 | 553 | 47 | 11.77 | 4/19 | 3 | 2.11 | 1963–73 |
| A.W. Greig | Sussex | 28 | 260.5 | 914 | 47 | 19.45 | 5/42 | 4 | 3.50 | 1967–78 |
| R.H.M. Cottam | Hants/Northants/Devon | 24 | 267.2 | 816 | 46 | 17.74 | 4/9 | 3 | 3.05 | 1964–78 |
| R.A. Woolmer | Kent | 28 | 299 | 911 | 45 | 20.24 | 4/28 | 2 | 3.05 | 1970–82 |
| J.A. Snow | Sussex/Warwicks | 34 | 359.2 | 982 | 45 | 21.82 | 4/35 | 1 | 2.73 | 1963–80 |
| D.P. Hughes | Lancs | 43 | 299.2 | 1161 | 44 | 26.39 | 4/61 | 2 | 3.88 | 1969–82 |
| C.M. Old | Yorks | 28 | 286.1 | 799 | 43 | 18.58 | 4/9 | 2 | 2.79 | 1967–82 |
| A.S. Brown | Gloucs | 27 | 282.1 | 962 | 43 | 22.37 | 4/17 | 2 | 3.41 | 1963–76 |
| P.J. Sainsbury | Hants | 31 | 342 | 1061 | 43 | 24.67 | 7/30 | 2 | 3.10 | 1963–76 |
| Khalid Ibadulla | Warwicks | 22 | 213 | 723 | 42 | 17.21 | 6/32 | 2 | 3.39 | 1963–71 |
| F.J. Titmus | Middlesex | 30 | 333.2 | 908 | 41 | 22.15 | 5/26 | 3 | 2.72 | 1963–76 |
| R.D.V. Knight | Surrey/Gloucs/Sussex | 30 | 272 | 934 | 41 | 22.78 | 5/39 | 2 | 3.43 | 1970–82 |
| J. Garner | Somerset | 16 | 171.5 | 432 | 40 | 10.80 | 6/26 | 6 | 2.51 | 1977–82 |
| M.A. Nash | Glamorgan | 26 | 280 | 815 | 40 | 20.38 | 5/31 | 1 | 2.91 | 1967–82 |

## JOHN PLAYER LEAGUE

### Winners and Runners-up, 1969–82

| 1969 | Lancs | 49 pts | Hants | 48 pts |
|---|---|---|---|---|
| 1970 | Lancs | 53 pts | Kent | 48 pts |
| 1971 | Worcs | 44 pts★ | Essex | 44 pts |
| 1972 | Kent | 45 pts | Leics | 44 pts |
| 1973 | Kent | 50 pts | Yorks | 44 pts |
| 1974 | Leics | 54 pts | Somerset | 52 pts |
| 1975 | Hants | 52 pts | Worcs | 50 pts |
| 1976 | Kent | 40 pts★ | Essex | 40 pts |
| 1977 | Leics | 52 pts† | Essex | 52 pts |
| 1978 | Hants | 48 pts★ | Somerset | 48 pts |
| 1979 | Somerset | 50 pts | Kent | 48 pts |
| 1980 | Warwicks | 46 pts | Somerset | 44 pts |
| 1982 | Essex | 50 pts | Somerset | 44 pts |
| 1981 | Sussex | 58 pts | Middlesex | 46 pts |

★ won on run-rate
† won with more victories

## Cumulative League Table, 1969–82

| | P | W | L | T | NR | Pts | Winners | Runners-up |
|---|---|---|---|---|---|---|---|---|
| Kent | 224 | 130 | 77 | 3 | 14 | 554 | 3 | 2 |
| Leicestershire | 224 | 124 | 80 | 1 | 19 | 536 | 2 | 1 |
| Essex | 224 | 125 | 84 | – | 15 | 530 | 1 | 3 |
| Hampshire | 224 | 121 | 83 | 3 | 17 | 524 | 2 | 1 |
| Somerset | 224 | 118 | 88 | 1 | 17 | 508 | 1 | 4 |
| Lancashire | 224 | 110 | 93 | 4 | 17 | 482 | 2 | – |
| Worcestershire | 224 | 107 | 98 | 2 | 17 | 466 | 1 | 1 |
| Middlesex | 224 | 103 | 100 | 1 | 20 | 454 | – | 1 |
| Sussex | 224 | 99 | 100 | 1 | 24 | 446 | 1 | – |
| Yorkshire | 224 | 94 | 102 | 1 | 27 | 432 | – | 1 |
| Surrey | 224 | 95 | 108 | 2 | 19 | 422 | – | – |
| Derbyshire | 224 | 93 | 111 | – | 20 | 412 | – | – |
| Warwickshire | 224 | 90 | 111 | 1 | 22 | 406 | 1 | – |
| Nottinghamshire | 224 | 86 | 119 | 2 | 17 | 382 | – | – |
| Northants | 224 | 82 | 124 | 1 | 17 | 364 | – | – |
| Gloucestershire | 224 | 74 | 120 | 2 | 28 | 356 | – | – |
| Glamorgan | 224 | 75 | 128 | 1 | 20 | 342 | – | – |

## Batsmen with 3500 Runs or More

| Player | | Mtch | Inns | no | Runs | HS | Av'ge | 100s | |
|---|---|---|---|---|---|---|---|---|---|
| G.M. Turner | Worcs | 177 | 174 | 10 | 6144 | 147 | 37.46 | 3 | 1969–82 |
| C.T. Radley | Middlesex | 200 | 195 | 18 | 5351 | 133* | 30.23 | 3 | 1969–82 |
| Younis Ahmed | Surrey/Worcs | 198 | 191 | 20 | 5300 | 113 | 30.99 | 3 | 1969–82 |
| D.L. Amiss | Warwicks | 176 | 174 | 13 | 5250 | 117* | 32.61 | 4 | 1969–82 |
| S.B. Hassan | Notts | 186 | 181 | 19 | 4875 | 120* | 30.09 | 4 | 1969–82 |
| J.H. Hampshire | Yorks/Derby | 167 | 164 | 18 | 4868 | 119 | 33.34 | 6 | 1969–82 |
| B.A. Richards | Hants | 132 | 129 | 11 | 4770 | 155* | 40.42 | 9 | 1969–78 |
| A. Jones | Glamorgan | 189 | 188 | 17 | 4587 | 110* | 26.83 | 1 | 1969–82 |
| D. Lloyd | Lancs | 179 | 167 | 27 | 4576 | 103* | 32.69 | 2 | 1969–82 |
| D.R. Turner | Hants | 179 | 176 | 15 | 4568 | 109 | 28.37 | 1 | 1969–82 |
| K.W.R. Fletcher | Essex | 189 | 174 | 20 | 4512 | 99* | 29.30 | – | 1969–82 |
| G.R.J. Roope | Surrey | 188 | 175 | 27 | 4434 | 120* | 29.96 | 1 | 1969–82 |
| G. Boycott | Yorks | 135 | 130 | 22 | 4413 | 108* | 40.86 | 2 | 1969–82 |
| C.G. Greenidge | Hants | 142 | 141 | 5 | 4405 | 163* | 32.39 | 5 | 1970–82 |
| R.W. Tolchard | Leics | 194 | 179 | 36 | 4264 | 103 | 29.82 | 2 | 1969–82 |
| P. Willey | Northants | 171 | 166 | 13 | 4179 | 107 | 27.31 | 6 | 1969–82 |
| C.E.B. Rice | Notts | 116 | 114 | 19 | 4153 | 120* | 43.72 | 6 | 1975–82 |
| P.W. Denning | Somerset | 172 | 166 | 15 | 4105 | 112* | 27.19 | 2 | 1969–82 |

## Batsmen with 3500 Runs or More, JPL (continued)

| Player | | Mtch | Inns | n.o. | Runs | H.S. | Av'ge | 100s | |
|---|---|---|---|---|---|---|---|---|---|
| Zaheer Abbas | Gloucs | 123 | 118 | 15 | 4087 | 129* | 39.68 | 5 | 1972–82 |
| K.S. McEwan | Essex | 138 | 136 | 13 | 4061 | 156* | 33.02 | 7 | 1974–82 |
| C.H. Lloyd | Lancs | 142 | 136 | 34 | 3995 | 134* | 39.17 | 5 | 1969–82 |
| J.A. Ormrod | Worcs | 180 | 174 | 17 | 3890 | 110* | 24.78 | 1 | 1969–82 |
| M.J. Smith | Middlesex | 145 | 142 | 4 | 3807 | 110 | 27.59 | 2 | 1969–80 |
| T.E. Jesty | Hants | 193 | 175 | 27 | 3779 | 110* | 25.53 | 2 | 1969–82 |
| B.F. Davison | Leics | 176 | 164 | 25 | 3691 | 85* | 26.55 | – | 1970–82 |
| R.D.V. Knight | Gloucs/Sussex/Surrey | 185 | 179 | 18 | 3604 | 127 | 22.39 | 1 | 1969–82 |
| M.J. Procter | Gloucs | 159 | 149 | 9 | 3585 | 109 | 25.61 | 1 | 1969–81 |
| I.V.A. Richards | Somerset | 106 | 104 | 12 | 3534 | 126* | 38.41 | 6 | 1974–82 |

## Bowlers with 150 Wickets or More

| Player | | Mtch | Overs | Runs | Wts | Av'ge | B/B | 4inn | RPO | |
|---|---|---|---|---|---|---|---|---|---|---|
| J.K. Lever | Essex | 204 | 1419.4 | 4956 | 277 | 17.89 | 5/13 | 10 | 3.49 | 1969–82 |
| D.L. Underwood | Kent | 176 | 1199.4 | 4304 | 276 | 15.59 | 5/19 | 20 | 3.59 | 1969–82 |
| S. Turner | Essex | 203 | 1464 | 5689 | 261 | 21.80 | 5/35 | 9 | 3.89 | 1969–82 |
| R.D. Jackman | Surrey | 177 | 1289.2 | 5402 | 234 | 23.09 | 6/34 | 7 | 4.19 | 1969–82 |
| J.N. Shepherd | Kent/Gloucs | 178 | 1207.5 | 4599 | 223 | 20.62 | 4/17 | 5 | 3.81 | 1969–82 |
| H.R. Moseley | Somerset | 147 | 1105.3 | 4493 | 222 | 20.24 | 5/40 | 9 | 4.06 | 1971–82 |
| K. Higgs | Lancs/Leics | 160 | 1135.1 | 4089 | 217 | 18.84 | 6/17 | 6 | 3.60 | 1969–82 |
| T.E. Jesty | Hants | 193 | 1096.1 | 5033 | 217 | 23.19 | 6/20 | 9 | 4.59 | 1969–82 |
| R.A. Woolmer | Kent | 167 | 1111.1 | 4248 | 214 | 19.85 | 6/9 | 5 | 3.82 | 1969–82 |
| J. Simmons | Lancs | 205 | 1304.4 | 5230 | 209 | 25.02 | 5/17 | 6 | 4.01 | 1969–82 |
| M.A. Nash | Glamorgan | 187 | 1281.5 | 4667 | 210 | 22.22 | 6/29 | 6 | 3.64 | 1969–82 |
| N. Gifford | Worcs | 184 | 1203.1 | 5281 | 202 | 26.14 | 5/28 | 7 | 4.39 | 1969–82 |
| B.M. Brain | Worcs/Gloucs | 139 | 961.5 | 3847 | 195 | 19.73 | 4/27 | 8 | 4.00 | 1969–81 |
| C.M. Old | Yorks | 143 | 1038.3 | 3872 | 192 | 20.17 | 5/33 | 9 | 3.73 | 1969–82 |
| B. Wood | Lancs/Derby | 170 | 1044.1 | 4045 | 190 | 21.29 | 5/19 | 3 | 3.87 | 1969–82 |
| M.W.W. Selvey | Middlesex | 147 | 1052.1 | 3961 | 188 | 21.07 | 5/18 | 10 | 3.77 | 1972–82 |
| A.A. Jones | Sussex/Somerset/Middx/Glam | 135 | 952.1 | 3995 | 187 | 21.36 | 6/34 | 5 | 4.20 | 1969–81 |
| M.N.S. Taylor | Notts/Hants | 162 | 1136.5 | 4868 | 187 | 26.03 | 4/20 | 8 | 4.28 | 1969–80 |
| K.D. Boyce | Essex | 108 | 780.1 | 2721 | 179 | 15.20 | 8/26 | 10 | 3.49 | 1969–77 |
| V.A. Holder | Worcs | 120 | 864.5 | 2970 | 176 | 16.87 | 6/33 | 6 | 3.43 | 1969–80 |
| R.E. East | Essex | 172 | 1011.5 | 4086 | 174 | 23.48 | 6/18 | 5 | 4.04 | 1969–82 |
| R.D.V. Knight | Gloucs/Sussex/Surrey | 185 | 987.4 | 4472 | 174 | 25.70 | 5/42 | 4 | 4.53 | 1969–82 |
| M.J. Procter | Gloucs | 159 | 1016.3 | 3670 | 173 | 21.21 | 5/81 | 8 | 3.61 | 1969–81 |
| G.G. Arnold | Surrey/Sussex | 148 | 1063.1 | 3670 | 173 | 21.21 | 5/11 | 6 | 3.45 | 1969–82 |
| G.I. Burgess | Somerset | 146 | 1020.3 | 4235 | 172 | 24.62 | 6/25 | 3 | 4.15 | 1969–80 |
| P.I. Pocock | Surrey | 169 | 1155.2 | 4475 | 166 | 26.96 | 4/27 | 4 | 3.87 | 1969–82 |

| Player | | Mtch | Overs | Runs | Wts | Av'ge | B/B | 4inn | RPO | |
|---|---|---|---|---|---|---|---|---|---|---|
| A.E. Cordle | Glamorgan | 150 | 1016 | 4061 | 164 | 24.76 | 5/24 | 4 | 4.00 | 1969–82 |
| E.E. Hemmings | Warwicks/Notts | 157 | 1003 | 4519 | 163 | 27.72 | 5/22 | 8 | 4.51 | 1969–82 |
| D.P. Hughes | Lancs | 206 | 786.1 | 3387 | 161 | 21.04 | 6/29 | 9 | 4.31 | 1969–82 |
| J.C.J. Dye | Kent/Northants | 123 | 918.1 | 3472 | 161 | 21.57 | 4/18 | 5 | 3.78 | 1969–77 |
| R.G.D. Willis | Surrey/Warwicks | 120 | 865.5 | 3345 | 158 | 21.17 | 4/12 | 3 | 3.86 | 1969–82 |
| J.A. Snow | Sussex/Warwicks | 111 | 787.3 | 2973 | 153 | 19.43 | 5/15 | 6 | 3.78 | 1969–80 |
| P.G. Lee | Northants/Lancs | 139 | 979.5 | 3800 | 153 | 24.84 | 4/17 | 6 | 3.88 | 1969–82 |
| J.F. Steele | Leics | 161 | 941.2 | 3661 | 152 | 24.09 | 5/22 | 5 | 3.89 | 1970–82 |

# BENSON & HEDGES CUP

## Finals, 1972–82

| 1972 | Leics | beat | Yorks | by 5 wkts |
|---|---|---|---|---|
| 1973 | Kent | beat | Worcs | by 39 runs |
| 1974 | Surrey | beat | Leics | by 27 runs |
| 1975 | Leics | beat | Middlesex | by 5 wkts |
| 1976 | Kent | beat | Worcs | by 43 runs |
| 1977 | Gloucs | beat | Kent | by 64 runs |
| 1978 | Kent | beat | Derby | by 6 wkts |
| 1979 | Essex | beat | Surrey | by 35 runs |
| 1980 | Northants | beat | Essex | by 6 runs |
| 1981 | Somerset | beat | Surrey | by 7 wkts |
| 1982 | Somerset | beat | Notts | by 9 wkts |

## Table of Results

| County | P | W | L | NR | Cup Winners | Losing Finalists |
|---|---|---|---|---|---|---|
| Derbyshire | 50 | 25 | 22 | 3 | – | 1 |
| Essex | 54 | 29 | 25 | – | 1 | 1 |
| Glamorgan | 49 | 22 | 25 | 2 | – | – |
| Gloucestershire | 49 | 23 | 25 | 1 | 1 | – |
| Hampshire | 50 | 22 | 26 | 2 | – | – |
| Kent | 60 | 40 | 20 | – | 3 | 1 |
| Lancashire | 54 | 33 | 19 | 2 | – | – |
| Leicestershire | 58 | 37 | 20 | 1 | 2 | 1 |
| Middlesex | 54 | 28 | 22 | 4 | – | 1 |
| Northants | 49 | 22 | 25 | 2 | 1 | – |
| Nottinghamshire | 52 | 31 | 19 | 2 | – | 1 |

Table of Results, Benson & Hedges Cup (continued)

| County | P | W | L | NR | Cup Winners | Losing Finalists |
|---|---|---|---|---|---|---|
| Somerset | 55 | 34 | 20 | 1 | 2 | – |
| Surrey | 56 | 33 | 20 | 3 | 1 | 2 |
| Sussex | 51 | 27 | 23 | 1 | – | – |
| Warwickshire | 55 | 35 | 19 | 1 | – | – |
| Worcestershire | 54 | 26 | 27 | 1 | – | 2 |
| Yorkshire | 52 | 27 | 22 | 3 | – | 1 |

## Batsmen with 1100 Runs or More

| Player | | Mtch | Inns | no | Runs | HS | Av'ge | 100s | |
|---|---|---|---|---|---|---|---|---|---|
| R.D.V. Knight | Gloucs/Sussex/Surrey | 54 | 51 | 7 | 1936 | 117 | 44.00 | 1 | 1972–82 |
| G.A. Gooch | Essex | 41 | 41 | 3 | 1828 | 198★ | 48.10 | 5 | 1973–82 |
| G. Boycott | Yorks | 46 | 44 | 8 | 1752 | 142 | 48.67 | 2 | 1972–82 |
| J.C. Balderstone | Leics | 48 | 46 | 10 | 1720 | 113★ | 47.78 | 4 | 1972–82 |
| S. Mohammed | Gloucs | 43 | 43 | 1 | 1583 | 128 | 37.69 | 3 | 1972–82 |
| B.F. Davison | Leics | 58 | 55 | 5 | 1583 | 158★ | 31.66 | 1 | 1972–82 |
| J.A. Ormrod | Worcs | 51 | 51 | 6 | 1572 | 124★ | 34.93 | 1 | 1972–82 |
| K.S. McEwan | Essex | 44 | 43 | 3 | 1480 | 133 | 37.00 | 2 | 1974–82 |
| D. Lloyd | Lancs | 49 | 48 | 3 | 1474 | 113 | 32.76 | 3 | 1972–82 |
| G.M. Turner | Worcs | 47 | 47 | 3 | 1433 | 143★ | 32.57 | 2 | 1972–82 |
| B. Wood | Lancs/Derby | 46 | 44 | 4 | 1413 | 106 | 35.33 | 1 | 1972–82 |
| D.R. Turner | Hants | 46 | 46 | 6 | 1410 | 123★ | 35.25 | 1 | 1972–82 |
| C.G. Greenidge | Hants | 41 | 41 | 2 | 1404 | 173★ | 36.00 | 3 | 1972–82 |
| Asif Iqbal | Kent | 58 | 54 | 4 | 1386 | 75 | 27.72 | – | 1972–82 |
| K.W.R. Fletcher | Essex | 51 | 49 | 8 | 1366 | 101★ | 33.32 | 1 | 1972–82 |
| D.W. Randall | Notts | 48 | 47 | 7 | 1296 | 103★ | 32.40 | 1 | 1972–82 |
| Younis Ahmed | Surrey/Worcs | 52 | 50 | 7 | 1287 | 115 | 29.93 | 1 | 1972–82 |
| A. Jones | Glamorgan | 48 | 47 | 1 | 1255 | 89 | 27.28 | – | 1972–82 |
| A.W. Stovoid | Gloucs | 34 | 34 | 5 | 1251 | 123 | 43.14 | 2 | 1975–82 |
| D.L. Amiss | Warwicks | 48 | 46 | 6 | 1239 | 105★ | 30.98 | 1 | 1972–82 |
| P.W. Denning | Somerset | 53 | 52 | 7 | 1219 | 129 | 27.09 | 1 | 1972–82 |
| M.J. Procter | Gloucs | 39 | 39 | 5 | 1205 | 154★ | 35.44 | 2 | 1972–81 |
| T.E. Jesty | Hants | 47 | 46 | 3 | 1201 | 105 | 27.93 | 1 | 1972–82 |
| Zaheer Abbas | Gloucs | 40 | 40 | 6 | 1192 | 98 | 35.06 | – | 1973–82 |
| C.T. Radley | Middlesex | 51 | 50 | 7 | 1189 | 121★ | 27.65 | 2 | 1972–82 |
| B. Dudleston | Leics/Gloucs | 42 | 42 | 5 | 1171 | 90 | 31.64 | – | 1972–81 |
| I.V.A. Richards | Somerset | 36 | 32 | 6 | 1148 | 132★ | 44.15 | 1 | 1974–82 |
| M.J. Smith | Middlesex | 43 | 43 | 0 | 71142 | 105 | 26.55 | 1 | 1972–80 |
| A.G.E. Ealham | Kent | 48 | 45 | 8 | 1141 | 94★ | 30.83 | – | 1972–81 |

| Player | | Mtch | Inns | no | Runs | HS | Av'ge | 100s | |
|--------|--|------|------|----|------|-----|-------|------|--|
| J.H. Edrich | Surrey | 33 | 31 | 2 | 1135 | 83* | 39.13 | – | 1972–78 |
| F.C. Hayes | Lancs | 42 | 42 | 8 | 1123 | 102 | 33.03 | 1 | 1973–82 |
| G.P. Howarth | Surrey | 40 | 38 | 1 | 1123 | 80 | 30.35 | – | 1973–82 |
| A.I. Kallicharran | Warwicks | 40 | 37 | 5 | 1115 | 109 | 34.84 | 1 | 1972–82 |
| B.C. Rose | Somerset | 42 | 40 | 5 | 1114 | 137* | 31.83 | 1 | 1973–82 |
| G.R.J. Roope | Surrey | 55 | 52 | 13 | 1108 | 115* | 28.41 | 1 | 1972–82 |

## Bowlers with 50 Wickets or More

| Player | | Mtch | Overs | Runs | Wts | Av'ge | B/B | 4inn | RPO | |
|--------|--|------|-------|------|-----|-------|-----|------|-----|--|
| R.D. Jackman | Surrey | 55 | 561 | 1981 | 101 | 19.61 | 4/24 | 5 | 3.53 | 1972–82 |
| J.K. Lever | Essex | 54 | 544.3 | 1615 | 97 | 16.65 | 5/16 | 7 | 2.97 | 1972–82 |
| K. Higgs | Leics | 51 | 502 | 1578 | 86 | 18.35 | 4/10 | 4 | 3.14 | 1972–82 |
| J.N. Shepherd | Kent/Gloucs | 54 | 533.1 | 1702 | 81 | 21.01 | 4/25 | 2 | 3.19 | 1972–82 |
| S. Turner | Essex | 53 | 530.2 | 1533 | 76 | 20.17 | 4/19 | 3 | 2.89 | 1972–82 |
| M. Hendrick | Derby/Notts | 44 | 428.1 | 1015 | 73 | 13.90 | 6/33 | 3 | 2.37 | 1972–82 |
| R.A. Woolmer | Kent | 55 | 512.2 | 1405 | 73 | 19.25 | 4/14 | 4 | 2.74 | 1972–82 |
| D.L. Underwood | Kent | 57 | 568.2 | 1549 | 72 | 21.51 | 5/35 | 3 | 2.73 | 1972–82 |
| C.M. Old | Yorks | 47 | 463.1 | 1171 | 71 | 16.49 | 4/17 | 2 | 2.53 | 1972–82 |
| R.G.D. Willis | Surrey/Warwicks | 40 | 404.2 | 1178 | 70 | 16.83 | 7/32 | 5 | 2.91 | 1973–82 |
| M.J. Procter | Gloucs | 39 | 362 | 1049 | 68 | 15.42 | 6/13 | 5 | 2.90 | 1972–81 |
| N. Gifford | Worcs | 51 | 494.2 | 1633 | 67 | 24.37 | 6/8 | 3 | 3.30 | 1972–82 |
| H.R. Moseley | Somerset | 47 | 468.1 | 1292 | 66 | 19.58 | 3/13 | – | 2.76 | 1972–82 |
| A.A. Jones | Somerset/Middx/Glam | 39 | 352.2 | 1116 | 65 | 17.16 | 5/16 | 2 | 3.17 | 1972–81 |
| M.W.W. Selvey | Middlesex | 50 | 456.1 | 1377 | 63 | 21.86 | 5/39 | 2 | 3.02 | 1972–82 |
| P.I. Pocock | Surrey | 54 | 544 | 1727 | 61 | 28.31 | 4/11 | 3 | 3.18 | 1972–82 |
| B. Wood | Lancs/Derby | 46 | 428.1 | 1154 | 59 | 19.59 | 5/11 | 3 | 2.70 | 1972–82 |
| I.T. Botham | Somerset | 43 | 398.5 | 1320 | 59 | 22.37 | 4/16 | 2 | 3.31 | 1974–82 |
| M.A. Nash | Glamorgan | 43 | 394 | 1067 | 58 | 18.39 | 4/12 | 3 | 2.71 | 1972–82 |
| S.J. Rouse | Warwicks | 35 | 331 | 1109 | 58 | 19.12 | 5/21 | 2 | 3.35 | 1972–81 |
| B.M. Brain | Worcs/Gloucs | 39 | 383.3 | 1124 | 57 | 19.72 | 4/30 | 1 | 2.93 | 1972–82 |
| K.B.S. Jarvis | Kent | 39 | 372.1 | 1285 | 57 | 22.54 | 4/34 | 2 | 3.45 | 1976–82 |
| T.E. Jesty | Hants | 47 | 383.4 | 1313 | 56 | 23.45 | 4/22 | 4 | 3.42 | 1972–82 |
| G.B. Stevenson | Yorks | 30 | 291.3 | 963 | 54 | 17.83 | 5/28 | 4 | 3.30 | 1975–82 |
| J. Simmons | Lancs | 50 | 441.4 | 1217 | 54 | 22.54 | 4/31 | 1 | 2.76 | 1972–82 |
| Sarfraz Nawaz | Northants | 32 | 330 | 1006 | 53 | 18.98 | 5/21 | 2 | 3.05 | 1974–82 |
| G.I. Burgess | Somerset | 37 | 370.4 | 1195 | 53 | 22.55 | 4/12 | 3 | 3.22 | 1972–82 |
| Imran Khan | Worcs/Sussex | 37 | 354.3 | 994 | 52 | 19.11 | 5/8 | 3 | 2.80 | 1976–82 |
| G.G. Arnold | Surrey/Sussex | 39 | 389 | 1098 | 52 | 21.11 | 3/19 | – | 2.82 | 1972–81 |
| G.D. McKenzie | Leics | 26 | 247.2 | 794 | 51 | 15.56 | 5/34 | 4 | 3.21 | 1972–75 |

# A Comparison between Pace and Slow Bowlers in Domestic Limited-Overs Cricket – Seasons 1979, 1980, 1981, 1982

*(1979–81 by John Stockwell, 1982 by Robert Brooke)*

| Year | Type | No. of Bowlers | Overs | Runs | Wkts | Av'ge | RPO |
|------|------|------|------|------|------|------|------|
| 1979 | Fast/Fast-medium | 52 | 5933.5 | 20635 | 959 | 21.52 | 3.48 |
| | Slow Left-arm | 18 | 1227.2 | 4500 | 196 | 22.96 | 3.67 |
| | Off-break | 24 | 1983.5 | 7443 | 285 | 26.12 | 3.75 |
| | Medium-pace | 78 | 5382.1 | 20731 | 786 | 26.38 | 3.85 |
| | Leg-break | 6 | 105.3 | 499 | 17 | 29.35 | 4.73 |
| | TOTAL | 178 | 14632.4 | 53808 | 2243 | 23.99 | 3.68 |
| 1980 | Fast/Fast-medium | 63 | 6814.5 | 24614 | 1107 | 22.23 | 3.61 |
| | Slow Left-arm | 19 | 1331 | 5222 | 188 | 27.77 | 3.92 |
| | Off-break | 25 | 1778.1 | 6937 | 213 | 32.56 | 3.90 |
| | Medium-pace | 83 | 5864.4 | 23666 | 859 | 27.55 | 4.03 |
| | Leg-break | 3 | 17.2 | 81 | 0 | – | 4.67 |
| | TOTAL | 193 | 15806 | 60520 | 2367 | 25.56 | 3.82 |
| 1981 | Fast/Fast-medium | 67 | 6536.4 | 24401 | 1040 | 23.46 | 2.73 |
| | Slow Left-arm | 17 | 1074.1 | 4196 | 148 | 28.35 | 3.90 |
| | Off-break | 25 | 1753.5 | 6585 | 249 | 26.44 | 3.75 |
| | Medium-pace | 72 | 4802.4 | 19690 | 744 | 26.46 | 4.09 |
| | Leg-break | 5 | 49.4 | 241 | 8 | 30.12 | 4.85 |
| | TOTAL | 186 | 14217 | 55113 | 2189 | 25.17 | 3.87 |
| 1982 | Fast/Fast-medium | 65 | 6955 | 27185 | 1151 | 23.62 | 3.91 |
| | Slow Left-arm | 17 | 1130.3 | 4311 | 148 | 29.13 | 3.81 |
| | Off-break | 25 | 2260.5 | 9138 | 285 | 32.06 | 4.04 |
| | Medium-pace | 91 | 5362 | 23117 | 853 | 27.10 | 4.31 |
| | Leg-break | 4 | 15 | 89 | 2 | 44.50 | 5.93 |
| | TOTAL | 202 | 15723.2 | 63840 | 2439 | 26.18 | 4.06 |
| All Seasons 1979–82 together | | | | | | | |
| | Fast/Fast-medium | 247 | 26240.2 | 96835 | 4257 | 22.75 | 3.69 |
| | Slow Left-arm | 71 | 4763 | 18229 | 680 | 26.81 | 3.83 |
| | Off-break | 99 | 7776.4 | 30103 | 1032 | 29.17 | 3.87 |
| | Medium-pace | 324 | 21411.3 | 87204 | 3242 | 26.90 | 4.07 |
| | Leg-break | 18 | 187.3 | 910 | 27 | 33.70 | 4.85 |
| | TOTAL | 759 | 60379 | 233281 | 9238 | 25.25 | 3.86 |

# Gate Attendances 1950–82

*(not including members)*

| Season | Touring Side | County Champion- ships | Gillette Cup | John Player League | Benson & Hedges Cup | Total |
|--------|--------------|------------------------|--------------|--------------------|---------------------|-------|
| 1950 | W.I. | 1,978,750 | | | | |
| 1951 | S.A. | 1,808,396 | | | | |
| 1952 | India | 1,943,165 | | | | |
| 1953 | Aus | 1,616,156 | | | | |
| 1954 | Pak | 1,40,571 | | | | |
| 1955 | S.A. | 1,640,565 | | | | |
| 1956 | Aus | 1,174,079 | | | | |
| 1957 | W.I. | 1,197,979 | | | | |
| 1958 | N.Z. | 983,820 | | | | |
| 1959 | India | 1,369,673 | | | | |
| 1960 | S.A. | 1,046,104 | | | | |
| 1961 | Aus | 969,382 | | | | |
| 1962 | Pak | 933,871 | | | | |
| 1963 | W.I. | 719,661 | 54,898 | | | 774,559 |
| 1964 | Aus | 832,993 | 82,653 | | | 915,646 |
| 1965 | N.Z./S.A. | 659,560 | 96,787 | | | 756,347 |
| 1966 | W.I. | 513,578 | 94,556 | | | 608,134 |
| 1967 | Ind/Pak | 614,444 | 110,558 | | | 725,002 |
| 1968 | Aus | 583,117 | 83,007 | | | 666,124 |
| 1969 | N.Z./W.I. | 326,927 | 101,663 | 280,608 | | 709,198 |
| 1970 | (R.O.W.) | 355,714 | 90,099 | 276,205 | | 722,018 |
| 1971 | Pak/Ind | 324,482 | 116,332 | 341,406 | | 782,220 |
| 1972 | Aus | 224,713 | 100,422 | 281,839 | 50,315 | 657,289 |
| 1973 | W.I./N.Z. | 233,718 | 97,178 | 330,688 | 62,891 | 724,475 |
| 1974 | Ind/Pak | 218,245 | 99,790 | 281,621 | 64,634 | 664,290 |
| 1975 | W.C./Aus | 278,483 | 127,588 | 374,299 | 62,215 | 842,585 |
| 1976 | W.I. | 216,834 | 117,609 | 345,473 | 71,044 | 750,960 |
| 1977 | Aus | 178,903 | 94,273 | 260,251 | 69,150 | 602,577 |
| 1978 | Pak/N.Z. | 190,788 | 104,149 | 238,281 | 59,982 | 593,200 |
| 1979 | W.C./Ind | 174,229 | 105,732 | 252,274 | 49,957 | 582,192 |
| 1980 | W.I./Aus.C. | 160,105 | 76,694 | 258,432 | 57,014 | 552,245 |
| 1981 | Aus | 198,011 | 78,891 | 241,592 | 54,941 | 573,435 |
| 1982 | Ind/Pak | 156,181 | 66,212 | 189,900 | 58,678 | 470,971 |

Gate attendances at the Prudential World Cup:

in 1975: 117,809;  in 1979: 132,768.

# Index

Cahn, Julian 14
Cairns, Lance 74, 106
Cambridgeshire 24, 32–3
Cambridge University 77
  *see also* Combined Universities
Campbell-Johnson, Alan 18
Canada 101–4, 106
Cardus, Neville 2–3, 9
Carr, Donald 89, 125
Carrick, P. 81
Carter, R.G.M. 23
Cartwright, Tom 28, 37, 51, 52, 85
Cavaliers *see* Rothmans Cavaliers
Chappell, Greg 10, 54, 72, 92–3, 97–9, 136
Chappell, Ian 92–3, 95, 97–9, 137
Chappell, Trevor 10
Cheatle, Giles 8, 124
Cheshire 24
Clarke, Sylvester 126
Clarke Report 75
Clarkson, J.A. 56
Clayton, Geoff 26–7
Clinton, G.S. 119
Close, Brian
  England 33, 71; on one-day cricket 1;
  Somerset 83, 84–5, 116, 121; Yorkshire
  22, 29–30, 39–41, 42, 46
Club cricket 11, 12, 22
  *see also* Lancashire League
Coleman, Bernie 142
Coles, 'Mister' 13
Combined Universities 77, 127
Compton, Denis 2, 15, 46, 48
Constantine, Learie 47–8
Cook, Geoff 114, 128
Cornell, John 134
Cornhill Insurance 69
Cornwall Senior League 12
Cosier, G.J. 72, 104
County Championship
  crises 15–17, 43–4, 75; disadvantages 26,
  67–8; origins 14; overseas players and 35;
  rules 16; Sunday cricket and 50; 1967 31;
  1968 35; 1969 52; 1975 112; 1976 114;
  1977 117, 120–1; 1979 126; 1980 132
Cowdrey, Colin
  England 35, 88; Kent 33, 79, 81, 82; on
  Close, Brian 40; on Dexter, Ted 21
Cowgill, Bryan 47
Cowley, N.G. 118
Cozier, Tony 136
Croft, Colin 28, 103, 107–9

Daniel, Wayne 103, 117, 130–2
Darling, Rick 101
Davey, J. 60
Davie, Michael 5
Davison, Brian 62, 84
Denness, Mike
  England 73, 81, 91, 97; Kent 32, 79, 81,
  83
Denning, P.W. 122, 126, 128
Derbyshire
  Benson & Hedges Cup 77; 1979 126;

Gillette Cup 1963 21; 1969 39–40; 1979
  127–8; Midlands Counties Knock-Out
  Cup 17; Nat West Trophy 1981 117
Dexter, Ted 1, 21–4, 25–6, 37, 46–9, 88
Dixon, A.L. 32–3
D'Oliveira, Basil 82, 88
Dooland, Bruce 35
Doshi, Dilip 114, 129–30
Douglas-Home, Alec 33
Doust, Dudley 84–5, 139
Drabble, David 3
Dredge, C.H. 117, 123
Dudleston, B. 78–9
Dunbar, Jim 18
Durham 5, 24, 81
Dye, J.C.J. 62, 114–15

Ealham, A.G.E. 119
East, R.E. 123
East Africa 89, 91–2, 96, 101
Edgar, Bruce 104–5
Edmeades, B.E.A. 38
Edmonds, Phil 108, 131
Edrich, Bill 15, 122
Edrich, John 85–6, 88
Edwards, M.J. 29
Edwards, Ross 92, 96, 98, 114
Emburey, John 120, 131
Engineer, Faroukh 41, 53–7, 59, 115
England *v.* Australia
  1948 42, 73; 1968 35, 71; 1975 89, 111;
  1977 72; 1981 11, 130; one-day *see under*
  Prudential Trophy, Prudential World
  Cup
England *v.* India
  1967 31, 33; 1974 74, 90, 91; one-day *see*
  *under* Prudential Trophy, Prudential
  World Cup
England *v.* New Zealand (one-day) *see under*
  Prudential Trophy, Prudential World
  Cup
England *v.* Pakistan
  1967 31, 33; 1982 7; one-day *see under*
  Prudential Trophy, Prudential World
  Cup
England *v.* West Indies
  1963 35; 1966 35; 1969 38, 39; 1973 73;
  1976 73; 1980 73; one-day *see under*
  Prudential Trophy, Prudential World
  Cup
Essex
  record 117; Benson & Hedges Cup 77;
  1973 81; 1975 113; 1979 126–7; County
  Championship 1979 126; Gillette Cup
  1963 20; 1967 33; 1969 38; 1970 56; 1971
  58; 1973 80; 1976 114; 1978 122–3; John
  Player League 1969 52, 54; 1976 116–17;
  1977 120; 1978 123, 124–5, 126
Evans, Godfrey 32, 48
Eyre, T.J.P. 39

Fagg, Arthur 63
Fairey, David 32
Flavell, Jack 22–3

Walker, Peter 99
Walters, Doug 93, 97, 99
Ward, Alan 39
Ward, B. 52
Warner, Pelham 9, 14
Warwickshire
    expenses 17; record 110; Benson &
    Hedges Cup 1972 78–9; 1974 84; 1975
    112, 113; 1979 127; Gillette Cup 1963 26;
    1964 25–7; 1965 28–9; 1966 28; 1968 36–
    8; 1971 59, 62; 1972 79; 1976 115; 1978
    122; John Player League 129; 1969 52,
    1972 27; 1975 111; 1979 112; 1980 129–30
Washbrook, Cyril 36
Wasim Bari 106
Wasim Raja 92, 95–6, 104–5
Watney Mann Knock-Out Shield 12
Wellings, E.M. 70
Wells, 'Bomber' 25
Wessels, K.C. 131–2
West, Peter 48, 59, 75–6
West Indies v. England 1967–8 33
    (one-day) see under Prudential Trophy,
    Prudential World Cup
Wettimuny, S. 93–4
Whitbread, Samuel 12
White, Crawford 67
Wilkinson, J.S. 81
Willey, Peter 54, 74, 114, 116, 128
Williams, R.G. 128
Willis, Bob 73, 105, 107, 129
Wilsher, 'Mister' 13
Wilson, Don 51
Wilson, Hugh 127
Wilson, Peter 23–4, 138
Wiltshire 24
Wood, Barry 7, 53, 55–9, 62–3, 115–16

Wood, Jack 49
Woodcock, John 4, 30–1, 141–2
Woolley, Frank 20, 23
Woolmer, Bob 62, 119
Worcestershire
    record 110; Benson & Hedges Cup 1972
    86; 1973 82; 1974 84; 1978 121; 1979
    125–6; County Championship 1964 22;
    Gillette Cup 1963 22–4, 55; 1964 24–5;
    1966 28, 34; 1968 35–6; 1971 58, 64; 1973
    80–1; 1974 83; John Player League 1971
    65; 1975 111
World Cup, Prudential see Prudential World
    Cup
World Series, Benson & Hedges see Benson
    & Hedges World Series
World Series cricket see under Packer, Kerry
Worsley, D.R. 26
Wright, Douglas 2
Wright, J.G. 106

Yallop, Graham 104
Yeabsley, D.I. 113
Yorkshire
    decline 41, 52, 78; expenses 16, 46;
    record 110; Benson & Hedges Cup 77;
    1972 79; 1974 84; 1975 113; 1976 116;
    County Championship 1966 34; 1967 34;
    1970 42–3; Fenner Trophy 111; Gillette
    Cup 1963 22; 1964 25; 1965 28–31; 1967
    32–3; 1969 38–41; 1971 61–2; 1973 5, 81;
    1974 83; John Player League 1969 54;
    1970 64; 1971 65–6; 1973 82; 1978 123
Younis Ahmed 5

Zaheer Abbas 80, 95, 107, 117